The Teacher's Attention

The Teacher's Attention

Why Our Kids Must and Can Get Smaller Schools and Classes

Garrett Delavan

 TEMPLE UNIVERSITY PRESS
Philadelphia

Temple University Press
1601 North Broad Street
Philadelphia PA 19122
www.temple.edu/tempress

Copyright © 2009 by Temple University
All rights reserved
Published 2009
Printed in the United States of America

Library of Congress Cataloging-in-Publication Data
Delavan, Garrett, 1973–
  The teacher's attention : why our kids must and can get smaller schools and classes / Garrett Delavan.
       p. cm.
  Includes bibliographical references and index.
  ISBN 978-1-59213-893-7 (cloth : alk. paper)—ISBN 978-1-59213-894-4 (pbk. : alk. paper)   1. School size—United States.   2. Class size—United States.   I. Title.
  LB3012.5.D45 2009
  371.2'51—dc22   2008043762

2 4 6 8 9 7 5 3 1

Contents

Introduction   vii

1 First and Foremost   1

2 Getting the Crisis Right   40

3 The Racial Relationship Gap   54

4 Defining the Harm: Adult Attention Deficit   61

5 The Four-Piece Relationship Load Solution   78

6 The Core of the Relationship Load Effect   103

7 The Counterarguments   116

8 The Costs and Savings   127

9 Implementation at the School and District Levels   145

10 Implementation at the State and Federal Levels   163

11 Help from the Private Sector   178

12 Implementation at Kid Level   180

Conclusion   185
Appendices   189
Notes   197
References   203
Index   219

Introduction

Just one: great public schools with classes of twelve or smaller.

—**Kurt Vonnegut** (1922–2007) when asked, "If you were to build or envision a country you could consider yourself a proud citizen of, what would be *three* of its basic attributes?" (*Infinite Mind* 2006, emphasis mine)

In Philip Jackson's classic study, *Life in Classrooms*, he writes, "The crowds in the classroom may be troubling. But there they are. Part of becoming a student involves learning how to live with that fact" (1990, p. 19). Class size is easy to take as a given of schooling if you've always taught or seen classes of relatively equal size. That's not my experience. I've taught for eight years at a public school with fluctuating enrollment, which makes for fluctuating class sizes. It's been a laboratory of sorts, a laboratory particularly suited to the formation and testing of hypotheses about class size. The genesis for this book came when I began to observe myself reacting to some students differently in large classes. I began to notice that I tend to throw up my hands sooner in a large class and say to myself, "This student doesn't belong here." Meanwhile, I noticed a similar student in a smaller class doesn't appear so beyond help. Instead, I feel up to the challenge of meeting his or her needs by offering a more basic option or a slower-paced plan—or something more tied to the student's interests or background rather than simply the mandated curriculum—allowing both of us to feel a sense of success. The same tendency held true for the done-in-half-the-time disruptors—they seemed to me not to belong only in the context of larger classes. In a small class I was more able to successfully engage them in additional or more challenging work.

After some self-study, I came to believe it's not simply a function of the amount of extra time I have in a small class to do that sort of accommodating or individualizing, much less of being a "bad" person or teacher. There is also a change in my attitude and outlook that is a product of having less time per student. In a large class I unthinkingly retreat from a sense of responsibility to each and every student. Because I perceive I can't much help this student in this particular situation (a large class), I fear that the student will create a sense of failure for me or endanger the standard I am attempting to set, whether academic or behavioral. In anticipation of that, I retreat from my duty to the student so I can protect myself from that feeling. I rationalize it by the belief that the problem resides in the student, not in me. (It really resides in the situation.) So instead of thinking, "I can't help this student," which makes me feel powerless, I think, "This student can't be helped." And, especially in my first several years of teaching, I often vented my frustration on that student for being in my class and not "belonging" in it. In a small class, all of a sudden, every student is transformed, by the magic of the situation, into someone I can help and who deserves it. With very few exceptions, I end up enjoying the company of every student in my small classes.

I tried to find a book on the issue, one that didn't just skim the obvious surface of things. It turns out there wasn't one.

Relationship Load Reduction

Bluntly put, our schools are neglecting our children, depriving them of the adult attention that is the cornerstone of their development into happy and responsible adults and parents. What's more, we're subjecting teachers to working conditions in which they are more likely to hurt our kids with the little attention they can pay them. This raises hints of abuse. The question of style of control is central to the question of nurturance in school. When truly faced with it, I suspect most of us find it hard to stomach that coercion is still an enormous component of teaching. I argue that large *relationship load*— the number of relationships we ask students and educators to sustain—is a predominant factor.

No, schools are not *completely* neglectful. Yes, our schools teach important information and skills. Yes, they are a chance for young people to be with and learn from each other. But these benefits come at a great cost when out of balance with adult attention. In this book you will find outrage but also hope. Obviously we *do* care about children, but in the case of schooling we fail to question assumptions that block that care from being apparent to them. By accepting that schools are *a part of* and not *a break from* childrearing, we can restructure them to be closer to what our children (future adults) need.

Mostly this book is practical in outlook, which means I may make compromises with—or departures from—the status quo that rub some readers wrong. Pedro Noguera, a prominent voice for educational equity, calls this kind of approach "pragmatic optimism" (2003, p. xiii). I would prefer, for example, not to have to resort to a supposedly universal human nature, or to resort to a philosophy of "development" to justify why we should meet children's needs *now*, or indeed to resort to a concept of "child" laden with assumptions that it is such a unique category of human being. But those are the frames within which research has been done and within which readers will respond. I would also like to include my worries about whether making the United States a healthier place to grow up might actually enhance the often selfish and harmful impacts of its superpower status in the world, but that would probably weaken my arguments. There are some philosophical compromises I refuse to make, however. Principally, the shift in outlook I am asking readers to consider is to see that schooling consists of relationships built around learning, rather than relationships valued only insofar as they benefit learning. That shift forces us to think outside our hyperindividualism (our philosophy of separation, as I'll call it), to see that we are embedded in a community and that the intentional or unintentional isolation of our children from the influence of nonparental adults is not only futile but also destructive. What it will take to make schools help rather than hurt childrearing is an up-front investment that will return to us with interest in the long run. My proposal is to restructure schools with positive adult attention as their primary goal and academics as their secondary but simultaneous goal.

I have tried to make this book the strongest case ever made for smaller classes, smaller schools, a maximum of continuity of teacher-student relationships, and fewer and deeper school relationships for parents and guardians. All these are aspects of what I'll call either *grouping size* or *relationship load*. The number of kids grouped together for learning purposes necessarily places a certain number of relationships on the educator's job description. Similarly, the number of teachers a student is asked to work with over the years makes for more relationships the student has to start "cold" and *to lose*. Parents and guardians, as well, are confronted with a certain number of relationships at schools that can either foster or impede cooperation and trust between the home and the classroom. I will show that the smaller these numbers, the better for our kids *and* their caregivers.

You'll notice that my arguments feature class and school size reduction—most prominently—and class size more prominently than school size. This is because the elements of relationship load seem to rank themselves in importance in direct proportion to the amount of sacrifice they would require and therefore the amount of resistance they'll face. So you'll notice that my arguments focus least on parent load reduction. This is because it is largely achieved as a by-product of implementing the other three elements. Because of its automatic nature, I could have defensibly left it out as a "mere" effect, but that would reinforce the mind-set that leaves parents out of the equation of schooling and schooling out of the equation of childrearing.

In making my case, I've refrained from promising gains in test scores. I do that *not* because I think humane schools won't get better academic results. I do it because I'm afraid that readers may hold to the mistaken belief that better academic results are the most legitimate reason for humane schools. That is a pervasive and damaging attitude shared by many of our citizens and their policy-makers. Academic achievement, such as we've measured it, has not declined in any overall way, despite myths to the contrary. Nor, as I will attempt to show, do changes in the economy demand better knowledge any more urgently than they demand better childrearing. Knowledge is not in trouble, but nurturance—and therefore our society as a whole—is. Let's ignore the fake crisis. The *real* crisis is that children are getting less-than-adequate adult attention, and it's partly the fault of schools. But schools can be a key to the solution—if relationships come first. Everything that is mature, ethical, compassionate, and responsible in our soon-to-be adults and parents depends on whether and how adults attend to them.

There is some talk in the education literature about the role of schools in mitigating the problem of neglect at home. Few dare suggest schools actually *participate* in the neglect of our children. It's a threatening concept that implies we are all accomplices in a culture-wide cruelty. If an individual did it, we'd prosecute or at least help that person. Since it's all of us, we call it "the way things are," and by implication, the way they have to be or should be. We all care about kids—I don't doubt that. But our school grouping size tells kids otherwise, and what *they* perceive matters more in the end.

Some may say this is all preposterous, perhaps pointing out that "emotional abuse is a pattern of behavior that impairs a child's emotional development or sense of self-worth. This may include constant criticism, threats, or rejection, as well as withholding love, support, or guidance" (Child Welfare Information Gateway 2006). Since schools try their best, they are not "withholding," they're just doing what they can with their resources. People who make this argument rarely acknowledge that we make decisions about how many resources to allocate—budgets are not accidents. From the child's perspective, the distinctions between school personnel and budget-makers and between intention and lack of intention are not significant (Daniel, Wassell, and Gilligan 1999, p. 131).

My proposal is based on both research and experience. On what wisdom have we based the status quo? Science? Tradition? Frugality? The squeaky-wheel principle? Since we are unable to advocate well for ourselves when we are children, it is relatively easy to subordinate childhood needs. But that can change. Admitting what kids really need—what we ourselves, who are now adults, needed—demands a fundamental questioning of relationship load (class size, school size, teacher continuity, and parent load) as a tradition of schooling. Kids need more adults (and adults more) than schools currently provide.

As already implied, I do have an answer to the above question. We've based the status quo on an underlying philosophy of separation. I didn't originally want to make this point because I was afraid it would keep the proposal from appearing down-to-earth and practical. In the end, ironically, it was practicality that forced me to discuss it. In order to make the proposal affordable in the eyes of enough of the public and enough policy-makers, the separation of services for special needs kids and the overspecialization of teachers—both of which come from this philosophy of separation—must change. Schools that have despecialized their teachers and included a greater percentage of children with special needs in mainstream classrooms have often reduced their class sizes by as many as ten students without finding new sources of funding. In other words, not only are despecialization and inclusion a more humane and natural way to educate children, they are also a practical means of reducing the costs and recruitment demands of class size reduction.

The Complete Set

Perhaps the most unique feature of this book is that it calls for the packaging of the four aspects I've grouped under relationship load. Most advocates of relationship-centered schools don't bundle them, or don't with any depth. I will argue that it's not any one piece of relationship load that's the key—it's the whole package. A truly relationship-centered school is one centered on relationships in all their dimensions: day-to-day interactions (class size); less being a stranger, as well as more teacher cooperation (school size); time to reap the rewards (continuity); and trust between school and home (parent load). I'll argue that the assumption that the parts do or should function in isolation is untenable. Ultimately, however, if forced to choose only one of the four aspects, I would choose class size because it tends to ameliorate the drawbacks of implementing changes to the other aspects.

Here are the recommendations I will provide support for over the course of the book:

- Classes of twelve for most students
- Classes of nine for students in areas beset with poverty and racism
- Classes of six for "disabled" or extremely troubled students who cannot be mainstreamed
- Secondary schools of no more than 500 students for most students
- Elementary schools of no more than 300 students
- Secondary schools of no more than 300 students in areas of poverty and racism

In Chapter 5 I will explain the reasoning behind these numbers. With regard to teacher continuity, I will propose elementary teachers stay with the same group for as many years as possible, and I will suggest we eliminate separate intermediate schools. I advocate universal use of the advisory model in schools where students learn from multiple teachers as a principal mechanism for promoting deeper parent-school relationships. (Advisories also benefit students and teachers, of course.) I also advocate full-service schools for impoverished and racially stigmatized communities that would offer parents and other community members a broader spectrum of services to make parenting and growing up a bit easier. I think this plan for relationship load reduction could be implemented within twenty-six years.

Organization of the Book

Nobody wants to be told they don't care about kids. The value of this book is not in its general appeals to demonstrating our concern for kids—I'm sure you've heard them all before. The value of this book lies in a marshaling of the evidence for using relationship load reduction toward that end. I've structured the book to prove in depth all that I've said so far in brief. I will advocate a notion that may seem uncomfortably radical or idealistic at first, but whose basis—that future adults are worth sacrifices on the part of current adults—is as conventional as one can get.

Chapter 1 will sum up the reasons behind the proposal. It summarizes the major arguments of the book by listing eighteen reasons we should reduce grouping size before bothering to do any other tinkering with public schools. It points out, for example, that in every other analogous theater of human interaction, including daycares with school-age children, groups tend to be much smaller than we find in our schools. If schools were considered daycares, they would break the law in most states. It also points out the many ways in which relationship load reduction is already a secret ingredient in other recommendations and "alternatives."

The next three chapters lay the groundwork for the proposal by defining the off-target—and then the on-target—aims of schooling. Chapter 2 clarifies the philosophy of separation that underlies both the imaginary test-score crisis and the real childrearing crisis, then attempts to dispel any lingering doubt about which crisis our schools should be helping to solve. Chapter 3 shows the symbiosis between a focus on relationships and a focus on racial justice. Chapter 4 gives a psychological explanation for why children need both parental and nonparental adult attention.

Getting to the heart of the proposal, Chapter 5 describes the four interconnected aspects of relationship load: class size, school size, teacher continuity, and parent load. It explains how they interact to meet the childhood needs identified in the previous chapter and why specialization and separation assumptions are interlaced with relationship load. I then lay out the reasoning behind my specific recommendations. Chapter 6 offers an in-depth look at relationship load reduction's effect on the teacher-student relationship. It provides particular detail on how teacher attitude and practice will change for the better.

Chapter 7 looks at the arguments most commonly used against relationship load reduction and shows where each one falls short. In Chapter 8, the "too expensive" argument is met with detailed cost projections that will surprise most readers. There you will find that to give our kids almost twice as much of their teacher's time, we'll only have to spend 20 percent more public money on education and only 0.8 percent more of the nation's wealth when all types of taxation are included. But that net increase will diminish in the long run as the costs of the effects of our neglect of children go down, for example, crime. Thus, halving the class size in the United States would cost between $0 and $420 a year for the average taxpayer, depending on how long one is willing to wait for savings to accrue. At worst, that upper figure is *a dollar a day* during the average worker's life between high school and retirement. I will try to show that dismissing the obvious solution as "too expensive" and dealing with the consequences is far more complex an undertaking than we pretend it is.

Chapters 9 and 10 discuss implementation issues not addressed earlier, including a timetable. They cover changes at the school, district, state, and national levels. Lest we forget that government is not the only entity with an impact on (and a responsibility to) the common good, Chapter 11 points out ways the private sector can help solve the nurturance crisis. Chapter 12 returns the focus to the parents and teachers who can turn the potential of smallness into the reality of nurturance.

I searched high and low for it, but a book like this simply hadn't been written yet. I can speak frankly and at length on the issue of relationship load because I've spent over eight years in the grouping size trenches and had my nose in a lot of books about education. The enrollment of the nontraditional public secondary school where I work fluctuates from year to year and as each year goes on. This means I've had an opportunity to teach classes that range from four to forty. And because of the satellite structure of my school, I've also taught at school sites that ranged from four to four hundred. My convictions on the effects of changes in relationship load are not conjectures but firsthand accounts. My arguments are supported by solid research, but at heart they are an expression of the most solid understanding my experience has left me with: School is not an exception to any rule, whether psychological or ethical; school is not separate from but is a part of childrearing—and it should behave as such.

How *Not* to Read This Book

I'm definitely not saying that relationship load reduction is a one-man show. There is clearly no such thing as a teacherless autopilot, but there are things that can make quality teaching easier and students happier and healthier. Doing something first and foremost does not mean doing *only* that thing. Small grouping size in schools is insufficient but necessary to solve the real crisis without bringing down average academic achievement or precluding its more just distribution, but although it's not the only ingredient, it's the most important and most easily fixed ingredient currently missing. And it does not imply that any other ingredients should be removed, such as teacher effort. Any reduction in teacher quality that comes with increasing the number of teachers to cut class size in half will be (a) inherently temporary and (b) counterbalanced by the job's becoming half as difficult. If you're worried about effort, research has indicated that educators tend to work *harder* in smaller schools and smaller classes, not *less* hard, despite the fact that success is easier to attain (Achilles 1999, pp. 38, 111; Jehlen and Kopkowski 2006; Toch 1991, p. 266). With that caveat in mind, let me try to chip away at any skepticism about whether relationship load reduction really should be first on our education reform "to do list."

The Teacher's Attention

1

First and Foremost

There are many good (and bad) ideas for changes in schools; I am convinced relationship load ought to be addressed first and foremost. For some it's a radical argument; for others it's a tired argument, supposedly long since shown to be simplistic. If you're skeptical, please read at least this chapter—I shall try to intrigue you. There are at least eighteen reasons grouping size reduction should be done first and foremost among (but not necessarily instead of) other good suggestions for school change. In Chapter 8 cost projections show that we'll spend 20 percent more on education than we currently do to implement my proposal—that's about 1 percent for each of these reasons. Surely many of them are worth at least a 1 percent spending increase in and of themselves.

Many have observed the fact that most education reforms fail to become widespread. An important reason is that many fixes actually complicate rather than simplify the jobs of educators (Cohen and Scheer 2003; Kennedy 2005; Tye 2000). This research lends credibility to relationship load reduction because it is a simplifying—rather than a complicating—reform in numerous ways.[1] As Deborah Meier, a leading figure of the small schools movement, suggests, we would be wise to reserve the complexity of schooling for the thinking that goes on in classrooms (2000b, p. 187). What follows are eighteen reasons we should reduce grouping size instead of looking for yet another apparently quick and cheap change that actually *increases* the complexity of both educating and growing up.

Eighteen Reasons to Reduce Relationship Load First and Foremost

1. First do no harm.
2. It furthers social justice in education.
3. It brings school into line with other human grouping sizes.
4. It's the simplest, most direct solution to the real nurturance crisis.
5. It has automatic results.
6. It simplifies teaching.
7. It requires little or no change to teacher training (initial or ongoing).
8. It facilitates other positive changes in education.
9. It immunizes kids against the drawbacks of what we can't change.
10. It accommodates local control.
11. It's simple to understand and noncontroversial.
12. It's simple to measure, regulate, and administrate.
13. It's preventative, which is kinder—and cheaper—than cure.
14. The arguments against it are simply wrong.
15. Simple-sounding alternatives to it only *sound* simple.
16. It's already a secret ingredient in many "alternatives."
17. It would prevent future Columbines.
18. It's simply an ethical imperative.

Reason 1
First Do No Harm

Doctors take the oath that they will "first do no harm" before trying to help. Likewise, before we seek to educate, we should vow not to hurt our students in the attempt. I believe the typical current relationship load does harm, in spite of our good intentions.

Reason 2
It Furthers Social Justice in Education

A focus on relationship load reduction does not detract from the fight for educational equity and equal outcomes for poor students and students of color. In Chapter 3 I will demonstrate how the racial achievement gap is due in part to the racial *relationship* gap.

Reason 3
It Brings School in Line with Other Grouping Size Norms

As a context for explaining why school should have small groupings, let's talk about the fact that it's pretty much the only place that doesn't. An opponent of relationship load reduction is in essence arguing that school is an exception to the rule of the negative impact of an insufficiency of adult attention. As we'll see, such opponents must also consider that school groupings are an exception to the rules of group dynamics that researchers have found to apply across groupings of all ages in Western societies. Perhaps most incredibly, schools are exempted from laws that govern how much adult attention children have a right to in daycares.

Daycare and "They *Don't* Care"

State laws regulate grouping sizes and ratios in public and private daycare centers due to compelling psychological research that foregrounds attachment theory and demonstrates the advantages of relationship-based care. One of the criteria used by an association that accredits daycares reads, "Sufficient staff with primary responsibility for children are available to provide frequent personal contact" (National Association for the Education of Young Children 1991, p. 40). Thus the social institution of daycare, imperfect though it often is, is informed not just by nineteenth-century tradition but by twentieth-century science. Daycares are regulated (if not run) with a clear understanding of all the research detailed in Chapter 4 and they have no reason to downplay or deny it. Take for example these two statements included in the Texas regulations:

> Research indicates direct, warm, social interactions between adults and children are more likely to occur with lower child/care giver ratios. According to the AAP, care givers must be recognized as performing a job for groups of children that parents would rarely be considered capable of handling alone. (Texas Department of Family and Protective Service 2006, p. 51)
>
> Research has shown that when care givers have fewer children to supervise and the group size is limited it reduces the likelihood of injuries and illness in children and increases opportunities for positive interaction with children. Excessive numbers of young children increase the danger of high care giver stress and loss of control. (p. 52)

TABLE 1.1   STATE CHILDCARE REGULATIONS IN 2006

AGE:	NUMBER OF CHILDREN PER ADULT					MAXIMUM GROUP SIZE				
	5	6	7	8	10+	5	6	7	8	10+
Mean	15.4	17.3	17.5	17.5	17.4	26.9	30.5	30.8	30.9	31.5
Median	15	15.5	16	16	16	28	30	30	30	30
Mode	15	15	15	15	15	30	30	30	30	30
States not regulating	0	0	0	0	0	17	21	21	21	21
24 with aide violates	7	2	2	2	1	0	0	0	0	0
24 with aide reaches	14	3	3	2	1	13	5	5	4	2
24 without aide violates	47	44	44	44	43	9	4	4	4	2

Source: LeMoine and Azer 2006.

Children who attend school often go to daycare during the afternoon as their parents finish work. And yet daycare grouping size for school-age children is limited by law to levels far below the classes where they have spent the rest of the day. Table 1.1 compiles state childcare regulations for school-age children.

From a cursory examination, it appears that about half of states do not lift ratio or group size rules at any time before the age of majority. Thus, the "10+" category often applies up to age seventeen. An average U.S. class of twenty-four students would violate the group size limits for ten-year-olds in only two states (plus Washington, DC), but without an aide it would violate the adult/child ratio law *in every state but eight*. Even with an aide it violates the law in Connecticut and is within two children of violating it in three other states. Incidentally, only every fourth or fifth U.S. classroom has an aide at any one time (Digest 2005, table 80).

Let's take the example of the youngest schoolchildren. The most recent national kindergarten data indicate that the average U.S. kindergarten had 17.5 students in 2003–2004.[2] The average kindergarten nationwide in 1993 was four students higher at 21.5; that same year, 61 percent of kindergarten classrooms had an aide for an average of 64 percent of the day (NCES 1993, section 5), which comes out to a 39 percent chance at any one time. Table 1.2 gives a picture of how kindergarten would fare legally if regulated like a daycare.

Texas public schools had kindergartens averaging 19.3 in 2005–2006 (Dallas Indicators 2007), and New York City's averaged 20.9 in 2003–2004 (Sweeting 2004). New York actually has the lowest daycare limit at nine five-year-olds per adult. That means that even with an aide, and even with only nineteen students, New York kindergartens would be illegal if they were considered daycares.

Public schools also teach preschool, serving 4 percent of U.S. three-year-olds and 14 percent of four-year-olds; the class sizes in public preschools

TABLE 1.2   NUMBER OF STATES (PLUS WASHINGTON, DC) WHERE
KINDERGARTEN CLASS SIZE EXCEEDED DAYCARE REGULATIONS

	2003 U.S. AVERAGE OF 17.5		1993 U.S. AVERAGE OF 21.5	
	AGE 5	AGE 6	AGE 5	AGE 6
Ratio limit without aide (61% of cases)	37	28	46	43
Ratio limit with aide	0	0	7	2
Group size limit	0	0	9	4

Source: LeMoine and Azer 2006.

TABLE 1.3   RECOMMENDATIONS OF THE NATIONAL RESOURCE CENTER FOR
HEALTH AND SAFETY IN CHILD CARE AND EARLY EDUCATION

AGE	CHILD/STAFF RATIO	STATES COMPLYING	MAXIMUM GROUP SIZE	STATES COMPLYING
5	8:1	0	16	0
6–8	10:1	2	20	4
9–12	12:1	1	24	2

Source: Fiene 2002; LeMoine and Azer 2006.

range from thirteen to fifteen, and aides appear not to be common (NCES 2003a). Though the class size finally drops for this group, the regulations drop also, making for more of the same. What's more, many consider current daycare regulations still too high. For example, one organization makes the recommendations in Table 1.3 for school-age children.

The discrepancy between daycare regulations and public school class sizes is a glaring double standard. In and of itself, this gap should be enough to prove that current school relationship load is ethically untenable. The double standard is heightened by the fact that schools are expected to accomplish even more with the fewer adults per child that they are allocated, that is, to prioritize learning over play. A prime example of the tacit acceptance of the double standard is found in Faye Steuer's *The Psychological Development of Children*. Steuer makes several recommendations for childcare facilities about how they might better foster child development. She writes, "We saw that class size appears to be an important sign of preschool quality. We might, then, expect it to be similarly important in the education of older children" (1994, p. 642). It appears she is prepared to apply a similar child development standard to schools. Instead, she changes direction:

> Educators, meanwhile, must make decisions about class size in the
> absence of total certainty about its *practical importance*. The argument

for smaller class size is intuitively appealing and has empirical support, but not everyone has yet been convinced of its merit. (p. 642,
emphasis mine)

This belies the mistaken philosophy that education is a practical affair, not a
part of childrearing.

Small groups and ratios are common sense for parents choosing daycares,
and common sense is right this time. Daycare researchers Alison Clarke-
Stewart, Christian Gruber, and Linda May Fitzgerald offer a good summary
of what's at stake:

> In day-care classes with more children per caregiver, it has been found
> that each child experienced less interaction with the teacher and the
> interaction was of lower quality than in classes with fewer children
> per caregiver; the classroom climate was less likely to be facilitative of
> social stimulation, positive in affect, or responsive to the child's needs,
> and was more likely to be restrictive and negative in tone. . . . In day-
> care programs with more children in a class, children have been
> found to be less cooperative, less talkative, and more hostile with their
> peers; their play was less complex; they had more conflicts, and spent
> more time in aimless activity. . . . Significant associations showing the
> detrimental effect of low adult-child ratios and high class sizes for
> children's behavior and development have been found in a substantial
> number of studies [twelve cited]. (1994, pp. 13–14)

I will argue in Chapter 6 that similar ratio and group size effects occur in
schools. They get no special exemption from human needs. By following the
recommendations in this book and placing school traditions under the same
scientific and ethical scrutiny as daycares have received, society can correct
this glaring oversight.

Other Groupings of Children
Ted Sizer, well-known school reform advocate and founder of the Coalition
of Essential Schools, points out the unlikelihood that anyone would ever group
kids as they're grouped in schools anywhere but in schools:

> Few parents want to spend, or can even rationally contemplate spend-
> ing, a full day all alone penned up in one room with twenty-seven
> twelve-year-olds, day after day. Indeed, the idea would reduce them
> to incredulous laughter. Most parents shrink at the prospect of run-
> ning a two-hour-long birthday party for a dozen twelve-year-olds. . . .

Most parents would gag at the prospect of asking those kids to do some serious sustained work rather than just have fun. (1996, p. 80)

My experience with destinations in the community that welcome school field trips is that they require the adult/child ratio to far exceed the norm in schools. These places aren't dumb; they're not going to let a class come with just their teacher—that's not enough adults! Here are some examples of places in my city where children often go in groups:

- Hogle Zoo did require a 1:10 adult/child ratio, but it is 1:5 as of July 2006.
- The Utah Museum of Natural History requires a 1:8 ratio.
- The Children's Museum of Utah requires a 1:5 ratio.

Scouting troops have guidelines that require adult/child ratios of anywhere from 1:3 to 1:8 (Boy Scouts of America 2004). Summer camps advertise similar ratios, sometimes allowing up to 1:10; the American Camping Association recommends summer camps have ratios between 1:6 for seven-year-olds and 1:12 for seventeen-year-olds (Safer Child 2008). State regulations tend to coincide with these numbers.

These activities are more consistently enjoyable for kids than school is. As Sizer suggests above, school is the only grouping of children not meant mainly for fun but for work, heightening the bitter irony of school grouping size. In Chapter 4 I'll argue that a child's need for adult attention rises during work as compared to play. Schools are structured as though we believed the inverse.

Adult Work Environments

Curiously, though frugality is the excuse given for our neglectfully large school groupings, organizations of adults that are more justifiably organized on the basis of monetary efficiency employ much smaller management groupings. Similar to what was noted above with daycares, formal discussion of the human limitations of management arose after the traditions of schooling were already firmly in place:

The concept of span of control was developed in the United Kingdom in 1922 by Sir Ian Hamilton. It arose from the assumption that managers have finite amounts of time, energy, and attention to devote to their jobs. In studies of British military leaders, Hamilton found that they could not effectively control more than three to six people directly. (Reference for Business 2008)

David Berliner and Bruce Biddle observe that the average number of workers per supervisor in representative industries in the early 1990s was just over seven workers per supervisor. "In contrast, education has *twice* that rate— 14.5 employees per supervisor or administrator" (1995, pp. 79–80). Though different industries vary, none come close to the average school class size of twenty-four:

> Historically, management effectiveness experts have recommended that individual managers should have no more than seven or eight people reporting directly to them. However, recent studies . . . show that the actual number varies considerably—by industry, company size, and type of work being done. The *Saratoga Institute Workforce Diagnostic System Benchmarking Reports 2001* found a median management ratio of one to 16 in the healthcare sector, but only one to four in the information services [sector]. (Davison 2003)

Charles Achilles, a class size researcher to whose work I am greatly indebted, points out in *Let's Put Kids First, Finally* the ludicrousness of the fact that these limits are recommended for adult employees who presumably have fewer emotional needs (1999, p. 130). Let's now turn to adult education.

Adult Learning Environments
It appears the average class size for community colleges across the United States in the mid- to late 1990s was twenty-one (Kwiatkowski 2002). Anecdotally, Salt Lake Community College plugs itself on my local public radio station by touting its average class size of twenty. Chatman (1996) found that the mean class size for postsecondary institutions overall was twenty-eight, and that the median was twenty-five (p. 7). Students at these schools are adults who presumably do not have as much need as children do for attention from their teachers, and yet their classes (which are highly subsidized with taxpayer dollars) are comparable to or smaller than most children's. Certainly these adults deserve small classes, but children deserve them more.

Although universities and colleges often do have large classes, they are not unaware of the value of small grouping size. Harold Howe, commissioner of education under Lyndon Johnson, writes,

> There is nothing novel about this strategy of restructuring organizations to create more intimacy. It was adopted by both Harvard and Yale universities in their undergraduate colleges seventy-five years ago, and it has spread to many other large institutions, both public and private. (1993, pp. 124–125)

As another local anecdote, this week's "help wanted" section of the local weekly in my city had four ads for training schools. Two of them listed small classes as a selling point. That advertising space—not to mention the small classes themselves—costs real money. The appeal of the teacher's attention must be worth that money. Students—regardless of age—see small classes as more likely to meet their needs.

Even the enrollments of postsecondary schools can be overstated relative to K–12 schools. Public colleges tend to be much larger than private, but taken together, the spectrum isn't a whole lot larger than U.S. high schools are. Of higher-ed institutions, 21.5 percent are between 1,000 and 2,500 students, but there are more schools that are smaller than this group (40.1 percent) than larger (38.4 percent) (Digest 2006, table 218).

Lower-Tech Learning Environments

Another way in which relationship load reduction is a simple solution is that it returns toward the forms of teaching used by ancestral societies and less politically complex contemporary societies. Before industrialization and schools came along, most children learned (and they still do learn in many parts of the world) by being surrounded by experts who model(ed) the important skills of the society on a daily basis. Schools invert an arguably more natural ratio of experts to novices, concentrating the novices in one place and surrounding them with only a few experts who must very deliberately teach society's now more hidden skills. Meier writes, "The way children best learn the complex skills and dispositions of adulthood is through keeping real company with the kinds of experts they hope to become. . . . The amazing thing is that we no longer trust these ways of learning" (2002, p. 16). Any reduction in grouping size will get us closer to the "natural" ratio of many adult experts surrounding a few child novices.

Thus, it's ironic that I speak of school relationship load as a tradition. Schooling has replaced the infinitely more rooted tradition of children learning by being in the company of adults, the practice of all human societies until very recently. Meier writes, "Since the schools we have today are a relatively new invention, and in fact the ways I'm proposing come from an older tradition, I believe we can reinvent schools to better conform to what we know about teaching and learning" (2002, p. 23). The grouping size aspect of our educational system, she writes elsewhere, is not "the inevitable product of our human nature" but "particularly in conflict with our humanity and everything we know about the rearing of the young" (2000b, p. 187).

Research into both past and current preindustrial societies supports Meier's contentions. Historian Peter Laslett found that prior to England's industrial revolution (the world's first) few persons "found themselves in groups larger than family groups, and there were not many families of more than a dozen members" (1984, p. 7). John Paul Scott writes,

> Anthropologists often refer to a set of "magic numbers" among human and primate groups. For example, 25 seems to be the average number of individuals in a gatherer-hunter band or a troop of primates, and 500 seems to be the ultimate size of a coordinated group such as a tribe. It is possible that 500 approaches the maximum number of individuals with whom recognition and some degree of familiarity is possible. (1981, p. 221)

Over 40 percent of our schools are larger than 500 (Digest 2006, table 91).

And what about the even deeper "traditions" mentioned by Scott of our evolutionary relatives, the other primates? Although primate groups max out at just above our current average class size of twenty-four, many more than one or two of those twenty-five monkeys are adults (Plutchik 1981, p. 135). No wonder kids monkey around in large schools and classes—we dedicate fewer resources to offspring care than even monkeys do!

Social Groups

Even in our postindustrial society, people tend to gather in groups far smaller than twenty-four. A. Paul Hare and colleagues give a good summary of group dynamics research:

> In field research that replicates early finding concerning the size of "natural groups," that is, casual work or play groups, most natural groups consist of only two or three members. However natural groups of children and adolescents are usually larger than those of adults, and larger for adult women compared with adult men. In free-forming groups, as in a conversation lounge, individuals are more likely to leave a group as group size increases. The optimum group size for many group discussion tasks is five members. As size increases individuals become less [ethically] self-conscious, there is less intermember interaction, and less satisfaction, members use less effort, with lower performance, with less cooperation, and more conforming behavior when judging an ambiguous stimulus. In larger groups, only a few members may actually take part in decision making and there will be more subgroups and cliques. (Hare, Blumberg, Davies, and Kent 1994, p. 147, citations omitted for readability)

Echoing a common theme of this book, Hare attests to the stark fact of the decrease in relationship quality as group size increases. Elsewhere he suggests six to seven as a normal maximum for social groups (1976, p. 217). In agreement with Hare's age distinctions, Clark points to higher numbers for adolescents, but we're talking ten, not twenty-four (2004, p. 79). Others have observed an upper size limit of twenty for informal groups in extreme cases (Robinson 1984, p. 117).

Group Therapy

Research into the optimal size of psychological therapy groups has yielded the number eight (Plutchik 1981, p. 143). Echoing the larger adolescent social groups above, some have put forth nine as the ideal for teen support groups (Vorrath and Brendtro 1974, pp. 58–59). These sizes harness the potential for complex interaction without sacrificing the individual's need to participate and be heard. Physical therapy appears to be similar. Research recommendations vary from three to twelve as a maximum per therapist (Gelsomino Kirkpatrick, Hess, and Gahimer 2000).

Incarceration

If schools don't resemble these other *positive* groupings, do they more closely resemble a prison, where enjoyment or getting things done is simply not at issue? "Ireland has the highest ratio of prison officers to prisoners in the world, a little over one-to-one," whereas the European Union on average has a ratio of about three to one (Coulter 2005). The U.S. Bureau of Prisons reports an average ratio of one guard employed to ten prisoners imprisoned in minimum-security prisons; in maximum security it's one to five (Camp and Gaes 2002). This is how such ratios are reported, but not all those guards are on duty at any one time, of course. Accounting for this we get actual on-duty numbers close to 1:42 for minimum security and 1:21 for maximum security. These numbers sound closer to K–12 class sizes.

But what about when prisoners go to class? A well-known critic of racial inequalities in schools, Jonathan Kozol (2000), observes that class size at New York City's Rikers Island jail and prison is "on average, twelve to fifteen students, as it is at schools like Groton and St. Paul's," expensive private schools, "but half of what it is in almost any elementary school in the South Bronx" (p. 130). If the children of the wealthy deserve small groups, if even prisoners deserve them, why doesn't every child?

Et Cetera

Meier urges us to "keep in mind that despite the cost we almost never try to teach anyone how to drive except one-on-one" (2002, p. 17). There are countless more examples of things that are simply too important to be done en masse. Certainly the vast majority of us do in fact consider schooling (and its contribution to our kids' quality of life) to be one of society's most important tasks. But just as certainly, one does not get that impression from a comparison of the numbers.

Reason 4
The Simplest Solution to the True Problem

In Chapter 2 I will explain more about why we need to get the crisis right. Meier describes it this way: "An even greater crisis than declining academic achievement—about which there is no [or] little real evidence—is a decline in the quality and quantity of long-term and stable personal relationships" (2000a, p. 33). Once one acknowledges the academic crisis as fake and the nurturance crisis as real, the solution of grouping size reduction takes on a crystal-clear simplicity. Our kids are lacking adult attention and nurturance because of postindustrial societal changes, but they're spending more than six hours a day with adults who also can't give them enough attention because of grouping size. It's simple: reduce grouping size. Teachers are clearly the most influential nonfamily adults already on the childrearing team (Deiro 2005, pp. 6–7). Since we already have an institution set up to care for our kids during a significant chunk of their waking lives, there is no need to create a new institution or perform any pie-in-the-sky miracles like reversing social and economic trends.[3] That also makes it the cheapest solution.

Using teachers as the missing attachment figures is the simplest of all possible sources of adults for such a purpose. An increase in the number of teachers is simpler to oversee and measure the effectiveness of than nonteacher mentoring systems such as those suggested by full-service school advocate Joy Dryfoos, who writes, "We have strong evidence that when children are attached to *well-trained and supervised* mentors, case managers, older peer tutors, their achievement and attendance levels improve" (1998, p. 201, italics mine). The training and supervising Dryfoos alludes to is where the rub lies—more complexity for educators. Furthermore, how would a third party verify whether such programs were operating in more than just name? A mentoring institution established outside the schools wouldn't complicate the jobs of educators, but it would compete for funds and would probably never reach as many children.

Nonteacher mentor proposals are worthy, but they make more sense as additions rather than alternatives to relationship load reduction. As I'll detail in Chapter 4, children would prefer to have attachment relationships with the most familiar and most powerful adults already in their lives rather than be given patching-up time with still other adults later in the day. In such a system, children would persist in getting their needs ignored in class, weakening the effect of external mentors.

Reason 5
Automatic Results

Perhaps the greatest benefit of relationship load reduction in terms of the nurturance crisis is that its benefits begin to accrue immediately for the student in the absence of any qualitative change in the teacher's method. Evidence from daycare research is particularly illustrative as to whether smallness acts as a catalyst to other developmentally positive indicators. One study notes, "Caregivers were rated as providing more positive caregiving when group sizes and child:adult ratios were smaller" (National Institute of Child Health and Human Development 1996). Another study finds, "Smaller group sizes and lower staff/child ratios have been found to be strong predictors of compliance with indicators of quality such as positive interactions among staff and children and developmentally appropriate curriculum" (National Association for the Education of Young Children 1991, p. 41).

Many have used the argument that because teachers don't automatically change method, smaller classes and schools do not have significant effects (for example, Swidler 2004, p. 115). This is a ruse, and a widespread one. What teachers do doesn't have to be different to be good for kids—it simply needs to be more plentiful. Higher-*quality* care will follow higher-*quantity* care. This is definitely true for nurturance effects and many argue that it's true for academic effects as well. "Observers have confirmed that in small classes teachers do more of what they already know to do" rather than magical new methods (Achilles 1999, p. 52). And yet there is a kind of difference inherent in *more*. Evertson and Folder write,

> There are predictable differences in class processes that follow simply from the numbers: students are more visible; each student is more likely to get a turn more often during class lessons; students don't have to wait as long for help; students initiate more contacts with teachers. (via Achilles 1999, p. 65)

This is what I'll call the "more of the same for each" phenomenon.

All other factors being equal, smaller classes are *in and of themselves* better for children—with no ifs or buts attached. Enough real-crisis results to make relationship load reduction well worth the money can be relied upon to come automatically. In contrast, if grouping size reduction is paid for on fake-crisis promises, there may be disappointment. Achilles concedes that it is possible to implement grouping size reduction poorly enough to lose its academic benefits, that is, to show little or no test-score gain (1999, p. ix). Again, though, the worst-case scenario is a *lack of improvement* in test scores after class size reduction; not even its staunchest opponents threaten *worse* academic results.

Reason 6
Good Teaching Is Easier

The nurturance crisis will automatically get better after relationship load reduction. That said, the benefits of grouping size reduction will *further* accrue and become *more* powerful if and when teachers qualitatively change their behavior and methods for the better, a change far more likely to occur *after* smallness arrives (Anderson 2002, p. 59). Staff development could be one source of enhancement, but research has suggested that in-service training did not show results that equaled the magnitude of the class size effect itself (Achilles 1999, p. 119).

Let me reiterate that small relationship load is not a teaching autopilot. I don't propose small groupings as a replacement for hard work and wisdom on the part of educators. I propose it as a climate that will allow the same amount of work and wisdom to bear more fruit. Sizer writes, "Of course, smallness is just the beginning, but it is a necessary precondition" (1996, p. 91). In this way, grouping size reduction is also a solution to the teacher quality "problem." Things will be better for kids no matter which end of the quality spectrum teachers are on: It will be easier to become excellent at teaching, and averageness or even mediocrity will be less damaging to kids. British researcher Peter Blatchford writes, "Small classes will not necessarily make a bad teacher better, but small classes seem likely to make it easier for teachers to be effective. . . . Conversely large classes inevitably present teachers with difficulties and the need for compromises" (2003, p. 150).

Those who argue that size is tangential to quality teaching fail to account for the ample evidence that better teaching has been found to flow automatically from (in the case of more of the same for each) or be made easier by (in the case of new methods) grouping size reduction and its various effects on teachers and students—without any miraculous change to teacher effort or skill. Lindbloom found that in smaller classes the following took place more often:

1. Frequent individualized instruction was geared to the needs and interests of students.
2. In addition to the textbooks, teachers used a wider variety of educational materials to enrich teaching.
3. Increased interaction occurred among pupils and between teachers and pupils.

4. Teachers made greater use of innovative or new materials and methods.
5. There was more student self-control and discipline with less teacher domination.
6. There was more small-group work than in larger classes.
7. Improved human relations occurred among students and with the teacher.
8. A greater number of instructional activities were used frequently.
9. Fewer discipline problems were observed.
10. There was improved morale among teachers (paraphrased by Achilles 1999, p. 115).

That's a lot of bang for a few bucks.

Reason 7
Little or No Additional Training

To solidify the points made above, training is not necessary to achieve benefits from class size reduction. "In the many class-size studies that have already demonstrated measurable student benefits," writes Achilles, "teachers in small classes did not have specific staff development . . . yet students achieved more, and behaved better" (1999, p. 112). Staff development is not essential, but it can enhance the academic effects of grouping size reduction. Does this mean that retraining teachers to take full advantage of smallness will increase the cost of relationship load reduction? No. The ongoing training teachers are already exposed to will suffice. In fact, it will become more cost-effective (and simply effective) because smaller classes and schools will make it easier and less intimidating for teachers to reflect on and improve their practice. As class size researcher Jeremy Finn argues, it will give them "opportunities to relearn strategies that may have been lost in years of teaching larger classes" (2002, p. 219).

Considering that I advocate inclusion of special education students to the greatest extent possible and the despecialization of teachers, training issues will arise. Again, though, these needs for training are not far beyond our current level of ongoing training. Teaching nonresource teachers how to meet the specific needs of their one or two mainstreamed students would be an obvious choice for training (Achilles 1999, p. 113). Another strategy would be partnerships with local colleges to endorse committed teachers in extra (and hard-to-fill) subjects so that small schools can be more flexible in their course offerings and assured of their teacher expertise (see Chapter 10).

In sum, staff development should be an attempt to perfect one's skills at a doable job, not an attempt to stave off failure at a nearly impossible job. Training that aims to minimize the negative effects of large relationship load becomes yet another hidden cost of this "cost-saving" strategy.

Reason 8
Facilitation of Other Positive Changes

Relationship load reduction is a good first step to other changes because it makes them easier to implement. On the other hand, it's also a good place to have stopped just in case no other major changes ever happen. Obviously, it would be nice to resolve a lot of other issues in education; but in case we don't, at least we'll have done the most critical thing we could have *first*. Again, grouping size reduction doesn't *cause* other changes, but it *facilitates* them. As already discussed, small relationship load allows for the implementation of new methods at the classroom level, but wider-scale changes get easier as well. Bryk and Scheider write, "a substantial body of research now documents the positive impact of small school size on . . . the effectiveness of school change efforts" (2002, p. 97).

As we'll return to below, there is nothing inherent in grouping size reduction that obligates us to prescribe particular changes to local decision-makers beyond basic legal and ethical standards. Communities, schools, districts, and states can use the facilitating benefits of smallness to fit their particular circumstances.

Of course, I have my own list of hopes for change I would like to see smallness facilitate beyond the racial equality concerns already mentioned. They all go along with increasing a child's ability to find the nurturance they need in our communities. One is the outlawing of corporal punishment in schools, which is currently illegal in only twenty-nine states (Center for Effective Discipline 2008). Less apparent need for teacher control through smaller grouping size will certainly melt some of this ice-age thinking.

Another change would be to reduce the various forms of quasi-apartheid for the "not up to snuff" still practiced in schools: grade retention, expulsion, exclusionary special education and other targeted services, and long-term ability tracking. These are all outgrowths of an underlying philosophy of separation (see Chapter 2) whose benefits seem to outweigh their often race-based injustices only in the context of large grouping size. One case study of a school that virtually eliminated the "pull-out" teacher model reads,

A change in the delivery of academic services from a pull-out approach to an integrated services model was the innovation implemented at Farnham. It was devised to reduce the interruptions to the flow of the regular classroom day as well as address the issue of de facto segregation for students with special needs. (Odden, Archibald, and Tychsen 1999, pp. 27–28)

As I'll show further along, the mutual benefit of increasing inclusion and decreasing specialization is also a cost savings in implementing small classes for all. Thus, *smallness and inclusion facilitate one another*—this is why it makes sense to package them. Ending grade retention in particular will save a huge sum of money, approximately 22 percent of the cost of this proposal. More savings in social costs are probable considering the link between grade retention and dropping out.

A last change would be to help areas of concentrated poverty and racial stigmatization by integrating more services into neighborhood schools, what many term "full-service" schools (Dryfoos 1994). Caring for the kids *and their context* will doubly protect them (Noguera 2003, p. ix). Although it would certainly be dangerous to trust that schools can be expected to counteract the effects of racism and poverty all by themselves, it would be foolhardy to not maximize the opportunity schools present. Suggested additions to school services have included the following:

- Preschool, daycare, and before- and after-school care (employing community adults)
- Health care
- Empowerment, employment, and career help for community adults
- First-time parent skill-building
- Community center and multigenerational gathering place
- Community upkeep/beautification programs

Local decision-makers could employ whatever combination of these is needed in their community. In fact, these full-service schools can be thought of as a part of the parent or guardian aspect of relationship load reduction: By concentrating neighborhood services in one place, full-service schools would also function to reduce the number of relationships parents have to navigate within the various institutions that assist with childrearing and community life, making parenting that much easier. I believe the private sector could be asked to cover most of the investment in such projects.

Reason 9
Immunizing Kids against the Drawbacks of What Doesn't Change

As a counterpart to the previous reason, where good changes get easier, relationship load reduction would also help render bad changes it can't prevent (and bad traditions it can't unseat) less harmful. Let's be honest: Even after grouping size reduction is in place, some tinkering with public education will continue to hurt kids. The recent standardized testing movement is a prime example; there's reason to believe that it might get even more draconian than it's gotten so far, and, unfortunately, grouping size reduction may be no direct impediment to it. But the extra adult support of relationship load reduction could cushion the blows of such policies.

Many have railed against bureaucracy as the chief problem in our schools. In the next section I'll show that relationship load reduction accommodates decentralized control. Any aspects of bureaucratic impersonalization that grouping size reduction doesn't fix directly it can protect kids from through increased adult attention. As I'll show in detail in Chapter 4, we do not need to prevent all negative feelings in children to make them happy adults, but we do need to help them process their negative feelings by giving them our attention.

Reason 10
It Accommodates Local Variation and Control

My argument does not prescribe precisely how educators should structure their smaller schools and classes—relationship load reduction does not invite the drawbacks of top-down decision-making. Barbara Tye (2000) observes that despite the failure of many large-scale reforms "it in fact does appear that reform efforts at the unique personality level are alive and well" (p. 159). The reason, she argues, "is simply a matter of size" (p. 158). This suggests a large-scale, top-down relationship load reform would be of a different type, one that is not in conflict with the localized uses of the new smallness. Jacqueline Ancess argues that a key mistake in trying to accelerate the trend toward small, caring high schools is the faulty assumption that what we need are exact copies of existing successful schools rather than copies of the autonomous conditions that allowed these schools to figure out how to succeed with the educators, students, and communities particular to them (2003, p. 137).

Rather than prescribe one program of behaviors for educators and students to follow, relationship load reduction empowers all educators—not just the extraordinary—to make their schools and classes attentive and effective no matter what the method or style. Certainly there are poor approaches, but these will be easier to weed out once relationship load is smaller. In the panic large schools and classes create around classroom management, administrators have a low standard of quality as well: A teacher or principal who can keep the chaos at bay is a satisfactory one. In a climate without chaos, quality will grow unhindered, and lack of quality will be far more rare—it will stick out like a sore thumb.

Moreover, local control is in harmony with enhancing the nurturance aspect of schooling because it helps with creating strong attachment figures who the students can see are trusted with major decisions (Meier 2000c, pp. 19–20). One caveat deserves attention here: Local control should never extend to a tyranny of the majority that excludes or stigmatizes people. Any local decisions are subject to the equity concerns discussed in Chapter 3. Similarly, local control should not be used as cover for avoiding responsibility for "other people's children," for instance, by letting districts with fewer resources sink while others swim.

Reason 11
Noncontroversial and Nontechnical

The controversy about the issue of grouping size is likely to center on cost and teacher recruitment, as opposed to major shifts in attitude. There will be those who trump up its cost or ignore its savings in an attempt to defeat it, but that will only work if they succeed in convincing the public that it should be compared with other proposals that are purely academic in their goals. Getting the crisis right will guarantee people are not disappointed that test score gains are not proportionate to dollars spent.

I believe the willingness of the American public to embrace the sacrifices necessary for fixing the nurturance crisis has been far underestimated. Karen Hawley Miles (2000) writes, "Reducing class size is a politically popular remedy to improve student achievement." Kirk Johnson (2000) reports, "70 percent of adults believe that reducing class size would lead to significant academic improvements in public schools." The implication, of course, is that they're also willing to pay for it. Imagine the level of support once it's explained in a high-profile and consistent way that small classes will have a greater and more guaranteed impact on things people find even more important than academic achievement!

A revealing example is when Doug Harris and David Plank (2006), who are convinced that raising teaching salaries would be a cheaper means of achieving academic gains, speculate on why their strategy is less popular with the public:

One possible explanation is that class-size reductions have a much more immediate and identifiable impact on student performance. Teachers like class-size reduction because it has demonstrable effects on student achievement and allows them to focus more closely on each of their students. *Parents like the reductions because they want their kids to have personal attention.* This puts a great deal of pressure on school leaders to reduce class sizes, even if it is not the most cost-effective use of resources. In contrast, *changes in teacher quality are hard to observe*, and they might affect student achievement only over an extended period of time. Teachers might appreciate the importance of higher salaries, but making the case to parents and taxpayers is harder. Hiring fewer teachers and paying them more in order to raise teacher quality simply *lacks the intuitive political appeal* of hiring more teachers and reducing class size. (emphasis mine)

Perhaps smaller classes are more popular and intuitive because we know that children need and deserve more than just higher test scores—even if we rarely say so in discussions of schooling. Our neighbors to the north appear to agree with the American public:

In each of five National Issues in Education polls . . . between 1997 and 2004, Canadians cited class size reduction as the most pressing educational spending priority. In the October 2004 poll, some 76 percent of those surveyed said that public school classes are too large. (Guillemette 2005)

Yet again, these data are cited within a critique of class size reduction as too expensive for the likely test-score gain. The message: "Seventy-six percent of people are alarmingly unaware that test scores are the only part of a child's life worth spending money on."

A related reason grouping size reduction is politically feasible is that it's easy for the layperson to grasp. Although there is plenty of need for academics to discuss grouping size reduction, there is no need for jargon and lingo when telling the public about it. In sum, since grouping size reduction has popular appeal and is easy to talk about, I see no reason why it wouldn't bring electoral success to politicians who will dare to advocate that we put kids first by putting up the bucks.

Reason 12
Simple Measurement, Regulation,
and Administration

No matter what level of government mandates and enforces the rules (if rules are needed), no new structures or staff will be needed because it's a simple act of counting. Even opponents of class size reduction tend to grant this (e.g., Franciosi 2004, p. 193). The administration of schools also becomes easier with a decrease in grouping size (Littky 2004, p. 69) and not always more expensive: The 2003 report by the Commission on Business Efficiency of the Public Schools that studied New Jersey public schools concluded, "This shift in difference in cost when compared to the difference in achievement may indicate that the most efficient high school size is somewhere near or below 500 pupils" (p. xi). I will show evidence in Chapter 5 that the perception that large schools are cheaper is in large part due to their tendency to have larger class sizes.

Reason 13
Prevention Is Kinder—and Cheaper—Than Cure

The key to the monetary savings of giving attention to kids is that it minimizes the number of unhappy or antisocial members of society. Fisher observes that current social services cannot patch enough people up sufficiently, and that

> when treatment and other forms of intervention fail, the sequelae of child antisocial behavior are evident in the growing prison population, in the number of uneducated and unemployed individuals dependent on public assistance, in the increasing number of children in the child welfare system because of abuse and neglect, and in the overcrowded homeless shelters and substance abuse treatment programs nationwide. (2003, p. 6)

How much money is tied up in that one short list? By providing more attention, schools can clearly have an impact on such socially burdensome behaviors (Walberg and Biglan 2003, p. 164). The likelihood of more equal educational outcomes will be another source of savings. Linda Darling-Hammond, a well-known advocate of improving teacher training, writes,

> The savings would include the several billion dollars now wasted because of high teacher turnover as well as the costs of grade retention,

summer schools, and remedial programs required because too many children are poorly taught. This is to say nothing of the broken lives and broader societal burdens. (2006, p. 341)

Darling-Hammond sees these savings coming from better-trained teachers. I see them coming from a teaching situation that is easier to train people for. In Chapter 8 we'll return to social costs when we try to quantify the savings inherent in grouping size reduction.

Reason 14
The Arguments against It Are Simply Wrong

The principal argument used against grouping size—and particularly class size—is cost. It soon becomes ridiculous when subjected to any semblance of consideration. First, as alluded to above, class size reduction is one of the things wealthy districts and schools tend to spend their extra money on, suggesting that it is not seen as "too expensive" when discretionary funds are available. Kozol writes, "In richer neighborhoods, the parents of the students frequently raise money independently to purchase books or even hire extra teachers to reduce the class size for their children" (2000, p. 174). He adds,

> Suburban schools get worried when a second grade has more than 21 bodies in one class; people who send their children to expensive private elementary schools in New York City and New England grow concerned if class size rises much above 16 or 17. But Damian's class has 31. . . . This is not unusual in elementary schools in inner-city sections of New York. There are classes in the city that begin the year with 40, even 45 or 50. I've also been in classes in the Bronx that don't have classrooms of their own but share a large and noisy space with several other classes, maybe 80, 90 children in one room. (p. 215)

This is not a new trend. In the days of official (rather than de facto) segregation, black schools had larger classes than white schools. Educational historian Larry Cuban reports that in 1947, schools in Washington, DC, had average class sizes of thirty-nine for black kids but only thirty-two for white (1984, p. 87). In other words, class size reduction has never been "too expensive" for high-status children.

Second, the "too expensive" argument lies about the true costs of large grouping size and the savings to be gained in reducing it. Chapter 8 will detail these projections and will go on to show that even this so-called extra amount will in all probability pay for itself over time because well-nurtured children will be more productive and less tax burdensome once they become working adults. This is where ethics and practicality meet. Put simply, we're already spending the "extra" money—we're just not spending it on prevention. Chapter 7 will detail the flaws in the other major counterarguments.

Reason 15
Simple-Sounding Alternatives Are Either More Complicated or Simply Pipe Dreams

Unfortunately, there are many opponents of small grouping size (and public education in general, in many cases) who use deceptive forms of simplicity to argue their case. Here are a few principal examples, all of which attempt to provoke emotional reactions that conspicuously do not include nurturing.

Pseudosimplicity A: "What Educators Need Is Simply a Swift Kick in the Butt"
This view hinges on the belief that education's "problems" stem from the laziness that is miraculously pervasive only in public schools and somehow wholly absent from employees of private schools and other businesses. The argument's appeal is that it sounds so easy. If we just hold educators accountable, they'll snap out of the half-sleep in which they've spent the last 150 years. (Because proponents of this belief do not specify when the laziness began, we can only assume it began with the very first public schools, since its proponents appear to claim it's endemic only to this environment.) Relationship load reduction does not suffer from this clearly preposterous notion that teachers are proportionally any lazier than anyone else. Rather, it allows the current amount of work teachers do to bear more fruit. Unlike other reform proposals, it does not require that teachers work harder, much less accuse them of hardly working.

The problem of children not getting enough attention at school is too systematic to be explained by what the individuals in institutions aren't doing out of supposed willfulness. A simpler, therefore preferable, explanation is that the structure of the institution is making them tend to withdraw emotionally in the same way it's forcing our kids to withdraw emotionally—kids and teachers are both human, after all. Take the analogy of recycling: What appears a lazy and shortsighted community when recycling is inconvenient can come to look like a conscientious and farsighted community when recycling is made easy for them. Our institutions facilitate and discourage certain behaviors in us, but ultimately we are in control of those institutions—we can restructure them to facilitate behaviors we want and discourage behaviors we don't want. By making our schools and classes large, we're discouraging personalized interaction between students and teachers. By making them small, we'll be encouraging—virtually guaranteeing—frequent, positive interaction.

Structural change costs money, but let's not be naïve—so do attempts to make people behave differently that don't significantly change the odds. Eventually, billboards encouraging people to recycle on their own will cost as much as a curbside pickup program would have—and will never produce the same level of recycling. Most would agree it's best to make recycling easy. Why is there so much opposition to making teaching easy? Mark Goldberg cites data that 30 percent of teachers leave the field within five years, rising to 50 percent in cities (2002, p. 91). *That leaves the average stay of a teacher in the profession at about five years* (deMarrais and LeCompte 1999, p. 152). We're burning our bridges.

Pseudosimplicity B: "Let's Simply Teach Them and Quit Wasting So Much Time on This Emotional Stuff"

This sounds easy—just tell them the facts, then give them the test. And it seems to make sense so long as the reader can be made to think of children only in the abstract. As soon as you're with one, you're bound to worry about their emotions. Relationship load reduction recognizes the fact that children have emotional needs that are prior to academic needs but that those two types of needs can and should be met *simultaneously.* As Beth Bernstein-Yamashiro writes, "Curriculum is a medium through which intellectual curiosity and personal development can be shared" (2004, p. 55). She notes that public policy discussions are characterized by this mistaken view that emotions are tangential in education (p. 56).

Pseudosimplicity C: Nostalgia for a Mythical, Simpler Era

Honestly I don't know why this rhetoric works, but it does: "Let's simply return to a time that had fewer problems." For some reason, when we hear this argument we usually don't bother to doubt that such a time ever existed. Nor do we consider that if it had existed, going back to anything like it might actually be impossible. But we like to succumb because of the wistful streak in all of us—it comforts us that much. Consider this excerpt from the very subtly titled *The Conspiracy of Ignorance: The Failure of American Public Schools,* a prime example of the "*I* came out all right" line of reasoning:

> On the subject of class size, I am reminded of my own experience in Junior High School 52 in the Bronx, the same school attended by General Colin Powell. In the 8th grade, more than 40 boys were crushed into one classroom. For lack of a seat, I spent some time be-

tween the radiators on a wooden board that stretched across the room under the windows. I confess to my rear being heated excessively at times, but I'm convinced it did not damage me or my sardine-packed classmates intellectually, or disrupt the rigorous instruction of the day. (Gross 1999, p. 34)

Grouping size reduction does not rely on a return to any golden age when people needed neither chairs nor bodily comfort, let alone adult attention. In fact, it is half return and half progress. Class sizes were never humane and are getting more so as time progresses, but far too slowly. School size and teacher continuity *were* humane, but they became less so over the course of the twentieth century. Luckily, secondary schools have recently started to ebb back toward smallness. Chapter 5 summarizes this history.

Pseudosimplicity D: "We Simply Need to Emulate the Exceptional Schools and Teachers"

This is a seductive one. We hear of a school that succeeds against great odds or a teacher who gets amazing results and we think, "Let's just do that everywhere and all the time." As we listen, we forget that these are the exceptional cases for a reason, that this is the very best that the very best could do. Clearly it is naïve to instantly assume everyone else could do it too. And if everyone really *were* able to do it, doesn't that suggest that perhaps these exceptional schools and people are in fact being lazy? Shouldn't they be doing even *better* than what the average person could do? The circular logic could go on indefinitely. What it always comes down to is this: Though we ought to emulate our best and brightest, they will still be better than average. Grouping size reduction does not suffer from this pie-in-the-sky thinking; on the contrary, it promises to help the average teacher make a significant difference in each student's life—without assuming that averages can be pushed forever upward—and without assuming that not to push them forever upward is to fail.

Of course, the argument should not be taken to the other extreme. Some scoff at successful small schools as unrepeatable miracles, "boutique schools" that can't be emulated by a nonselect staff (Ancess 2003, p. 136). Ancess examined small schools with relationships as their core focus, writing, "While these schools may not be typical, to deny that they *can* be typical is an assertion of will to prevent them from being typical and a repudiation of the belief that environment can affect human behavior" (p. 131). In other words, what allows average schools and teachers to get better results is not a "swift kick in the butt" and not the mere emulation of the best examples, but to focus on creating an environment conducive to caring and quality.

Pseudosimplicity E: "Simply Butt out and Let
Parents Raise Kids"

This is appealing because we like the heroic thought that parents can (or at least could) raise kids single-handedly. Unfortunately, this is and was a myth. Historian Stephanie Coontz writes, "The historical evidence does suggest that families have been most successful wherever they have built meaningful, solid networks and commitments *beyond* their own boundaries" (2000, p. 288). By calling any attempt to help kids and parents "socialism" or a proposal for "government nannies," some writers attempt to scare us with the threat of a totalitarian state (Duffy 1995). This may be a wise fear, but it should not preclude us from fearing the consequences of our widespread neglect of our children (and the increased risk that might put us at for poor oversight of government). Incidentally, such writers seldom advocate that the private sector help (rather than simply entreat) our adults to spend less time at work and thus require less of our "government nannies." Relationship load reduction does not invade any parent's realm of influence; it merely allows teachers to act more effectively as the role models our childrearing system (whose chief component is—and should remain—parents) already relies on them to be. As detailed in Chapter 5, trust between parents and educators will be *enhanced* by relationship load reduction.

Another aspect of this "butt out of parenting" pseudosimplicity is anxiety about the potentially harmful influence of teachers. This may be a subset of a larger tendency to fear that nonfamily adults will do to our kids what predominantly happens at the hands of family members (Glassner 1999, pp. 31–35; Hodgson 1997, pp. 66–71). Even some teachers are wary of deepening their relationships with students. What I'm calling for is to make possible the kind of connections we already want between our teachers and students, not something that should threaten a rational parent. Bernstein-Yamashiro found that "most students felt that relationships did not have to extend beyond the classroom or be particularly intense" (2004, p. 59). Any potential for harm from closer relationships is dwarfed by the inevitable harm of the neglect inherent in having distant ones. Furthermore, smaller classes will increase the likelihood that home abuse of children—by far the most common variety of child abuse—will be either noticed and stopped or prevented through better social support of parents and better nurturance of future parents (current students).

Illogically, many "butt out of parenting" proponents endorse this fear of influences beyond the family while simultaneously citing research that shows how much more influential parents are than schools on many desired outcomes (e.g., Gatto 2001, p. 113). Although this finding *could* be used to argue that schooling should be abandoned, it *cannot* be used to argue that school should not approximate parenting. Quite the opposite, it instructs us that our institution of schooling, should we choose to keep it, needs to better resemble the childrearing that it is. Childrearing has only recently come to be seen as the nearly exclusive responsibility of the nuclear family (Coontz 2000, p. 210). There is also a subtext of aristocracy in this "butt out of parenting" stance, in effect asserting, "Schools shouldn't resemble effective nuclear parents because children who aren't from such homes don't deserve the effects of such homes." Neglectful schools and families stripped of social support work together to reproduce inequalities in the next generation; they help ensure, for instance, that the emotional inheritance stays in the families that "earned" it at some remote time in the past.

Members of this camp do make one very good point, however: Top-down prescription also tends to become inhumane. Ideally, we don't want to tell people what to do but give them the wherewithal to do the right thing themselves. This is why I've insisted that grouping size reduction fits with the principle of local control—even down to the classroom. The only thing I'd add to this is that to be done well the task still has to be doable. This is why relationship load reduction should come first and foremost in education reform: It makes autonomy work better—it makes kids easier to educate. The same goes for parents: Yes, we still want them to make their own decisions, but that's no reason to deny that modernity has made parenting harder and that we ought to think of ways to make it easier again. To reject any such measure sight-unseen as an invasion of parenting privacy or a police-state maneuver is to wish more difficulty—and failure—upon our society's parents. By making our schools and classes smaller, we'll help kids *and* their parents, as well as the parents these kids will likely become.

Notice that I'm not recommending that teachers teach any particular outlook or moral orientation to the world of the kind that will inevitably drive some portion of parents crazy or have too much cultural bias—some bias, after all, is inevitable. What I'm recommending is giving attention and care to children, which ultimately has more effect anyway. As I'll detail in Chapter 4, children draw from positive attention the sense that the world is a good (but improvable) place full of people who can (mostly) be trusted and who deserve (mostly) trust and kindness.[4] Explicit "character" education is more often a Band-Aid approach, since the more fundamental—and culturally inclusive—prosocial understandings built within attachment relationships are less available through large groupings.

Sadly, attachment security is by many accounts less and less available outside of schools as well, which is part of the nurturance crisis I'll describe in Chapter 2. As evidence of this and other aspects of the nurturance crisis, the "butt out of parenting" camp is matched by an ever-growing "butt in by actually helping" camp. Many describe a feeling among today's parents that they deserve more societal support (for example, Hewlett and West 1998).

One of the reasons I chose to include parent load as an aspect of relationship load was to head off the "only parents should raise kids" argument. To keep firmly in mind that parents and parenting can benefit from school change is also to keep in mind that schooling truly is a part of our society's childrearing system, like it or not. Regardless of whether that's an ideal situation to be in, we're in it.

Reason 16
Smallness Is a Secret Ingredient That Simply Doesn't Get the Credit

Because grouping size is so universally taken for granted or actively ignored, the difference it makes is often attributed to something else. Grouping size can sometimes be the secret ingredient in what we compare to schools—such as the example above where the effects of families are compared to the effects of schools without acknowledgment of the vastly different relationship loads— but more often it's a secret ingredient in things we recommend for our schools. For example, Achilles observes that certain researchers "found that only three of the 13 schoolwide reform models they studied met their evaluation criteria for achievement"; he notes that class size reduction was "strangely missing from that analysis." Meanwhile, "all three models that met the evaluation criteria use small classes. What part of their effect is left over for the 'model'?" (1999, pp. 164–165).

As Gerald Bracey (2003) notes, grouping size is also a secret ingredient in the charter school and voucher debates:

> Most students in charter schools or using vouchers attend small classes in small schools. Therefore, even if these students score higher on tests, the results might well be not because of some inherent qualities of "charterness" or "voucherness," but simply because the students sit in small classes in small schools. (p. 31)

TABLE 1.4   PUBLIC VERSUS PRIVATE CLASS SIZE, 1999–2000

SECTOR	AVERAGE CLASS SIZE		STUDENT/ TEACHER RATIO	PERCENT OF SCHOOLS WITH A STUDENT/ TEACHER RATIO OF LESS THAN 10:1
	SELF-CONTAINED	DEPARTMENTALIZED		
Public	20.9	23.6	15.6	9.7
Private	18.9	18.8	13.2	35.8

Source: NCES 2002, table 4.

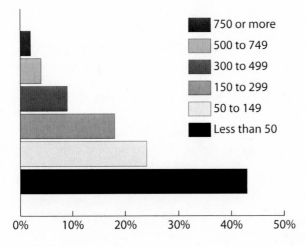

Figure 1.1 *Percentage of U.S. private schools within enrollment size categories, 2003.* Source: Digest 2006, table 55.

Meier notes that even regardless of test results, what parents often seek in vouchers but may not acknowledge is the chance to go to a smaller, more personalized school, a market that private schools have long had cornered (2000a, p. 37). Figure 1.1 shows the minuscule number of private schools that could be considered large.

Private school pupil/teacher ratio (a correlate of class size) hovers around two students fewer on average than in public schools (Digest 2006, table 61), but we'll see below that public schools of similar sizes have similar pupil/teacher ratios and classes. Table 1.4 is a public/private class size comparison that shows a difference of two to five students.

In other words, for those who would like to prevent future voucher campaigns—like a referendum my state recently rejected—my advice is to give parents what they want: small public schools. Even though it appears to many voucher supporters that what they want is "privateness" or even "charterness," what they really want is smallness. (In Chapter 2 we'll return to the issue of what exactly is and isn't better about private schools.)

Small Schools with Invisible Small Classes
Another important instance of the secret ingredient phenomenon is the fact that even the small schools movement has not given full credit to the participation of class size. Again, all four aspects of relationship load reduction are interconnected, and all are important in helping schools meet kids' needs for positive adult attention. Tony Wagner, codirector of Harvard's Change Leadership Group, writes of the catalyst school of the small schools movement, "The class sizes and student load of teachers [are] further reduced by the fact

that almost everyone teaches at Central Park East, even the principal" (2002, p. 89).[5] This fact is easily missed in the midst of a discussion that credits the smallness of the enrollment as the key ingredient. In contrast, Miles and Darling-Hammond (1998) credit Central Park East's success to its class sizes rather than its enrollment. After all, the former is a bigger accomplishment than the latter—eighteen in a district where the norm is thirty-three. "Students and teachers told us that the extraordinary outcomes achieved at CPESS [Central Park East Secondary School] were made possible by these small class sizes and the continuity" in teacher-student relationships and between special and regular education.

Figure 1.2 graphs data offered by *New York Magazine* in 2001 about its top picks for public high schools in the city. Though these data are neither a large nor a random sample, they are exemplary because New York City has been seen as the epicenter of the small schools movement (Raywid and Schmerler 2003, p. 11). As enrollment drops, so do class sizes. The trend line illuminates the relationship. Exceptions like schools 1 and 3 in this local situation become negligible on a national scale, as Figure 1.3 shows.[6]

In sum, small classes clearly tend to be an ingredient in successful—as well as average—small schools, but the credit tends to go entirely to school size—assuming even school size is credited rather than "privateness," "charterness," or "nontraditionalness." (Conversely, large class size tends to be the secret "money-saving" ingredient in larger schools.)

On top of small schools that deemphasize their small classes, there are successful small schools that even deemphasize their smallness in favor of their approach. Take the example of Urban Academy in New York City, one member of the Julia Richman Complex of small schools. The school's Web site (urbanacademy.org) features a self-description whose first heading is "It's

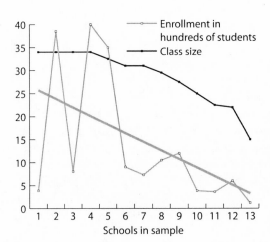

Figure 1.2 *Class sizes compared to school sizes in prestigious New York City public high schools, 2001.*

Note: All thirteen schools featured with both enrollment and class size data were included; when class size was expressed as a range, the two numbers were averaged.
Source: "Top of their class" 2001.

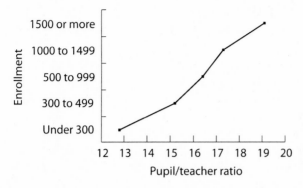

Figure 1.3 *Correlation between school size and pupil/teacher ratio in U.S. public schools, 2004.*
Source: Digest 2006, table 60.

not just our small size," which is a mere 120 students, and despite references to "personalization," the Web site makes no mention of class size. *New York Magazine* reports it as never above fifteen, making it the lowest of the schools included in the comparison above ("Top of their class" 2001) and nine students below the national average. The school's approach is certainly laudable and unique, but smallness is clearly a huge ingredient, and one that is strangely unacknowledged.

The Shift to Age-Grading

A historical example is how grouping size was the secret ingredient in the reaction to the introduction of age-grading in 1848. Henry Perkinson writes, "In the older, ungraded school teachers had spent much of their time trying to maintain order. . . . The power of the graded school to reduce problems of discipline became one of its most attractive features" (1995, p. 69). What Perkinson—and decision-makers at the time—failed to acknowledge was that the Quincy age-graded model called for classes of fifty to sixty rather than the *two to three hundred* (no typos here) in the schools they were replacing. Joel Spring writes, "Rather than the usual school construction of the same period—large rooms accommodating hundreds of students—the Quincy School contained a greater number of schoolrooms, each of which could hold fifty-six students" (1997, p. 152). He highlights

> a Providence, Rhode Island, grammar school in 1840, where each floor seated 228 students in a single room and was conducted as a single school. A master teacher and assistant teachers combined their efforts to teach the entire group within this large, ungraded classroom. In 1823, Boston schools were being built with rooms that seated 300 pupils, on the premise that three large groups would be taught by one master teacher and two assistant teachers. (pp. 150–151)

It appeared to reformers that grouping students by age was the solution to discipline and instructional efficiency problems. Clearly, though, the bafflingly ignored ingredient was class size reduction. Ironically, this misperception was possible because the drop, though drastic, wasn't drastic enough. Because the mid-fifties was still an inhumane number, age-grading was still functioning as a coping mechanism, not a true solution. Once you get near a class of twelve, personalized rather than uniform curriculum (including multiage curriculum) becomes truly possible for the average teacher, revealing that age-grading, with its inherent one-size-fits-all mentality and tendency to promote direct instruction, is not the true fix.

The deeper irony is that though 300 kids of various ages in a room may have been an unnecessarily chaotic experience, it probably wasn't any more emotionally damaging in terms of attachment needs as being with fifty-five age peers—especially if one considers the fact that pre–Quincy model schools also tended to be in session many fewer days of the year. Time is the other secret ingredient here. The average K–12 student's number of days in school doubled between 1870 and 1950 (Digest 2006, table 32). The trend appears to continue smoothly back in time. Church finds documentation of "a slow and gradual increase" in school days per year in New York, "from 14 days in 1800 to 20 in 1840. . . . to 40 in 1861" (1976, p. 57). These antebellum numbers make the experience sound more like a yearly conference than a school year. Since the length of the school year increased more or less simultaneously with a gradual drop in class size, the nurturance gains were not as pronounced as they appear when school year length is ignored.

What Is and Isn't Teaching?
At the most fundamental level, relationship load is a secret ingredient in our very definition of the word *teaching*. When people say to me, "Teaching? That must be hard!" my mind travels back to whichever of my classes is currently small, and I think, "No, it's not the *teaching* that's hard." So at this very basic level, when we discuss teaching, we have to suspect that we may be discussing the secret ingredient of relationship load rather than the thing itself. After all, few would respond, "Tutoring? That must be hard!" even though all that distinguishes tutoring from teaching are four letters and class size. Teaching and grouping size are tangled up in each other. In the course of this book, I hope to sort out what grouping size is and, in so doing, what teaching both *can be* and *does not have to be*.

What's So Special about Special Education?
A dispassionate observer will soon see that the essential difference between special education and "regular ed" is not the training of the teachers, though that is helpful. The key is that (a) each child is seen as unique and given an

"individual education plan," and (b) classes (and "pull-outs") are made small enough so that those individual needs can be met.[7] Regular ed, after all, treats children as groups and gives them what one might call "group education plans" that we prefer to call "the curriculum standards." In all honesty, then, special education is in large part a class size reduction program that's targeted to a particular subset of the school population, but class size is largely unrecognized as a chief ingredient.

Special education accounts for much of the increased cost in public education in recent years (Berliner and Biddle 1995, p. 81). Harris and Plank (2006) agree, citing figures that contradict claims that overhead costs (although they may indeed be too large) are *proportionally* the source of increased funding in recent decades. Thankfully, the proportional increase in spending has gone to teachers and students by way of salary increases and smaller classes—*especially* smaller classes for those classified as having special needs. This targeted class size reduction for those students in small special education classes has not been wasted money, but it's money we've spent in a problematic fashion because the essential problems with the separateness of special education are made more intractable by the now-entrenched two-track system of funding. That system also leads to a competition rather than collaboration for funds.

A thoughtful person has to question the assumption that there needs to be a separation between special and regular education. To a large degree, special education is a more humane remnant of an outdated ideology of isolating the "unfit" from the "fit." That's why in recent years the concept of mainstreaming or inclusion has been gaining momentum. Both regular and special education children are cheated by being separated. The disabled students lose because they are made to feel incompatible with society at large, and the rest lose because they are allowed to believe they don't need to include or respect all people. One might go so far as to say that both groups are cheated out of understanding that disability itself is an arbitrary concept, that everyone has his or her challenges to face. Inclusion has the goal of making students see that the similarities are far more numerous than the differences. It could be argued that large grouping size is what makes us think of only some students as special in the first place. Uniqueness should come before categories:

> In inclusive school communities, responding to and supporting student diversity becomes a shared responsibility of all school professionals. Rather than fitting students into categories that correspond to the roles of school professionals, the collective and individual needs and goals of students shape the daily decisions and actions of school professionals. That is, students, not professionals, drive the

organization and use of educational resources. (Sands, Kozleski, and French 2000, p. 24)

Miles and Darling-Hammond write,

> Not only are pull-out strategies extremely costly, they also segregate students in sometimes stigmatizing ways and provide services that are often ineffective due to their fragmentation and lack of connection to the students['] classroom experience. (1998)

The reorganization of staff to efficiently provide small classes should go hand in hand with the reorganization of special education.

The ideals are clear-cut—what makes inclusion impracticable is mainstream class size. Workable inclusion for special education students, therefore, is best seen as a partner of grouping size reduction—the former will never succeed without the latter, and the latter will not be very affordable without the former (see Chapter 8). As stated above, individualized needs-meeting through small classes is the essence of special education. You can't have inclusion without small classes for all, but you can't even have separate special education without small classes for those you've separated from the rest.

The national percentage of special education students is 13.8 percent (Appendix B). A class of twelve, therefore, could expect to have one or two mainstreamed kids—normally just one—hardly an unreasonable "imposition" on teacher and peers. Another way to think of it is that I'm actually advocating the *inverse* of mainstreaming. I'm advocating that regular ed students be included with special ed students in small classes that accommodate individual needs. Of course, there will always be a single-digit percentage of the population that needs to be separated because its needs can't be met in any mainstream scenario, but it should be far fewer than are currently isolated.

The Band-Aid Effect: Why Are Practices That Are Philosophically Hard to Justify also Hard to Prove as Nonfunctional?

Relationship load is also a secret ingredient in why philosophically indefensible practices (e.g., retention, tracking, etc.) often tend not to look as bad in the research as would make sense. I suggest that ethically questionable practices like these may appear to work only in the context of unquestioned large relationship load. That is, large grouping size is a secret ingredient in the "effectiveness" of practices like grade retention and tracking.

As an example, Karl Alexander, Doris Entwisle, and Susan Dauber (2003) find that researchers drawing definite conclusions about the academic and psychological negatives of retention in grade have overstated the case. They do not defend the practice, however, arguing that neither retention nor so-called social promotion are the "remedies" they claim to be (p. 247). The absence of retention by itself does not adequately deal with the problem of differing paces of learning. They write, "The challenge—a daunting one—is to build more flexibility into the system without the stigma and other problems associated with being" nonaverage or not on schedule (p. 250). They quote the National Education Commission on Time and Learning: "Students are caught in a time trap—processed on an assembly line to the minute. Our usage of time virtually assures the failure of many students" (p. 250).

As a better remedy for the unavoidably unequal pace of learning, Alexander and colleagues appear to push for personalization:

> The kernel of the problem is not grade retention so much as the institutional structure within which grade retention is embedded. At present, this structure makes deviants of otherwise "normal" children while failing to accomplish the aims it was designed to fulfill. (p. 263)

They point out several issues in school as currently structured that aggravate the problems of slow learners and present the need for the so-called remedy of retaining a student:

- Not enough extra time available for the slower students (p. 249)
- Too many transitions, for example, moving in and out of middle school (pp. 250–251) and changing teachers every year (p. 261)
- Weak attachment to school (p. 252) and "a broader need to help all students fit in comfortably" (p. 257)
- Lack of personalization (p. 250)
- A focus on remediation rather than prevention (p. 259)
- Age-graded classrooms and the equation of "age" with "grade" (pp. 261–262)

With the exception of the last item, every one of these issues is directly addressed by relationship load reduction, and multiage classrooms would be far easier to implement with smaller numbers. Alexander and colleagues provide support for this when they allow "retention coupled with other services such as one-on-one instruction and smaller classes" seems to work better (p. 255). In short, large relationship load is a secret ingredient in the short-term necessity for unethical and imperfect Band-Aids like grade retention.

Tracking and detracking research suffers from similar inconclusiveness. Kulik writes, "Sweeping statements about the effect of grouping and tracking may make good rhetoric but they make poor science. Recent accounts also suggest that . . . detracking American schools may be easier to achieve in theory than in practice" (2004, p. 179). The unacknowledged chief reason for this is large classes, which are seen as a constant in the equation. Several examples will be presented in the book of small schools with small classes that have effectively eliminated tracking.

In clear reference to critics of the philosophy of separation, Alexander and colleagues write, "Not all 'separations' are bad, and the reflexive inclination toward leveling can do more harm than good in the absence of superior alternatives" (2003, p. 247). Relationship load is that superior alternative. Without addressing the structural constraints of large groups that can make inclusion, detracking, and remaining with one's classmates harmful to academic outcomes, the philosophy of separation can be a self-fulfilling prophecy. Herbert Walberg feels we should "seek, where possible, avoidance of retention, grouping, and tracking largely by nipping problems in the bud before they are necessary" (2004, p. 206). The four aspects of relationship load reduction are the pruning shears to do that bud-nipping with.

What's Lurking inside the Teacher "Shortage"?

The National Academy of Education cites "the high attrition of beginning teachers" as "the real source of most teacher shortages" (2005, p. 63). Darling-Hammond (2006) argues that the problem with staffing some schools is that "there are distribution problems caused by production of and demand for teachers across states and communities (heightened by funding disparities which make teaching in some locations much more appealing than in others)" (pp. 337–338). She also concedes, however, that the conditions of teaching have a lot to do with the attrition rate; chiefly, "teachers are more likely to stay in schools where they feel they can succeed." To this end, she cites a need for better "learning opportunities for teachers and stronger teacher-student relationships" (p. 341). Richard Ingersoll (2003) agrees, arguing that what's hidden inside the "teaching shortage" is in fact a long-standing emphasis on recruitment over retention. He argues that the data don't point to a shortage of qualified graduates but to a turnover rate Keller (2007) puts at 30 to 40 percent within five years of entering the profession. Thus, it's not so much that we have a shortage of teachers but that we have a shortage of doable, sustainable teaching jobs. Ingersoll writes, "Lasting improvements in the quality and quantity of the teaching workforce will require improvements in the quality of the teaching job" (p. 18).

Class size in particular appears to be the secret ingredient lurking in the low quality of the teaching job. Katia Fredriksen and Jean Rhodes write, "Sadly, many adults who were initially drawn to the teaching profession out of a desire to establish meaningful connections with their students have become increasingly disillusioned by the structural impediments to relationships in schools" (2004, p. 51). In small-class experiments teachers spoke much more positively about their jobs (Achilles 1999, p. 47). McCaskill and colleagues found, "As class size and total student load increased, teacher work satisfaction decreased" (1979). But the other aspects of relationship load are also clearly involved in the attrition equation: Too many relationships with students, parents, and colleagues make for shallow relationships that give less of a sense of belonging and purpose to what is otherwise simply a job. As well, a system where relationships are limited to one school year makes leaving seem to have less consequence; after all, a teacher who doesn't return the next year is hardly "abandoning" students and parents he or she doesn't yet know.

One telling piece of evidence is that there is a very strange lack of correlation between why teachers say they left teaching or left a particular school and what they would do to make the job more worth keeping. Ingersoll, for example, found that only 7 percent of departing teachers cited large class size as a reason (11 percent of those leaving for good did, versus 3 percent who were only changing schools) (2003, p. 16). Compare that to the fact that 38 percent of departing teachers recommended smaller classes as a way the system could retain more teachers, which was bested only by better student discipline at 50 percent (arguably a class size effect) and better pay at 64 percent (p. 19). (The pay is hardly a surprise for those entering the profession, but finding out what one has to do to earn it is clearly disappointing to many.) This may speak to relationship load's indirect action on dissatisfaction: Perhaps it does not tend to come to mind immediately as directly dissatisfying (though its effects do), but when solutions are sought, class size comes up because the dissatisfactions it leads to cannot be solved directly in most cases. Put another way, when asked to express frustration, a significantly lower percentage of teachers mention class size than when asked to make constructive suggestions. It seems plausible that in the former case there is a tendency to discuss effects, and in the latter case, a tendency to search for causes.

Chapter 8 will estimate how much savings the proposal can gain by reducing teacher attrition, and Chapter 10 will estimate the reduced need for recruitment that better retention would provide.

What's Lurking inside the Aversion of Potential Teachers?
What is much more seldom discussed in the area of teacher attrition and recruitment is the question of exactly why *non*teachers choose *not* to become teachers. Although teacher interviews are revealing, I suspect that interviewing college graduates who earn a similar salary about why they *aren't* teachers would be fascinating. Public Agenda's 2000 report *A Sense of Calling* surveyed

nonteaching, young college graduates about their inclinations toward or away from teaching; unfortunately, salary was not accounted for. Eighty percent admitted that teaching made a more important contribution to society than what they were doing. When compared to teachers of similar age, 16 percent fewer loved their jobs. Eighteen percent said they would seriously consider becoming a teacher, and only 32 percent would never consider it. Eighteen percent of college grads make for a big pool of potential teachers that could be attracted by smaller grouping size.

The biggest reason cited for avoiding the profession was personal safety, another factor minimized by grouping size reduction, which we'll return to in the next section. After money (which ought to have been excluded as a variable), the third reason for not going into the profession was the feeling that teachers are scapegoated for all problems in education. This survey choice sounds at least in part like an expression of the fact that teachers are set up to look like failures because of large grouping size.

Why Isn't Teaching as Respected as the Other Professions Yet?

When we compare teaching to other professions, we need to recognize that there is a huge difference in relationship load. Small public high school pioneer Dennis Littky points out the obvious with doctors—they see one patient at a time.

> Can you imagine walking into a medical office and being shuffled off to a room of 20 to 30 other people who have the same complaint or disease, and then watching as the doctor discusses the treatment that all of you will receive before sending everyone out the door with carbon copy prescriptions? (2004, p. 74)

The same applies to social workers, therapists, and other counselors who seldom counsel more than a few people at a time (though their caseloads can be unethically enormous in many cases). Researchers have reached a consensus that a ratio of four to six patients per nurse is optimal (Curtin 2003). Calls to professionalize teaching have merit—they should simply move to a slower lane until the more important step of relationship load reduction is taken. Curtin reports research showing that patient-nurse ratios are a matter of life and death. "A 10 percent increase in the proportion of RNs across all hospital types was associated with five fewer patient deaths for every 1000 discharged patients." School grouping size is also a matter of life and death, as we'll now discuss.

Reason 17
Columbine

Though it was a high price to pay for awareness, the 1999 Columbine High School tragedy in Colorado did bring to the fore what countless scholars and educators had warned us of: that our school system was ripe for the most impersonal responses imaginable from students made to feel worthless. Daniel Duke writes, "Research has found that larger schools are more likely to experience discipline problems," and when problems arise, size slows the administrative response time and makes it "more difficult to recognize students by name or to distinguish between students and strangers" (2002, p. 184). Duke provides a series of recommendations that include two other aspects of relationship load reduction as well; he observes that the Safe School Study Report to Congress found, as far back as 1978,

> that school size was linked to student anonymity and alienation, factors that in turn were associated with school crime. The report called for efforts to "personalize" schools by *lowering teacher-student ratios and increasing the amount of continuous class time that teachers spend with groups of students.* It is much easier to promote constructive relationships and connectedness in small schools. (p. 113, emphasis mine)

Thus, although smaller schools have gotten most of the airtime (the last sentence being a case in point), all aspects of grouping size reduction are associated with increased safety (see also Achilles 1999, p. 164; Newman 2004, p. 297). Not getting into an Ivy League school is not a life or death situation— even figuratively—but large grouping size literally is. Let's get the crisis right before it's too late for too many more of us.

Reason 18
It's Simply Wrong Not to Pay the Piper

In Chapter 4, I will lay out the argument that children have a human right to develop autonomy while perceiving the availability of positive adult attention. I hope it is self-evident that by protecting the rights of children we protect everything about our society that we hold dear as well as make more possible everything about our society we would like to improve. There aren't that many clear-cut ethical choices in life, but this is one of them—it's a simple pick between right and wrong. Think about a kid you know. Does he or she deserve it? Case closed.

2
Getting the Crisis Right

Schooling is a part of childrearing.

—**Deborah Meier** (1995, p. 114)

B eneath the educational policy in the United States is an underlying philosophy that runs counter to a balanced, relational view of human existence. Nel Noddings, one of the best-known philosophers of education in the United States, refers to it as "the relentless cultural press for separation" (1989, p. 214) and "the orientation characterized by hierarchy, specialty, separation, objectification, and the loss of relation" (1984, p. 200); she contrasts it with an ethic of caring. Relational balance in education is misconceived in at least three dimensions that bear on this proposal: the individual and the community, achievement and nurturance, special needs and the need to belong. Figure 2.1 is an outline of the implications of a separation philosophy for schools.

In Chapter 5 I will return to specialization and sorting issues. In this chapter I will compare the real nurturance crisis with the fake academic crisis, one a consequence of the separation philosophy and one a figment of its imagination.

The Fake Crisis

"The central myth," writes Meier (1995),

> is the notion that in the past public schools taught more effectively and children learned more thoroughly. It's a given part of

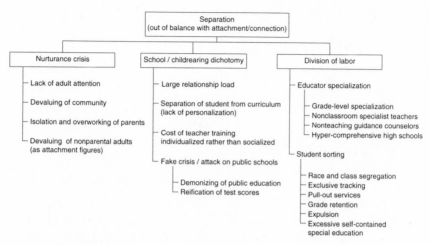

Figure 2.1 *Philosophy of separation underlying much of educational thought and policy.*

almost every conversation about schools and undermines every effort to understand what is wrong and thus what must be righted. The universally accepted story of a system "in decline," of the puzzling inability of a once strong system to do what it once did so well, would make disillusionment reasonable—if it were true. It's not. (p. 69)

We continue to hear accusations that American public schools are places of worsening academic standards that are threatening the nation's economy. Though patently false, these accusations garner credence from many citizens and policy-makers. Even staunch supporters of public schools often participate in the accusations in hopes of gaining more funding for education or sparking interest in improving it. Meier writes, "Attempts to bring these realities to light are generally hushed up, as though they were a threat to our resolve to undertake tough reforms" (p. 70). The problem is that we're unlikely to free ourselves from the pointlessly traditional and limited view of public education (narrowly defined as academic achievement) if we continue to hold to the myth that schools are failing even in this. The four principal myths of the public education bashers are the following:

1. Test scores are falling.
2. Our schools are hurting our international competitiveness and must improve test scores or we'll fall behind.
3. School isn't preparing our kids for the jobs of the future, which will require more math and science skills.

4. Society would be better served by a more effective, more efficient, private school system.

Even a cursory look at the research literature will show these statements to be false.

"Falling" Test Scores

Berliner and Biddle (1995) systematically dismantle the failing schools myth in their thorough study, *The Manufactured Crisis*:

> From the evidence, readers will learn that standardized test data reveal *no* recent drop in student achievement; indeed, many of the tests indicate modest recent *gains* in students' knowledge. In fact, we know of only *one* standardized test that ever generated falling aggregate test scores—the Scholastic Aptitude Test (SAT). . . . To be sure, *aggregate* total SAT scores . . . fell between about 1963 and 1975. (p. 14)

Not surprisingly, critics who assert that our schools are failing often cite the SAT as their only evidence, apparently satisfied that it's severe enough to be sufficient proof of their assertions (for example, Hanushek [2003], who is a senior fellow at the Hoover Institution of Stanford University). Unfortunately for these critics, SAT scores have (a) dropped overall because more students are now taking it, rather than the smaller, more elite group of the past, and (b) show similar results *or even gains* when comparing the more select group from the past with a similar group from today's test-takers. Moreover, scores rose for every minority group between 1976 and 1993, including an 8 percent jump for African Americans (Berliner and Biddle 1995, p. 22).

What about since Berliner and Biddle published their book in 1995? First, minority participation has continued to increase. "Between 1996 and 2006, the percentage of test-takers who were minority students increased by 7 percentage points, from 31 to 38 percent" (NCES 2007a, indicator 14). Second, SAT scores continue to climb in most cases. "Between 1996 and 2005, the average mathematics score increased for all racial/ethnic groups" and verbal scores fell slightly for one group (Hispanics who were non–Puerto Rican and non–Mexican American) but rose for white, Puerto Rican, and Asian/Pacific Islander students (NCES 2007a, indicator 14). So much for the SAT myth.[1]

In *The Way We Were?* Richard Rothstein (1998) comes to similar conclusions about the fake crisis. He even argues that it is much older than *A Nation at Risk*, the 1983 federal report that kicked off the contemporary school-bashing movement. He isolates four claims made by public school bashers:

1. Achievement has declined.
2. Urban, minority schools are getting worse the fastest.
3. Even if achievement is not going down, it's not getting better like it must to meet future demands.
4. U.S. public schools compare badly to other countries' schools.

Rothstein writes,

> These claims are similar, indeed nearly identical, to what has been said about American schools for a century or more. In each generation the claims proved false.... In part the claims are just plain wrong, and in part there is simply no credible evidence or adequate data with which to evaluate them. Without such evidence, assertions of school inadequacy are generally supported by selective invocation of anecdotes. (1998, pp. 1–2)

The next time you read an article or book that trashes our public schools, look closely at the evidence—unrepresentative exceptions in the data and isolated cases are probably all they're using. But we've heard so many repeat it that we suspect it's true. Even those of us who would never abandon a system of public schooling fall for lies about its quality.

Private Schools

Now take the assumption that private schools get better results. This is a myth that touches directly on the thesis of this book. If and when they do get better results, is it because they're private or because they tend to be small and have small classes?

> Evidence from the NAEP provides little support for the notion that private (or public) schools have a broad, substantial edge in average student achievement. All of which raises an interesting issue. Several reasons may be cited for why students in private schools *ought* to outperform those in public schools. (Berliner and Biddle 1995, p. 123)

A recent report by the U.S. Department of Education corroborates these findings. Braun, Jenkins, and Grigg (2006) found that when students of like background were compared, the differences between public and private achievement vanished. Harold Wenglinsky (2007) studied high school outcomes by controlling for middle-school achievement and parental involvement, finding similar results—no advantage of any school type over the traditional public high school.[2]

As examples of why students *ought* to perform better in private schools, Berliner and Biddle (1995) offer ideas such as selective enrollment (i.e., siphoning off the brightest public school kids and those least hampered by the multiple challenges of poverty and racism), the ability to enforce rules and more quickly expel problem students (i.e., making the local public school deal with their problems), and more chance "to create a sense of 'community,'" principally because private schools are not forced to be large (p. 123).

This raises the question, *What are parents paying for if it's not academic results?* My answer is that they assume their child will be more likely to get good modeling and less likely to come into contact with antisocial and otherwise inadequately parented peers. More cynically, it could be argued that private schools are primarily a method of keeping one's children away from "the wrong kind of people," which for many white parents happens to mean nonwhites. And, of course, parents want small relationship load from private schools (Finn, Gerber, Achilles, and Boyd-Zaharias 2001, pp. 145–146). As Clive Harber (1996) observes, private schools tout their smallness and intimacy in their brochures (pp. 18–19). As discussed, grouping size is often a secret ingredient to school successes credited to other factors, and private schools are no exception to this phenomenon—only 6 percent of them are larger than 500 students, and 67 percent of them have fewer than 150!

Interestingly, teacher continuity in private schools, though enhanced by their tendency to be small, is undermined by the fact that they experience higher turnover than public schools. Ingersoll found that public schools lose just over 15 percent of their teachers per year, while private schools lose nearly 20 percent (2003, p. 15).

Math, Science, and the Job Market

Issues around math and science in our schools—including test scores, "rigor," and teacher qualifications—are wrongly framed, in my opinion. I think we need to reconsider our assumptions about how much math and science we can teach in secondary as opposed to postsecondary schools. The math and science "crisis," which has been with us since the USSR launched Sputnik, also has jingoistic and xenophobic undertones in some cases. The effect of class size reduction on math and science expertise is arguably neutral because although less qualified teachers may be hired, the increased satisfactions of the job could attract and keep those who currently take their expertise elsewhere. Because the solutions are largely independent of the grouping size factor, I don't address them in the proposal. For what it's worth, my opinion is that we should explore giving math and science teachers more post-hiring training. Instead of struggling to recruit those who are qualified for higher-paying jobs, we could try teaching more math and science to committed teachers, which I'll discuss in Chapter 10.

As far as the seriousness of the math and science "crisis" goes, Berliner and Biddle find that "it is contradicted by *all* available evidence" (1995, p. 96). Like Berliner and Biddle, cultural critic Neil Postman (1996) questions the constant and unexamined linking of achievement (particularly in math and science) and the economy, particularly its ever-elusive "jobs of the future":

> Putting aside its assumption that education and productivity go hand in hand, its promise of providing interesting employment is, like the rest of it, overdrawn. There is no strong evidence for believing that well-paying, stimulating jobs will be available to most students upon graduation. Since 1980, in America at least, the largest increase in jobs has been for those with relatively low skills. (p. 30)

Noddings, a former public school math teacher, adds the observation that higher education (driven by this post-Sputnik mindset) appears to be exerting self-interested and unrealistic pressure on the secondary system. She rejects

> the claim that, because academic mathematics has served as a gateway to higher education, all children must now become proficient in mathematics so that they will not be deprived of educational opportunities. The alternative, of course, is to remove mathematics as a gatekeeper and insist on proficiency only for those who need it in order to pursue their interests. (2003, pp. 199–200)

For a thorough debunking of all the myths listed at the beginning of the chapter, refer to the two books I've mentioned as well as Bracey (2003). Many will argue that the purpose of this misinformation campaign is to dismantle public schools. That would fit with the separatist philosophy, which appears to see public schools as too indicative of our connectedness. But even firm supporters of public schools are misled by these myths. In believing them, even *they* are convinced that there is an academic crisis in our schools. Believing that, they are likely to accept the premise that schools have problems of their own and therefore don't have the power to help society with its real nurturance crisis. In its worry about "falling" test scores, our school system continues to neglect the truly unmet and more fundamental needs of our children.

The Real Crisis

The real crisis is an individual and social crisis, a nurturance crisis: Kids aren't getting enough attention *in or out of* school. Thanks to social, economic, and technological changes, our society's adults are no longer spending enough time with its children. We are doing our descendants and ourselves a disservice by not maximizing the number of kids who become positive adults—and by positive I am not suggesting blindly acquiescent or uncritical. Educational sociologists Kathleen deMarrais and Margaret LeCompte include factory-style schooling as part of the problem, arguing that it "has changed the way young people grow up and caused them to develop and function with only limited contact with adult culture" (1999, p. 102). In traditional societies, they write, "youth are closely supervised by adults, and there are no great concentrations of young people" (p. 104). Yet most who observe the problem are skeptical of the idea of simply abandoning schools altogether. This crisis in nurturance can be boiled down to the elements discussed below. This is only a scratching of the surface—for more details, read the sources I cite.

Before I proceed, however, let me address two questions some readers may be posing: Is this "crisis" just another form of the fear mongering I've criticized? Is it just another form of the nostalgia I've criticized? My assertion that the real crisis is not nostalgia or sensationalism is based on the premises of human biological theory, that is, that humans evolved in a social environment vastly richer in adult-child interaction than the social environment in the United States at the current time. I start from the assumption that we cannot possibly have had time to adapt *genetically* to a drastic reduction in adult attention, and I don't think any of us really prefer the *psychological* adaptations that neglected children are making. In Chapter 4 I use attachment theory to explain human needs for attention. This theory starts from the assumption that proximity-seeking was selected for in human evolution since individuals who were loners were more likely to have been killed by starvation, accidents, predators, or enemies (Bowlby 1988, pp. 60–61). There may be nonevolutionary premises to support the same conclusions about the nurturance crisis, but this is the premise I myself am working from.

Lastly, am I using nurturance as a cover for promoting subservience or puritanical moralizing? No. While I agree that far too many things children do in school are classified as "misbehavior" (largely as a result of large grouping size), I do not go as far as believing that adults should never critique what children do. As I've implied, I reject simplistic portrayals of our youth's every (mis)deed as heroic antiestablishment political action or healthy exploration. I think the goal of children's "misbehavior" is very often to protest lack of adult attention and respect rather than to make a statement about income disparity or institutional racism. I do not believe that neglecting children makes them more likely to fight for a more just society; on the contrary, it allows far too many to become unhappy, withdrawn, and even antisocial adults and parents who are unlikely to fight for justice. Neglect is at least as likely as nurturance—though I believe more likely—to create docility and manipulability in the populace.

The Adult Problem

First of all, let's not locate the problem in our kids. The handoff of responsibility involved in terms like "youth problem" is reminiscent of referring to racism in the United States as the "Negro problem." Not only is it just as much an adult problem as a teenage problem, it's also a whole-childhood problem (as well as both a home and school problem). It's only seen as a teenage problem because that's when it tends to become a problem *for adults*. Brigid Daniel, Sally Wassell, and Robbie Gilligan write,

> Problems that may already have been present can become much more obvious and disturbing in teenagers. They may be manifested because of the growth in the ability of the young person to challenge their parents, to make comparisons, and to articulate their thoughts better. (1999, pp. 281–283)

Others have also observed this blaming of the messenger (Clark 2004, p. 74; Males 1996, 1999; Young 1999, p. 280). The most obvious way in which the youth problem is really an adult problem, of course, is that youth is where adults are made.

Children's Testimonies of Adult Withdrawal

Many people agree that our kids are suffering from adult withdrawal—in both senses of suffering and in both senses of withdrawal. Once when I explained to a group of my students that I think elementary students should stay with the same teacher for seven years, one young woman responded, "That's a lot of time to spend with one person. What if you got sick of them?" I asked her if people got sick of their parents after so much time. "But that's way more time than I've ever spent with my parents," she responded. Apparently her parents have to work that much to pay the bills in our "land of opportunity." Chap Clark has a book called *Hurt: Inside the World of Today's Teenagers*, in which he writes, "We must recognize that we have abandoned our young for decades and it will take years to correct our indifference" (2004, p. 70). Wagner writes, "The conclusion from [the] data is inescapable: young people today are growing up profoundly alone—perhaps more than at any time in human history. They are being raised by each other, as much as by anyone" (2002, p. 34).

Attachment is a way to talk about the psychological process by which children rely on their ongoing relationships with adults in order to grow up feeling secure. Many have argued that attachment problems are at the root of *most* of the problems of troubled kids. Daniel, Wassell, and Gilligan, for example, write,

> The contention of this book is that in social work practice the majority of children encountered have difficulties that can be attributed to attachment issues. . . . There is great reparative potential in the improvement of existing relationships and the making of new, healthy relationships. (1999, p. 37)

In other words, attachment problems—and the problems that follow them—have attachment solutions. In Chapter 4 we'll explore attachment theory in detail, including its significance for schools.

Industrialization, Urbanization, and Schooling

It's easy to make a case that the industrial revolution and the resultant urbanization are the chief contributors to the lack of adults in children's lives these days. Historians speak consistently about the drop in quality of life for children that accompanied the arrival of the industrial economy (e.g., Stearns 2006, p. 58). But industrialization was gradual rather than immediate. Judith Deiro (2005) points out that most Americans were rural dwellers before the 1930s. Changes since then have continued to reduce opportunities for adult attention:

> Due to a combination of factors such as the baby boom, easy mobility, and postwar job opportunities in cities, the United States has become a nation of people who live primarily in large cities or suburbs. . . . With the migration to the cities, young families lost the nurturing support of extended families, lifelong friends, and close neighbors. . . . In short, children lost their network of caring adults who know them well, watch them grow up, and even help with their parenting. (p. 4)

Thus, though many of our problems may appear to some to be related to the social freedoms gained in the 1960s and 1970s, the real roots are much older—and *more a product of social structure than social mores.* Yes, changes like TV and video games do present ever-new challenges to raising kids, but, in my opinion, too much emphasis has been placed on resisting individual waves in the tide of change. Strengthening the structural conditions of child-rearing to meet whatever comes along makes much more sense. Maximizing children's opportunities for attachment relationships would be the proactive rather than the reactive route to sustainable social health and justice.

I don't see universal and compulsory schooling as a wonderful thing in and of itself. It came about as an adaptation to (some would say as a part of) industrialization and its various implications, especially urbanization (de-Marrais and LeCompte 1999, p. 73) and work's movement out of the home (Laslett 1984, p. 13). What the factory economy had to offer children in terms of quality of life made the universalizing of schooling look a lot less sinister a change (Cunningham 1995, p. 89, 103). In *A History of Childhood*, Colin Heywood takes the view that apprenticeship in the family and local community "was doubtless appropriate to a relatively stable, agrarian society, but not to a more restless commercial and urbanized one" (2001, p. 160). He also traces how popular resistance to compulsory schooling waned as industrialization completed its takeover of the economy (p. 166). Sadly, schooling today retains nineteenth-century structures based on long-outdated perceptions of how much attention kids deserve and what the consequences of too little attention really are. As pointed out in Chapter 1, schools were largely organized on the mass production model. In Chapter 5 I'll detail some of the early class size numbers—they may alarm you. Our kinder but still neglectful schools are thus a large part of our crisis in childrearing. Using the recommendations in this book, we can give them the feel of villages they should always have had.

Now It Takes More Than Just Parents and Families (and It Always Did)

Let's return to the "just let parents do the childrearing" argument. Many try to trace a childrearing crisis to the disappearance of the two-parent, one-earner family. As often as it's repeated, and as nice as it sounds, this theory just doesn't square with the research. As suggested above, more important is the disappearance of extended family and other secondary attachment figures in the community. The effect of their absence simply dwarfs the difference between a one-parent family and a two-parent family. Coontz writes,

> A growing body of research demonstrates that the crucial difference between functional and dysfunctional families lies not in the form of

the family but in the quality of support networks outside the family, including the presence of nonkin. (2000, p. 230)

Nor does a working mother's use of daycare, that is, reliance on other community adults, have negative effects on attachment or behavior (p. xxiv). (It would certainly be possible to take the use of daycare to an extreme and harm the primary attachment, but that is not how it is currently practiced or likely to be practiced in the future.)

Quite logically, adults are simply not significantly worse or better at bringing up other people's kids than they are at bringing up their own, with only one exception: *when relationship loads get large enough to make parenting and nonparenting significantly different situations.* Recall from the previous chapter that small grouping size is a secret ingredient in the power of parenting. There is one caveat to drawing this similarity: Nonparental attachments will tend to be less intimate and rely to a large degree on the fact that a core of parent-child intimacy exists. I do not argue that nonparental or nonguardian attachments should replace the primary attachment; indeed, they couldn't be very effective without it. Conversely, the primary attachment can't be as effective without the secondary attachments.

In light of such research, many argue that even *two*-parent nuclear families left to their own devices can no longer compensate for both modern and perennial assaults on growing up healthy—whether or not they ever really should have. Psychologist James Garbarino writes,

> The idea of raising a child by yourself in isolation is unnatural to us as social animals; yet when the community takes the view that parents are, or should be, wholly responsible for their children, parents are isolated from the kinds of support that only a community can give. We need to identify the support parents might need and take community as well as individual responsibility for children. (1995, p. 132)

Our notion that two parents are plenty just doesn't take into account how many adults it really takes (and took) to show a kid how to be an adult. Coontz writes, "As a historian, I suspect that the truly dysfunctional thing about American parenting is that it is made out to be such a frighteningly pivotal, private, and exclusive job," adding that our discussions of American childrearing "are distorted by the myth that parents can or should be solely responsible for how their children grow" (2000, p. 210).

In other words, we should also avoid the trap of scapegoating "bad" parenting for the nurturance crisis in a context that does little to support parents. It is more productive to focus on the lack of social support for parenting than the shortcomings of those who don't have such support. This lends credence to my hunch that we should improve (rather than discard) our schools as a childrearing institution. Could schools be made at least as good for children as villages were? We shouldn't rule out the possibility. With enough adult support, we can make our kids strong enough to handle—and hopefully improve—this brave new world that gets braver by the day.

The On-Target Aim of Schools

The summary of a report called *Voices from the Inside: A Report on Schooling from Inside the Classroom* by Mary Poplin and Joseph Weeres reads,

> By far our most consistent and striking finding is this: Students, parents, teachers, administrators, and other staff members believe the crisis in schools is directly linked to human relationships. . . . Teachers report their best experiences in school take place when they connect with students, and students describe their best teachers in similar ways. Teachers also say they regret having so little time in the day to seek out individual students. (1993)

Threatening though it may be to educators like myself, we would be wise to recognize that teaching our subjects per se is not the most important thing we do. Poplin and Weeres add that they had "predicted issues such as what to teach, how to measure it, how much a teacher knows, and choice of school would have surfaced; they did not" (via Clinchy 2002, p. 45). In other words, as I'll reiterate frequently, *relationships trump academics*. As Daniel, Wassell, and Gilligan put it, school's "socio-emotional effects provide more protection than intellectual effects" (1999, p. 229). Well-being research points to a similar conclusion, that education's correlation with life satisfaction "may be largely instrumental, acting mainly through its effects on human and social capital," that is, improved relationships (Helliwell and Putnam 2005, p. 437). Richard Layard, an economist who has turned his eye on well-being research, argues that amount of education exerts its influence on happiness mainly in that it controls access to relative income advantage; he concludes from the research that family relationships, steady work, community and friends, and health are the predominant external factors in order of importance (2005, pp. 62–63).[3] This book's proposals touch on every one of these aspects to a greater or lesser degree, but particularly on that of community.

Knowledge should be gained in addition to, not at the expense of, the other things a child needs. School is a large part of a child's life and, for far too many children, a necessary supplement to the insufficient positive adult attention in their families (Rockwell 1997). But again, my proposal is not about scapegoating "bad" parents but about helping more parents be effective by increasing their social support. By focusing on their role in childrearing, schools can serve society better than they currently do. James Comer, the child psychiatrist behind the Comer School Development Program at Yale, writes,

> Schools of education should be called schools of child development and education, which could help establish the importance and give focus to the discipline of education at the university level. A child-development focus would suggest appropriate community-family-school policy, preparation and selection of teachers, and the organization, support, and management of schools and school systems. This in turn would affect curriculum and instruction, and promote needed attitudes among all in a school. (1997, p. 173)

Schools are, after all, one of "the key public institutions commissioned with responsibility to create social environments which make it possible for healthy personality to develop" (Cotterell 1996, p. 214). By focusing on healthy development, schools will be perfectly poised to help maximize the number of prosocial adults in society without sacrificing intellectual rigor.

Despite our best intentions, our relationship loads send the message that our institution of school subordinates childrearing to principles of efficiency purloined from the world of business. Influential psychiatrist William Glasser argues that we're requiring families to give their children enough adult attention to *overcome* the effects of school (1969, p. 14). Schools and families should be on the same team. In sum, schools should be places designed with relationships in mind.

Indeed, one could say there are three levels of conceptualizing school knowledge, each of which correlates with a different level of belief in home-school compatibility: On the first level, those who fear the school's destabilizing effect on what is taught in the home tend to promote the idea that knowledge does or should consist of "facts." On the second level, those who frame knowledge as "critical thinking" often express defensiveness at the idea that teachers are involved in childrearing, suggesting an acceptance of ideological questioning but a fear of emotional involvement. The third level is that knowledge is relational; only by parents and teachers collaborating in childrearing will schooling meet academic, emotional, and democratic or pluralistic needs simultaneously. Relational knowledge does not exclude facts and critical thinking; rather, it admits that participants are embedded in a community where these things are negotiated through dialog. Educational philosopher Alexander Sidorkin (2002) writes,

Let us try to imagine that all curriculum, all knowledge and skills that students acquire have no independent worth or meaning. All of these are simply means of entering the world wide web of relations; these are simply tools, tokens, or signs that allow students to enter the relational fabric of human existence. (p. 88)

Relationship load reduction is the logical conclusion of this more complete conception of knowledge.

Some claim that proposals like mine are intended to "just" make kids feel better about themselves and therefore undermine the academic goals of our schools. On the contrary, small groupings will be more effective at making students feel good about themselves (and others) *through* competence, not *instead* of it. For various reasons detailed in Chapter 6, small groupings will actually enable teachers to *raise* their academic expectations. Here are three examples of the many reasons:

1. Schoolwork will not need to be simplified to serve the purpose of crowd control.
2. Schoolwork can be personalized and thus better matched to each student's skills and interests.
3. Attachment relationships will enhance motivation and time on task.

I'll admit there is a counterintuitiveness to letting go of the philosophy of separation and its imaginary achievement crisis. Challenging schoolwork will still be the *content* of better school interactions—it just won't be (and never should have been) their only *purpose*. Teachers of small classes in small schools will focus on academics, but *through* nurturance rather than *at the expense of* it. We can reach both goals simultaneously because nurturing conditions are also conducive to learning. Let's get our aims on target by getting the crisis right.

3

The Racial Relationship Gap

Just as academic achievement is not equitably distributed across races, relationship load is not equitably distributed. A major factor in the achievement gap is that students of color tend to be placed in schools that are "understaffed and overpopulated" (Williams and Land 2006, p. 583). Consider the four aspects of relationship load as experienced by two racial groups who tend to experience less school success. African Americans and Latinos are more likely to be in large schools and classes. As Figure 3.1's trend line demonstrates, smaller pupil/teacher ratios (a correlate of class size) are disproportionately an entitlement of white students.

One study suggests, "Hispanic teens are more likely than Blacks and Whites to attend public high schools that have the most students" as well as the "highest student-teacher ratios" ("Pew Report" 2005). Other data suggest that the pupil/teacher ratio indeed correlates with class size in this case, leaving urban classes about two students larger on average (Ballou 1997). Lee and Wong (2003) report that predominantly African American schools also have larger classes on average than predominantly white schools. This continues a historical trend. Cuban reports that in 1947, segregated schools in Washington, DC, had an average class size of thirty-nine for black kids but only thirty-two for white (1984, p. 87). Even in public pre-K classrooms, an intervention purportedly targeted to poor students of color, those in schools with 50 percent or more minority students are three

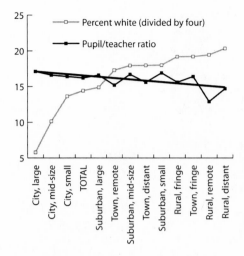

Figure 3.1 *Pupil/teacher ratio in U.S. public schools compared to percentage of white students by community type, 2004.*

Source: Digest 2006, table 86.

students larger—which is 23 percent in this case—than in schools that have 6 percent to 20 percent minority students (NCES 2003a, section 5).

As Figure 3.2 shows, white students also disproportionately attend smaller schools. A trend line makes the relationship clearer. Teacher continuity is also lower on average in schools in which blacks and Latinos are the majority. These schools tend to have the highest teacher turnover, leaving black and Latino students with shorter relationships with their teachers, on average, than white students get. Figure 3.3 suggests that teachers are twice as likely to transfer from a high-poverty school. As mentioned, the reduced experience and training of teachers in mostly minority schools is a chief factor in the

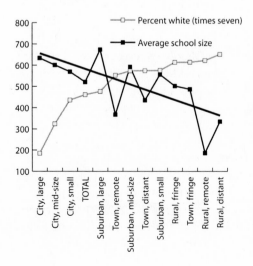

Figure 3.2 *Average school size in U.S. public schools compared to percentage of white students by community type, 2004.*

Source: Digest 2006, table 86.

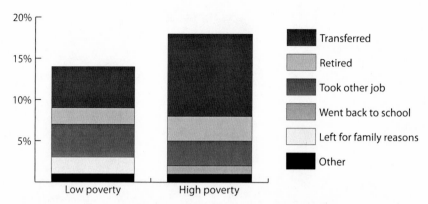

Figure 3.3 *Percent of teachers leaving for various reasons from public K–12 schools where they have taught, 1999 to 2000. The low poverty category comprises those schools where fewer than 15 percent of the students qualified for free and reduced lunch. The high poverty category comprises those schools where 75 percent or more qualified.*
Source: NCES 2005, figure 8.

achievement gap (Darling-Hammond 2006, p. 335). Here poverty is a correlate of race. Let's discuss the connection.

Poverty in and of itself also correlates with large relationship load, and poverty is not equally distributed across races. Members of all minority groups but continental Asians are two to three times more likely to live in poverty than whites (NCES 2007a, indicator 4). Students of color are more likely to have impoverished schoolmates. Nearly half of African American and Latino fourth graders were in schools where more than 75 percent of students were eligible for free or reduced lunch. Only Asians and Pacific Islanders were more likely than whites to be in schools where fewer than 10 percent of students were eligible for lunch subsidy (NCES 2007a, indicator 7). Poverty (as indicated by lunch subsidy) is 14 percent higher in the 100 largest districts, which tend to have larger schools and classes (NCES 2003b). As with race, this is true even for the youngest kids. Although the opportunity for free pre-K correlates with being poor and minority because it's a targeted intervention (NCES 2003a, section 3), the numbers remain discriminatory, higher class size correlating with higher concentrated poverty (section 5).

Poverty has additional implications for teacher continuity and parent-teacher communication. The jobs available to people in poverty are often temporary; this and other correlates of poverty make families less geographically stable, causing children in these groups to have shorter stays at schools, which decreases the continuity of their relationships with school adults (Orfield

1996, p. 54). Poverty also frequently forces parents to work more and to have jobs that allow less leeway for interacting with educators.

Families that work more also have less time together. This is one of several arguments that could be made to show that the nurturance crisis—lack of adult attention in children's lives—affects our society inequitably by race and class just as much as academic achievement. It could be argued that because the poor, who are disproportionately people of color, live in neighborhoods with additional challenges to growing up, they are in fact asked to be *better* parents to get the same results. Berliner writes, "A 'good' zip code can make a bigger difference than good parenting" (2006). In other words, nonpoor parents are more able to rely on (and take for granted) the nonnuclear family support human parents have consistently had until very recently.

It could also be argued that racism and economic hardship leave poor and minority children with *greater* needs for positive adult attention because of greater suspicion that teachers disapprove of them (which may sometimes, unfortunately, be true) and more negative emotion that needs to get heard because of the negative experiences that go along with racism and classism. William Smith (2008) has coined "Racial Battle Fatigue" to explain "how the social environment (e.g., institutions, policies, practices, traditions, groups and individuals) perpetuates race-related stressors that adversely affect the health and academic achievement of Students of Color." For similar reasons, poor urban parents tend to be those most deprived of the help of other adults in raising their kids. Joyce Epstein and Mavis Sanders cite research that finds that "urban families had limited natural support systems and placed heavy importance on their connections with the children's schools" (2000, p. 293). Hence, I propose classes of nine for the communities with the most concentrated poverty and the effects of this country's historical and contemporary racism.

I believe it would be unwise to opt out of using relationship load reduction to solve the nurturance crisis in the fear that it will detract from a focus on the racial achievement gap, the largest reason being that they are not mutually exclusive choices. Smallness will undoubtedly have *some* impact on the achievement gap and arguably a great deal of impact. Reason A: Some researchers claim it already has. Grissmer, Flanagan, and Williamson (1997) write,

> The often-quoted evidence that real per-pupil resources doubled in education from the late 1960s to early 1990s while NAEP scores stagnated is flawed. . . . When disaggregated, scores for all racial-ethnic groups rose in reading and mathematics for all age groups. Non-Hispanic whites' scores rose by smaller amounts, while scores for Hispanics and blacks rose dramatically.

They claim "a disproportionate amount of resources was directed toward minority and lower income students." They find more evidence to credit gradual class size reduction with narrowing the racial achievement gap than the many other changes during the period, including that the average teacher was better educated and more experienced. Christopher Jencks and Meredith Phillips (1998) argue that further class size reduction is one of two policy responses most likely to reduce the black-white test score gap (p. 44).[1] Moreover, many who argue against class size reduction because of its cost relative to test score gain acknowledge that the gains for racially stigmatized students are significant (e.g., Allen and Lynd 2000).

Others cite evidence that school size reduction has similar effects for racially stigmatized students, not least of which because they tend to be in larger schools:

> There is evidence that size is a more important issue for students from disadvantaged social backgrounds, both directly in terms of learning and indirectly in terms of differentiating environments that seldom favor minority and low-income students. Thus, it is often the case that the students who would benefit from smaller high schools the most—minority and low-income students—are actually educated in the largest schools. (Ready, Lee, and Welner 2004)

Reason B: Racially unequal education is in many respects a *relationship* gap—inequitable treatment, expectations, and social support. Although relationship load reduction won't solve age-old white supremacy single-handedly, it is my conviction that relationship load reduction will help in the incremental breaking down of racism, sexism, classism, homophobia, and the like, through deep relationships in the public sphere that challenge assumptions and assuage fears. Although I do not argue that group size reduction alone will overwhelmingly make teachers and administrators less discriminatory, there are several reasons to believe that it could be an important piece of such progress.

First, relationship load reduction facilitates the efforts of those educators already inclined to address the challenges of "disadvantaged" groups. Second, it offers educators and students more opportunity to know and trust one another and thus transcend stereotyping one another. Not all will automatically take advantage of this opportunity, of course, and probably children are more likely to do so than adults. But as I'll revisit in Chapter 6, large groups tempt us to focus attention on a smaller subgroup, and in our anxiety we tend to seek out those most like us; this helps explain the common case of a white, middle-class teacher feeling justified (whether consciously or not) in giving more attention to white, middle-class students. Smaller groups are likely to reduce this tendency. Again, though, grouping size reduction will by no means be a complete solution to inequity—nor will schools ever get much further past it than the rest of society. Educators—particularly white ones—need to become conscious of how they treat students of different backgrounds and appearances than their own and seek to overcome their prejudices. Open acknowledgment of inequality is central to fighting it, and teachers need to be willing to talk about inequality in education with students and others. Well intentioned or not, acting as if we're already all equal, as if we no longer see race, is a copout. As Cris Mayo (2004) warns us, we do not want to set our sights on making relationships in education "less difficult" as yet another way for whites to avoid confronting the realities of race and racism.

Third, though racist interactions and outcomes certainly don't disappear completely because of smallness, there is evidence that smaller schools and classes have an equalizing effect on discriminatory achievement outcomes (Achilles 1999, p. 81; Ready, Lee, and Welner 2004). Miraculously fixing the injustice of the minority achievement gap through the memorization of test-score answers will not solve the injustice of how unfairly the real nurturance crisis impacts people of color; but truly addressing the real crisis in those communities with the recommendations in this book *will* help close the achievement gap (Achilles 1999, p. 81; see also Rice 2002, p. 92) and a whole lot more that stands in the way of minority Americans. Universal small classes would help those less empowered by society and school to learn better for the same reason they would help all kids learn better—the reason being that *getting taught curriculum* is secondary to *being raised*. Again, if we get them in the right order, we can do both.

This leads us to yet another reason a focus on the achievement gap should not overshadow the need for fixing the nurturance crisis—reason C: Research has shown that smallness is more consistently effective at raising college enrollment and graduation rates than test scores (Funk and Bailey 1999). If you had to choose one of the two, which would it be? Clearly rates of college completion will change the social and economic status of stigmatized groups more than test scores will. Research also suggests that the test-score gap can close without much effect on the college-going gap:

> High schools with large numbers of poor students send a smaller proportion of their graduates to college than do high schools with fewer poor students. Further, impoverished high schools that manage to perform well on the accountability tests lag well behind like-performing affluent schools in postsecondary enrollment. (Price and Reeves 2003)

Small schools (which tend to have smaller classes), not test score increases, are the intervention that's been found to increase college enrollment and completion among stigmatized students, and hence closer income and social respect parity for stigmatized groups. Again, if we get the crisis right, we may solve achievement concerns in ways that make better sense simply because our priorities are straight. We are working for people, not test scores.

Let me conclude by explaining why my proposal seeks to help racially stigmatized kids and communities first, but not exclusively. There is another flaw in the attempt to close the achievement gap without relationship load reduction, and it's a flaw shared by many arguments in favor of the "disadvantaged" that include issues of mental health and happiness: The assumption of a zero-sum game. Briefly, it is sometimes assumed that those with more privilege, opportunity, or power would hoard their increased happiness if given equal opportunity to mental health gains and use it to widen or maintain socioeconomic divides. Common sense points to the contrary, as does evidence. Huppert cites research indicating that, similar to physical health phenomena, population-wide mental health improvements appear to "trickle down" to those with the most risk factors (2005, p. 327). A simple explanation for such a process is contained in attachment theory, which posits that the predominant (fixable) source of a lack of mental health is a lack of access to functional relationships. Thus mental health is not a zero-sum game: Better relationships can multiply. It is a rare person who will disagree that the human tendency to oppress weaker groups is aggravated by unhappiness and reduced by happiness. In short, a happier majority is likely to be a less oppressive majority.

We should not confine our efforts toward educational racial justice to relationship load reduction, nor should we leave it out.

4

Defining the Harm: Adult Attention Deficit

I n this chapter I hope to make clear what children need from adults and how it harms them not to get it. I will also discredit three damaging myths:

- Less attention makes kids more self-reliant.
- Parents are the only adults whose attention matters.
- In all circumstances, older children have less need for attention.

All kids want and need attention from adults, and schools don't provide nearly enough of it.

Attention Balanced with Autonomy

The reasoning in this proposal is grounded in the understanding that the two overarching needs perceptible to children in their relationship to adults are *autonomy*, that is, getting to do what they want (explore the world, seek pleasure, play) and *attention*, that is, getting help from caregivers when they're hungry, bored, unsure, lonely, afraid, hurt, and so on. Support for this assertion lies at the heart of attachment theory, which began with the work of John Bowlby. The work of Bowlby and his colleague, Mary Ainsworth, asserts that children explore the world from the "secure base" of the caregiver. When the base is not felt to be secure, the exploration suffers, and thus healthy development suffers. This need to explore the world equates with the notion of autonomy, while the secure base or "the need for a particular person if distressed" equates with the notion of adult attention (Daniel et al. 1999, p. 17). Bowlby echoes my choice of terms when he writes,

> Those who are most stable emotionally and making the most of their opportunities are those who have parents who, whilst always encouraging their children's *autonomy*, are none the less *available and responsive when called upon*. Unfortunately, of course, the reverse is also true. (1988, p. 12, emphasis mine)

Many present a more complex picture of needs. For example, Sands and colleagues (2000) isolate seven needs listed in Figure 4.1. They add, "These purposes or outcomes become the reinforcers for our behavior. The higher the probability that we will meet our needs in one of these seven areas, the more likely we are to perform the behavior" (2000). These needs can be seen to correspond to a simplified explanation derived from attachment theory. By arguing that autonomy and attention are the principal perceived needs of children, other needs should not be understood to have been erased. The simpler picture of just two labels can be expanded with more specificity when necessary.

Attachment theory demonstrates that when you hurt one half of the autonomy-attention balance, you also hurt the other. If you impair the availability of attachment figures, you "impair a child's security and the associated exploratory behavior" (Daniel et al. 1999, p. 18). Christine Stephen (2003) writes, "Children need adult support, comfort and company. However, their need for this (particularly for individual attention) is not constant throughout the day, but is an immediate and pressing need when experienced." In other words, children are not *constantly* checking for caregiver attention, but when they do check, the answer matters to them (Fraley 2004).

It is worth noting that urgent needs for attention do not always involve negative emotions. For example, "Three-year-olds can be observed to demonstrate pleasure and pride in solving problems and will call an adult's attention to their accomplishments" (Slentz and Krogh 2001, p. 158). This is a prime illustration of the interplay: A child wants adult attention in order to show off her growing independence, to give it meaning. British educational psychologist Mia Pringle writes, "Competence brings its own reward while the mother's or other adults' pleasure in the child's newly acquired skill further reinforces his willingness to seek new fields to conquer" (1980, p. 42). Here Pringle also provides support for a concept we'll return to later in this chapter: With chores (as opposed to child-directed play), where competence

Commonly cited needs	Autonomy	Adult attention
Freedom		
Power		
Fun		
Self-expression		
Safety/security		
Recognition		
Affiliation		

Figure 4.1 *The overlap between attachment theory and theories of multiple needs.*
Source: Sands et al. 2000.

in the eyes of the adult world is a central issue, a child needs an adult to be more directly and consistently involved. Pringle also portrays the pleasure inherent in receiving adult attention as the child's incentive in the face of disappointments. When a proper balance is struck between these two principal child-perceived needs—autonomy and attention—children thrive.

Far from Fostering Dependence

The balance between autonomy and attention also relates to the balance between society and the individual. The hyperindividualism that shapes so much of our public policy has a dangerously tilted view of these balances. It is part of a philosophy of separation that places too much emphasis on autonomy. Meier writes, "It's not true that the best way to learn to deal with adult change and trauma is to know nothing but change and trauma. In fact, it's quite the opposite; greater, not less, intimacy between generations is at the heart of all the best school reform efforts around today" (2002, p. 13). The "tough-love" notion accepted by some that too much attention will breed dependence is not supported by research. Some might argue, for example, that a self-regulated learner has no need for teacher attention. Research disagrees: "Self-regulated learners feel autonomous. This does not mean they are self-sufficient and isolated from others. On the contrary, they feel comfortable asking for assistance when necessary" (R. S. Newman 2002).

Hyperindividualist assertions that an increase in adult attention in our children's lives will create overly dependent adults are simply wrong. Daniel, Wassell, and Gilligan argue that this is not true even for adolescents categorized as insecure or anxious, who tend to have a "preoccupation with the presence or availability of adults or carers." The evidence suggests that meeting a teen's needs for adult availability "will not make the young person over-dependent; rather, the reassurance of the carer's availability will allow them to become more self-reliant" (1999, pp. 279–280). Daniel and colleagues summarize research on the effects on children of psychologically unavailable parents by stating, "When seen later at 54 months of age, these same children demonstrate poor impulse control, extreme dependence on their teachers and other generalized behavior problems in the classroom" (p. 132). In other words, overdependence and negative or antisocial expressions of autonomy tend to come from too little attention, not from too much.

No Rules?

Another objection may come from the opposite direction: Am I advocating *too much* autonomy, no setting of limits with children? Adults clearly meet many more of children's needs than those that children can perceive, what Noddings (2003) calls "expressed" needs, but these other "inferred" needs are often overemphasized in schools (p. 243). Adult attention is not restricted to meeting children's expressed needs. Attention that appears negative to children in the short term may be positive in its long-term effects. I am not naïvely arguing that all forms of negative attention are eventually beneficial to children, but the fact remains that adults must do things for children—because they care about them—that children see as negative. Fortunately, children tend to accept those things in exchange for enough of what they do find satisfying. Again, a balance is what is called for.

I am advocating a balanced and simultaneous approach to meeting the needs for both autonomy, on the one hand, and, on the other, children's inferred and expressed needs for their autonomy to be limited in the interest of social compromise that offers some measure of predictability and fairness. In a way it's silly to posit an attachment relationship that doesn't offer children limits, let alone a child that doesn't want any. Certainly there are adults and schools that take rule-making too far, but no one functions without some semblance of rules or interpersonal compromises. Attachment theory's "exploring the world" is not meant to posit a world empty of other people; it includes exploring the *social* world and its limits and possibilities—and even its injustices that cry out for fixing.

Only through comprehensive care—balanced between autonomy and attention, that *feels* to children like care—will children become the sort of adults we want them to be and that they most often aspire to be. The limits set by parents and other caregivers are just as important as meeting the perceived needs. Together their effect is to create adults who are autonomous in the prosocial sense, neither selfish and hyperindividualistic at one extreme nor unquestioningly compliant and conformist at the other. According to Smetana, Campione-Barr, and Daddis (2004), "recent definitions of autonomy have focused on self-governance of behavior in the context of supportive guidance, relational ties, and social commitments" (p. 1418). Again, the goal is a balance.

Where Does Attachment Go at Adulthood?

Though attachment theory began as an explanation for why infants who were deprived of care showed alarmingly negative impacts (Bowlby 1988, p. 21), and though it still is discussed most often in infant and toddler issues, attachment theorists have always applied it beyond the infant-mother pair (p. 119). Scholars continue to use it to explain all forms of social bonding and belonging, from teacher-student relationships to equal-status adult relationships like marriage, which appear to stick close to the "internal working model" formed in childhood relationships (Daniel et al. 1999, p. 18). Though adults also shift between needing autonomy and attention, maturity allows us to be more patient in times of need and more conscious of the cyclical shifting between the two. Adults still need attention, but usually it's without regard to how old others are.

Attachment is lifelong and, many argue, transfers to society or humanity at large (Holmes 1996). In other words, attachment can be seen as precisely the mechanism by which children become prosocial and even justice-seeking adults, by which they come to see others as deserving the same respect their parents and siblings do. It is through promoting secure attachment that society can ethically expect adults to abide by laws; well-treated children become adults who've generalized positive, justice-seeking social behaviors from their family to humanity.

An example of adult attachment is friendship or partnership. Through relationship load reduction, parents and teachers can better form this sort of adult attachment. An improved educator-guardian partnership is valuable for the student but also for its own sake as a deeper relationship in the two adults' lives.

Age Differences

Although attachment is lifelong, its nature does change with age. But it does not vary in ways that justify large school groupings, even in high school. Bowlby himself finds more similarities than differences among attachment behaviors at various ages. "When an individual (of any age) is feeling secure he is likely to explore away from his attachment figure" (1988, p. 121). There are several points that need to be made:

First, after the age of three or so, separation anxiety gradually appears less acute and intense (Bowlby 1988, p. 179). This reduction in observable separation anxiety is a sign of ongoing healthy attachment; it does not mean that attachment becomes less important. Anxiety still occurs when people's attachment figures are needed but unavailable—it's simply less acute for older people, especially those who had a secure primary attachment in those first three years.

Second, though primary attachments are most critical in the first three years of life, the need for them does not suddenly vanish. Benson writes, "The demand for attention to developmental needs does not end at age five, or ten or fifteen" (1997, p. 89).

> Children typically do not begin to have the cognitive or emotional abilities to internalize certain behaviors, values, and competencies— the internal assets—until ages six to nine. They develop these ... through a slow process of observation, social learning, and internal- ization, a process that continues through early and middle adoles- cence. (p. 80)

This means that we jeopardize an essential developmental opportunity if we leave school-age children outside of secure attachments for six to seven hours a day.

Third, much of a child's development is determined by attachments that are not primary. "By the time young people enter middle school, we hypoth- esize that a young person's development is heavily, if not largely, shaped by influences beyond the family" (Benson 1997, p. 89). Judith Harris (1998) dem- onstrates that peer influence on identity and development is far underesti- mated. Attachment theory would see these peer relationships as secondary attachments. As I'll argue below, only in the context of secure attachments to adults will these peer attachments tend to be positive for development.

Fourth, the longer a child goes without secure attachments, the harder it becomes to remedy their difficulties (Dryfoos 1998, p. 105). Appendix C goes into more detail on this issue. Fifth, evidence of early attachment problems can be hidden until much later. "Indeed it can often be during adolescence that attachment problems become most pronounced" (Daniel et al. 1999, p. 278). As discussed earlier, this has led to the false perception that what we have is a "youth problem" when it's really an adult problem.

Sixth, children need and seek a greater number of attachments as they age. Edward Zigler, namesake of the Edward Zigler Center in Child Develop- ment and Social Policy at Yale, and Mary Lang write, "A child needs to relate to a limited number of adults in the course of a day, a number that increases with the age of the child" (1991, p. 63). Though it may seem counterintuitive, the more securely attached a child is to the primary caregiver, the more at- tachment figures he or she tends to seek and the more secure these other at- tachments become; nor do these other attachments weaken the original bond

(Bowlby 1982, p. 308). In other words, lack of other attachments beyond parents is a sign of weak attachment to them, not strong. It's a sort of winner-take-all system: When security rains, it pours. Again, this suggests that society would be best served if each individual adult had had ample opportunity to form multiple attachments—parental and nonparental—throughout their lives, but at the very least throughout the entirety of their childhood.

Seventh, adolescence is a time when secondary attachments can become more attractive than primary attachments. Though adolescents often reject *parental* attention (because they are separating their identities from them) they still want *adult* attention. School is the logical place to provide such adults. Fredriksen and Rhodes write that teacher-student relationships "can be particularly important to early adolescents, who are often undergoing profound shifts in their sense of self and are struggling to negotiate changing relationships with their parents and peers" (2004, pp. 48–49). Let's address nonparents in more detail.

Squandered Adults: Attachment to Nonparents

Parents can't do it all. For example, one study found "that children with more frequent and high quality contact with non-parental adults have fewer behavior problems" (Rishel, Sales, and Koeske 2005). As shown above, attachment is not a zero-sum game. An increase in nonparental attachments does not result in a loss of parental attachment. To argue that nearly all children attach most strongly to their parents is quite reasonable. Clearly, the ideal situation is for a child to have a healthy attachment to a guardian (or two) that far exceeds the importance of any other attachment. "This is the single most important resource you can have to promote resilience in childhood: having someone who is crazy about you" (Garbarino 1995, p. 158). But to argue that attachment relationships to parents are essentially different from attachments to other adults, rather than just more intense, is silly. It is especially dangerous to carry on this misconception when parents leave their children for extended periods with adults who act, in legal terms, *in loco parentis*, "in place of the parent." To argue that such an adult either can't or shouldn't have an attachment relationship with the child that approximates a parental one is to advocate for neglect.

Although many have left teachers out of the attachment equation, there are plenty who have included them. Benson writes,

A second kind of necessary support is provided by sustained contact with adults other than parents. . . . This could be an aunt or uncle, a teacher *who pays attention to and takes an interest in a child across more than one school year.* It is the adult in a congregation who develops a long-term friendship with a child. It is a neighbor who always acknowledges a child's presence. (1997, p. 36, emphasis mine)

Notice that the teacher gets the longest qualification. This speaks to the tacit understanding that in large classes it is out of the ordinary to get significant attention from a teacher. The next qualifier, "across more than one school year," speaks to the need for greater continuity of teacher-student relationships. Others have been less cautious: Fredriksen and Rhodes summarize research that correlated "perceived decreasing teacher support" with "increased depressive symptoms and decreased self-esteem" among middle school students (2004, p. 46).

Many researchers have found support for the notion that any prominent adult in a child's life is a potential (and much-needed) attachment figure. "Strong, healthy connections with prosocial adults have been identified as the key protective factor buffering children against the negative influence of adversity" (Deiro 2005, p. 3). Many point out that other adults, often teachers, can serve as "pinch-hitter" parental figures for children whose parents prove inadequate in a childrearing system that puts its eggs in too few baskets. Richard Williams and Colin Pritchard (2006) write,

After the family and peers nothing is more important or influential to children than their school. It is . . . not only where, hopefully, they can maximize their potential, but where society meets the child in trouble and can go some way to compensating them for any disadvantage. Indeed, irrespective of socio-economic and family structure, if a child likes school, this is a formidable barrier against being involved in many problematic behaviors. . . . One issue that continues to bedevil schools, however, is that of class size. (p. 21)

But it is not only "misparented" children who need other adults, of course—it is all children. In sum, the parents-only mindset is both naïve and dangerous—by placing all our chips on this one relationship, we give "misparenting" its power.[1]

Peers: The Keyword Is Balance

The influence of peers can be negative when out of balance with adult influence (Clark 2004, pp. 110–111). One of the benefits of smaller school grouping size would be, according to British psychologist Penelope Leach, to "replace some of the peer influence with adult influence and enthusiasm" (1994, p. 164).

Notice that she did not say *all*. Research into ideal daycare arrangements has yielded results that support this notion of balance:

> For cognitive development, sociability with a friend, and social competence with adults, a moderate amount of interaction with peers in day care was best. This moderate amount of interaction offered children the best of two worlds: an adequate opportunity to learn about peers by interacting freely with them, without at the same time losing the benefits of frequent interactions with an adult caregiver. (Clarke-Stewart et al. 1994, p. 239)

In the context of kids in daycare and not yet of school age, the researchers specify some precise numbers by recommending a situation "that offers the child opportunities to interact with a moderate number of diverse other children—four or five—under the supervision of one adult" (p. 240). The result of too many peers is negative and may even make later adult attention (from teachers) less effective. It is *ongoing adult attention* that allows children to interact positively with peers. Research like this fits perfectly with attachment theory's contention that only a secure attachment to an adult allows a child to explore the environment confidently and benefit from other attachments (Daniel et al. 1999, p. 243).

The desire for peer attention is quite natural. There is only one caveat: In the absence of secure adult attachment, children tend to approach peer relationships with an unhealthy level of insecurity. In such a frame of mind, peers can more easily lead one another astray. Nicole Gnezda writes,

> Young people who lack the affirmation of being loved are often willing to sacrifice everything for peer acceptance. Gangs and pregnancy fill the empty spaces in the hearts of underloved teenagers because they seem to offer "someone who's got my back" and "someone who will love me." (2005, p. 34)

Kids tend to get plenty of peer attention in our schools—it's adult attention that's the missing piece.

Older Peers, the Forgotten Role Models

Does the age of peers make a difference? In the same study already mentioned, Clarke-Stewart and colleagues discuss how they observed older children's presence to have a positive effect on development, but the researchers go on to emphasize that the effects of attention from adults dwarfs that of older peers (1994, p. 201). Such evidence suggests that we might move away from age-group isolation in our schools, but without smaller groupings as a first step, we are unlikely to get significant benefits. Adjusting age grouping to better serve child development could be a relatively easy and inexpensive add-on, but it's not a substitute for increased adult attention.

Play versus Work

Beyond limiting dangerous and unhealthy behavior, limiting children's freedom includes the assigning of work or chores, which include much of what happens at school. As discussed above, the level of involvement from adults needed to assure that adult attention is perceived to be available diminishes with age, which is reflected in group-size and adult/child-ratio limits in most state regulations of childcare facilities. I now need to add one qualifier to that: It applies primarily to play rather than work. Though ratios at daycares change as children age, I believe school class size should not change between kindergarten and twelfth grade. One main reason for this is that children generally *play* at daycares and *work* at schools. As work gets harder and less like play, adult attention remains at a constant level of importance. Let me explain.

Figure 4.2 is an attempt to classify the spectrum of childhood activities, each of the four quadrants marking off different levels of need for adult attention. The *low-support chores* quadrant is highlighted because it is the danger zone where schools fail children. Too much time in this quadrant at the expense of the others is emotionally neglectful and developmentally harmful. Play tends to be children's primary use of their much-sought-after autonomy. In play, the adult is usually uninvolved but available when needed, such as when the child becomes bored. As a typical parenting guide advises, "Naturally, you should intervene when it looks like someone could get hurt, when they seem to be having difficulty working out a problem, or when they specifically ask for your assistance. But otherwise, butt

↑ Increasing amount of adult involvement	Coplay	High-support chores
	Free play	Low-support chores
	Decreasing amount of child choice →	

Figure 4.2 *Childhood activities in a two-dimensional spectrum. The quadrants variously combine autonomy and attention.*

out" (Steinberg 2004, p. 121). One should "butt out" because free play is extremely valuable to cognitive and emotional development (Garbarino 1995, p. 12).

Caring adults will occasionally "coplay," that is, offer to join the play or plan fun activities as a way to demonstrate their availability. Daniel and colleagues (1999) offer support for these two levels of adult involvement in play. They argue that attachment develops as the result of two cycles of interaction between child and caregiver that correspond closely with my labels of free play and coplay. The first, the "arousal-relaxation cycle," is initiated by the child in times of need. By responding appropriately (i.e., paying attention and attempting to meet the need), the caregiver allows the child to develop feelings of trust and security—a restatement of attachment theory. As alluded to earlier, the authors note that "some parents and alternative caregivers feel that children need to be shielded from all discomfort, however, the arousal-relaxation cycle suggests that it is the *soothing* process that is crucial, rather than the attempt to anticipate all discomfort" (p. 38). In other words, it's okay to leave children alone to play for a while and put them at risk for negative feelings as long as the perception that the adult is available to soothe remains strong. The second cycle of interaction they call the "positive interaction cycle" where the adult initiates positive interactions, which the child enjoys, leading the adults to continue initiating such interactions. The result for the child of such unconditional displays of positive attention—through coplay— is a sense of self-worth and increased security in the availability of the caregiver.

Chores, on the other hand, are necessarily an adult-chosen activity; thus an adult needs to be more involved to ensure efficiency and to offer help, comfort, correction, or challenge. According to another childrearing guide, children like to do chores because it makes them feel useful (Taylor 2003, p. 144). I would change that slightly but significantly: Children like to do chores *so long as* it makes them feel useful. Adult attention makes that possible. Susan Kohl writes that the Child Development Project's research

> has shown that one of the best things parents can do is take the time
> to peel carrots, fold clothes, or clean the kitchen with their child. The
> more children engage in cooperative activities, the more motivated
> they become to help and work with others harmoniously. (2004,
> p. 119)

"As a child," Kohl confesses, "I resisted having to wash the dishes or being sent to clean up my room. . . . Yet I enjoyed working with either of my parents on projects" (p. 118). She relates that once while running a workshop, she asked the participants to draw a favorite activity from childhood:

> I was amazed that almost every one of us drew ourselves working on a project with a parent, like baking cookies or gardening. . . . I think part of the pleasure of shared work is that the adult sees the child as having the competence for collaboration and wishes to include him in the activity. (pp. 118–119)

She therefore recommends shared work as part of good childrearing.

This working together on chores is what I've called *high-support chores* in the above diagram. Certainly some amount of low-support chores is necessary to develop sufficient autonomy in our children. Caring adults support children's development of prosocial independence by assigning them age-appropriate unsupervised duties; the culmination of this increasing chore independence might be a teenager's first job, where the reward structure is the same one operating on the parent. Unfortunately, low-support chores can quickly become excessive and approach the unethical. At the extreme is the loss of true childhood entirely. The sharing of work between adults and children is precisely what's missing in industrial and postindustrial societies; hence the nurturance crisis. Though most play can and maybe ought to be free rather than coplay, the balance is reversed with chores; most chores ought to have high rather than low support. Getting this balance wrong is the part that makes our schools neglectful: The perception of attention-availability is undermined if low support for chores is done repeatedly for adult convenience.

High-support chores are clearly more beneficial as teaching situations than low-support chores. In the course of the school day, there may be activities that fit in any of the four quadrants of activity, but chores will tend to predominate, especially as children age. The ideal may be to have students engage in sustained educational play. But the chief problem with proposing to increase autonomy without increasing attention is that only exceptional schools and teachers can probably pull it off.[2] Most schools—most of the time—won't be able to reach that ideal because of pressures from tradition and standardization. Large grouping size makes it such that few will ever dare try such freedom. Sidorkin (2002) writes, "Not all learning can be fun, and the older students are, the more this is true. The search for intrinsically motivating learning activities is a worthy one and should continue; we just need to be clear that it has very definite limits" (p. 87).

Consequently, kids will usually perceive school as work because most of them will be in work-based schools, so they'll naturally prefer to have high rather than low adult support. Play-based schools clearly have benefits for development, but, luckily, work-based schools will also "work" for child development so long as the work is (a) in the context of strong attachment relationships and (b) as personalized as possible. Both of these conditions are facilitated by relationship load reduction. Work *won't* "work" if school remains impersonal as a result of large relationship loads. Miles and Darling-Hammond observe that nonacademic classes are often smaller in public secondary schools than academic ones (1998). This is clearly backward when considering the work-play distinction.

A last factor that makes work require more adult attention is the simple fact that it raises the danger of feelings of failure, which free play does not normally raise. Glasser (1969) believes that our schools' tendency to ascribe failure to children is their chief problem. Relationship load reduction should decrease this tendency.

In sum, children see themselves on the path to adulthood. In play they mimic adult scenarios. In chores, though, they usually cannot act independently because they aren't adults and don't see the value of chores except by trusting the authority of adults. Adults have a number of ways of understanding and prioritizing chores based on feedback and consequences from the outside world—principally from relationships, incidentally. Children can only rely upon the assertions of their caregivers to know what they should do besides play. Their motivations in chores are necessarily linked to adult approval and attention. Much of the time they're not interested in the work per se; what they want out of the experience is to do the work *with* the adult. Gradually children gain a sense of independent accomplishment, but at each stage the work (especially intellectual work like schoolwork) gets harder, requiring them to continue to need the guidance of adults no matter how much independence those adults have fostered.

As an example, one study where student teachers joined classrooms in teams for a month notes, "For these children, it did not seem to matter to them what the help was about, in which subject, in what project, with what skill, or with what problem, only that it was there" (Lythcott and Schwartz 2005, p. 150). The irony of this observation is that the adults pointed to other benefits of the situation. The authors emphasized that the team nature of this student teaching experience was helpful for the teachers in developing their curriculum-writing skills and practicing their management of teacher-centered classrooms. Like the child who saw that the emperor had no clothes, these children saw the obvious for what it was: more adult attention to make their schoolwork meaningful.

The Limits on an Adult's Ability to Care

Children need a certain amount of attention. Adults, conversely, have an attention-paying threshold, a certain number of kids they're asked to pay attention to beyond which they cannot operate without becoming defensive and beginning to depersonalize the children. Simply put, there is a point at which even the kindest caregivers lose patience. Sadly, teachers usually operate at or above this threshold of caring. Garbarino notes, "Conventional economic thinking does not fully consider the true costs of caring for children. There are limits to the number of children that one caregiver can serve" (1995, p. 117). One consequence of the overload is that instead of blaming the relationship load teachers often blame the kids for being "too needy" or blame their parents for not having parented well enough. It is foolish to argue that what we need are simply better teachers rather than conditions that allow the average teacher to be more effective.

Consequences of Lack of Positive Adult Attention

It follows from other ideas presented above that children often "misbehave" as a way of calling for what they're lacking (Gnezda 2005, pp. 22, 75; Williams and Pritchard 2006, p. 186). This understanding certainly reflects my experiences as a teacher. Thanks to the perceived meeting of needs, behavior improves—the child's *and* the adult's behavior—in smaller groupings.

Of course, the "bad" that stems from calling for attention often becomes much more serious than simply playing the class clown. Many interconnected consequences flow from emotional neglect. First of all, the undernurtured tend to hurt themselves. Suicide has been linked strongly with insecure attachment. West, Spreng, Rose, and Adam (1999) see "suicidal behavior as an extreme attachment behavior." Second, lack of attention simply makes "bad" people with underdeveloped senses of responsibility to others. Garbarino writes, "We pay the price each time a marginal kid goes bad for lack of a positive experience of being needed, wanted, and affirmed" (1995, p. 100). These "bad" people hurt so much they take it out on others. This is because lack of attention leads to anger, withdrawal, and a lack of empathy. Glasser writes of neglected children,

> Because they can't fulfill their needs adequately, because they can't find love and self-worth, they become angry and frustrated, reacting against a society that they think is depriving them of a chance to fulfill their needs. Becoming hostile and aggressive, they try to gain their needs forcefully. (1969, p. 16)

Unfortunately, the myth that "bad" people are born that way persists partly because it does such a great job of letting our childrearing and penal systems off the hook.

The third consequence interrelates with the second: Attention-deprived children tend to be chronically unhappy and lack self-worth. Whether or not this leads to reperpetration on others, it is something to be avoided in and of itself. Fourth, children who are denied secure attachment have difficulty forming other relationships (Daniel et al. 1999, p. 34). As discussed earlier, all other relationships tend to be modeled on a child's attachment relationships, for better or for worse. This is the double jeopardy of insecure attachment: The potential for ameliorative relationships is reduced to the same degree that the need is increased.

Fifth, lack of attention has physiological consequences. As neuroscientists are coming to understand, the physical development of the brain is inhibited by lack of positive attention and attachment (Cozolino 2006). Sixth, secure attachment is related to overall health. For example, one study's findings "suggest that adolescents' perceptions of connectedness with teachers are an important correlate to engagement in fewer health risk behaviors" (Voisin et al. 2005). More and more health researchers are finding evidence of emotional factors in disease.

Lastly, perhaps the most serious consequence to lack of attachment is its endangerment of the rearing of future children. Neglected children often impact society when they have kids themselves. By improving childhood, relationship load reduction will help to minimize the number of inadequate parents because, very logically, inadequate parents are often the products of inadequate childhoods.

Ignored Costs of Ignored Kids

Prevention of attachment problems not only benefits those individuals affected but also their relationships with others. It is also the better way to go in terms of our monetary relationship as taxpayers. Pringle speaks to the fact that few have seriously considered how much money could be saved by a systematic, child-development-focused, prevention-based public policy (1980, p. 154). Elliott Currie writes,

> We have programs for youth who are already abusing drugs or throwing up their food or who have tried to kill themselves, but we do not have many that are designed to offer the sustained nurturance and attention that might keep these things from happening in the first place. (2005, p. 275)

As argued throughout this book, schools are the logical point of delivery for this investment. Rather than paying for more crisis responders, let's start by paying for more attentive schools and preempt more of the crises we're allowing to arise.

Truly to take to heart the evidence that lack of attachment is at the root of social ills and unethical or antisocial behavior demands that schools and public policy take on some of the burden of increasing the likelihood of happy childhoods for all (Noddings 2003, p. 2). As it stands, we are spending vast sums on curing (or at least isolating) adults to whom the damage is long done, with a higher percentage of our people in prison than any other nation.

The Chance to Undo Harm

Luckily, many of the effects of neglect can be undone. However, it gets harder the longer we wait (Garbarino 1995, p. 159). That's why our current system of waiting until kids are troubled to give them small classes isn't adequate— there's too much harm to undo too fast. It's early and unending second chances at attachment that gradually undo the harm (Daniel et al. 1999, p. 15). Again, even a kid with less-than-satisfactory parents can be saved from dysfunction by one outside adult:

> Children value adults who value them. Thus children who are living in seemingly intolerable situations but have a prosocial adult outside their [negative] home environment who cares about them will adjust their behavior to carefully safeguard that relationship. In doing so, the child begins to internalize the prosocial value system of the caring adult. (Deiro 2005, p. 3)

We need to fill our children's school careers—and not just the early years— with unending chances at attachment to adults. And we need to do it for all our children, not just the ones who've already been cheated so badly they act out.

The On-Target Aims of Schooling Reiterated

Now that we've discussed childhood needs in detail, let's return to the essential question: What does recognition of the importance of adult attention and attachment mean for schooling? The answer is self-evident: Schooling needs to accept that it is a part of childrearing—not an interlude from it—and it needs to act accordingly by reducing relationship load. Caring and academics are not a mutually exclusive dichotomy. Ancess (2003) writes of one small school she studied:

> Close, caring intense relationships between teachers and students, and among faculty who share students, are the central, most powerful driving force of the schools. These relationships teach students that they matter and that their learning matters. (p. 127)

She stresses that these relationships were not a lucky accident but an intentional educational strategy:

> The organization of the schools creates the possibility for belonging, for the kind of interpersonal engagement that facilitates these intense, caring relationships—easy access, opportunities for serendipitous and intentional attachments, watchfulness over student work and behavior, expectations for teachers to know students well as learners and individuals, teacher push, shared beliefs and goals, and faculty collaboration and dialogue. (p. 128)

In this conception you'll notice recognition of the compatibility of behavioral limit setting, high academic expectations, and plentiful, positive attention.

As will be outlined in the next chapter, relationship load reduction is the simplest, most direct means of reunifying schooling and childrearing—in one fell swoop.

5

The Four-Piece Relationship Load Solution

The Sephardic thinker Maimonides grappled with the issue of class size in the twelfth century (Achilles 1999, p. 22). In 1693 John Locke argued that private tutors were preferable to schoolmasters in their moral influence because a tutor "was likely to have only three or four children to supervise, compared with the three or four score of the schoolmaster" (Heywood 2001, p. 160). Relationship load in education is hardly a new topic, yet it continues to be seen as secondary to fake-academic-crisis concerns. Brevity has been a chief culprit. Because of the obvious value of small classes, for example, we don't tend to linger on the details, which gives the impression that the issue is of less importance. In an 1899 lecture, John Dewey said as much. The fourth of four keys to his laboratory school was "individual attention":

> This is secured by small groupings—eight or ten in a class. . . . It requires but a few words to make this statement about attention to individual powers and needs, and yet the whole of the school's aims and methods, moral, physical, intellectual, are bound up in it. (1990, p. 169)

Let's give the subject more than a few words.

What Each Piece Does

Let me briefly describe the effects of each of the four aspects of my conception of relationship load. **Class size** affects the number and length of day-to-day individual interactions students can engage in with teachers. As will be described in the next chapter, small class size also increases the positivity and personalization of each interaction. It has the most direct impact on the child's ability to perceive the availability of adult attention, as well as the teacher's ability to balance that with the child's need for autonomy.

School size affects the depth of nonclassroom relationships students and educators have at school. The larger the school, the more relationships are required, and thus the more like strangers students and educators will feel and treat each other. Another effect is how closely teachers can coordinate their efforts when members of small rather than large faculties. Miles and Darling-Hammond (1998) emphasize the tendency for teachers to coplan in small schools as one of the greatest benefits. Indeed, they found that by despecializing teachers and programs schools could actually reduce class size *and* increase coplanning time.

Continuity is the time dimension, the length of relationships, which affects how deep they become and how effectively they can work to optimize attachment security. The effects of all three other dimensions are enhanced by increased continuity.

Parent, guardian, or family load is a way to consider how many home-school relationships guardians and teachers have to sustain with one another, as well as how deep and trusting they can become. In large part, family load varies in tandem with the other aspects. The smaller the classes and schools, and the more continuous the teacher-student relationships, the fewer, deeper, and more cooperative family-educator relationships can be. In addition, full-service schools would offer other services to parents and lighten the load of institutions and personnel with which they need to interact in order to raise their kids.

Relationship Load from the Outside In

According to Beth Simon and Joyce Epstein, school-home communication as a key factor in school success and climate has been well documented (2001, p. 5). Less acknowledged is how parenting becomes easier with more school connection and social support. Earlier I discussed how the social isolation of parents is one of the factors in the nurturance crisis. A secret ingredient in our perception that parenting was easier or better in the past is that "There was nearly complete 'overlap' of home, school, and community influence on children's learning" by many community adults rather than our current trend toward parents performing their duties in isolation (p. 21). Simon and Epstein point to the mutual benefit of school-home connection when they write,

> These connections are likely to result in "family-like schools" where educators welcome parents and community partners, and treat each student as an individual; and "school-like families," where parents guide their children to fulfill their roles and responsibilities as students. (p. 4)

Home visits appear to be particularly helpful in drawing reluctant or overworked parents into a relationship with the school (Hiatt-Michael 2001, p. 43; Williams and Pritchard 2006, p. 159).

Clearly, such outreach on the part of schools (and parent-school connection in general) will be more likely the smaller relationship loads become. An elementary-school case study observes that one rationale for reducing class size "was that teachers would have better communication with parents if there were only 15 students in a classroom" (Odden, Archibald, and Tychsen 1999, p. 4).

From the perspective of a teacher, developing so many parent relationships doesn't seem to be easy. One survey found that new teachers felt relationships with parents were both the hardest aspect of the job and the least satisfying school relationships (MetLife 2005, p. 5). From the perspective of a parent, meanwhile, what do *big* and *many* do for me? Not much. Teacher continuity would clearly give me a better chance to develop more trusting and mutually beneficial relationships with my children's teachers. Why throw away a level of trust built over nine months between parents and teachers to start the next year with minimal trust again? What exactly are the supposed advantages in teacher "variety?" If a teacher-parent or teacher-student relationship really isn't working, a switch could be arranged. But why mandate switches as if they were somehow natural or inherently beneficial? It's a shameful waste of human investment. "Trust is an intangible characteristic that develops *over time*," write Sandra Christenson and Susan Sheridan. "The need to allow a trusting relationship to develop often runs counter to practices in schools wherein quick and efficient solutions are sought" (2001, p. 114). They also argue that the quality of the relationship between parents and teachers is more important for outcomes than the performance of specific (often ceremonial) activities on either side (p. 66). Low relationship load would clearly seem to foster an emphasis on the former over the latter and allow teachers and guardians to surmount class, race, and other cultural divides.

Research on both class size and school size suggests that parents and educators are more likely to communicate with one another in smaller schools or schools with smaller classes and that fewer and longer relationships between parents and teachers build trust on both sides. After one class size reduction program, researchers observed, "Most teachers felt that the levels of communication and interaction with parents increased notably" (Munoz and Portes 2002; see also Achilles 1999, p. 145; Bohrnstedt and Stecher 1999, p. 110). Kathleen Cotton's (2001) review of the research leads her to conclude, "Levels of both parent involvement and parent satisfaction are greater in small than in large school environments" (p. 17). The Met, a beacon high school of the small schools movement, "advertises that it enrolls families, not simply the child" and has the intimacy available to make it more than just a slogan (Hiatt-Michael 2001, p. 41).

Conversely, research into trust within schools suggests causal connections with relationship load. Christenson and Sheridan (2001, pp. 115–116) cite research on parent-teacher trust that found the following:

1. Parents trusted teachers more than vice versa.
2. Teacher and parent trust for one another was stronger in elementary than in high school.
3. Parents whose children received special education services expressed more trust the more intensive the services were.
4. Parents expressing more trust were also more involved.
5. Parents whose children got better grades, more credit, and attended more, trusted teachers more.
6. Income, ethnicity, and regular versus special ed were not significant variables (which went against the researchers' hypothesis).
7. Both teachers and parents cited communication as a means to building trust.

I've rearranged the findings to tell a sort of narrative—you may have already guessed the plot.

The first three findings could be explained by relationship load. In each case the less trusting are those burdened with more relationships, and the more trusting are those allowed to deepen fewer relationships. As well, in each case where parents are more trusting, their children have also been given the opportunity to have fewer and deeper relationships. Findings 4 and 5 suggest a kind of feedback loop, either positive or negative: Either school success breeds more parent trust and involvement, which breeds more success, and so on, or school failure breeds less parent trust and involvement, which breeds less success, and so on. Like the chicken and egg problem, it is fruitless to assert where the cycle actually began. The point is that low relationship load would seem to make the positive loop more likely than the negative one. Finding 6 implies that teachers and parents who may see each other as quite different nevertheless may be just as likely to have trusting relationships as teachers and parents who see each other as more similar. The last finding points to the obvious solution: Time to interact, that is, relationship load reduction.

Parenthood and teacherhood ought to operate symbiotically for children rather than competing for influence. Parents provide both support and accountability to teaching, just as the presence of teachers in children's lives provides both support and accountability for parenting. Longer and deeper relationships between these two will remove the inherent anxieties of negotiating over precious young people and allow for a more collaborative, productive, and equity-inducing accountability. Diana Hiatt-Michael writes, "Open and regular home-school, two-way communication will replace . . . fears with knowledge, confidence, and caring" (2001, p. 39).

"School" Defined

Before discussing school size any further, let me clarify from the start that by "school" I do not necessarily mean "school building." As will be detailed in Chapter 10, current buildings can be subdivided to create more than one school, each of which is below the applicable maximum size. Such a situation may in fact be preferable, particularly for secondary education, because specialized resources can be shared in such arrangements (Harber 1996, p. 27). Examples of shared resources would be space, technology, highly specialized teachers, sports programs, and student organizations like gay-straight alliances that are more effective when they can draw on a larger pool of potential members. Even noncontiguous small schools can be networked with one another to provide mutual support and accountability (Meier 2000b, pp. 189–190). In Chapter 10 we will return to this issue, stressing that the research shows autonomous (but networked) small schools to be more effective and long-lasting than subschool learning communities.

Interconnectedness

Though there are important exceptions, the four aspects of grouping size reduction have most often been treated separately. Revealingly, there has been no term created to encompass all four aspects, which is why I've had to use *grouping size* and *relationship load* to be able to discuss them less cumbersomely. The lack of an overarching concept shows both *that* and *why* they haven't been grouped. In several ways, the four aspects of grouping size reduction are not nearly as separate as they may appear. The assumption that they function in isolation from one another has to overcome the following facts:

One, small secondary schools all but automatically increase teacher continuity through reduced specialization. Continuity is essentially a built-in advantage of small secondary schools where students often return to the same, less specialized teachers for several years. Not surprisingly, as reported by Alain Jehlen and Cynthia Kopkowski (2006), recently formed smaller schools seem to be capitalizing on this opportunity by keeping "teachers and students together for several years to strengthen their relationships" (p. 24).

Two, both advocates and researchers of small schools argue that those that do not maximize teacher continuity waste much of their value. The National Research Council found,

> Small schools that do not also adjust their organization and instruction may have few advantages. Note that in studies finding positive effects of small schools on student engagement and learning, the schools also implemented a variety of other innovations, such as . . . teachers seeing fewer students and students seeing fewer teachers. (2004, p. 116)

Similarly, Nancy Mohr argues that a small school can reduce pupil load and keep teachers and students together over several years, "and if it does not, it is losing an invaluable opportunity" or even "missing the point" (2000, p. 150).

Three, smaller schools tend to have smaller classes (Harber 1996, p. 6). This aligns with the general tendency for larger organizations to have larger managerial loads. "By company size, the median result also varies considerably—one manager to four employees in companies with 500 or less employees and one to nine in companies with 2,000 to 5,000 employees" (Davison 2003).

Four, recently downsized schools in the United States tend to have smaller classes and put effort into reducing them as much as possible. I showed evidence of this in Chapter 1 when I used them as an example of the "secret ingredient" phenomenon. Ancess also emphasizes the ingredient of small classes in caring small schools that are committed to their students (2003, pp. 30, 57).

Five, parent relationship load is automatically smaller when any of the other three aspects are in place. When the number of teachers a child has a relationship with is reduced, the same is true for the child's guardians. Conversely, the number of guardians a teacher needs to build a relationship with is reduced, facilitating greater depth and quality.

Any serious attempt to have schools help solve the nurturance crisis will not split up the four aspects of relationship load reduction but use them all in unison. I will show that significant class size reduction is paramount because it fixes the complications that come with the three *apparently* cheaper aspects. As a preface to that, we need to recognize that a philosophy of teacher specialization undergirds our use of large classes.

Separation Philosophy

Beneath an acceptance of large relationship load lies an acceptance of a separation/specialization philosophy that justifies it and keeps it in place. DeMarrais and LeCompte regard the "social efficiency" approach as the most prevalent in U.S. public education, citing its emphasis on "discrete," "stratified," "departmentalized," or "differentiated curricula," and its view of teachers as "subject matter specialists who work alone in isolated rooms" (1999, p. 236). Many have addressed the philosophical problems with the increasing specialization of educators and other caregivers. For instance, Sidorkin (2004) writes,

> The idea that the roles of a teacher, of a social worker, of a school counselor, and of a neighborhood club organizer should belong to different people has to be reconsidered. While market economies always benefit from division of labor, in the nonmarket relational economies the opposite is true. (p. 68)

Not only are schools artificially differentiated from the rest of the community, there is rampant differentiation within schools. "Role differentiation among school professionals," argue Sands and colleagues (2000),

> assumes that students' differences are more important than their shared traits and that one school professional cannot have adequate competencies to work with more than one type of child. . . . This rigidity makes it difficult to re-allocate resources in response to the shifting needs of learners and communities. An alternative to an expert-based role differentiation model would be collaborative, transdisciplinary teaming, in which professionals assume that it is their professional obligation to share their expertise and help others develop the skills to work effectively with students. (p. 16)

But can "regular" teachers really teach kids with "special" needs? Case studies demonstrate that they can. For example, a study of one school that despecialized its staff and reduced class sizes notes that teachers did seek help and advice from teachers with special training, but the classroom teacher is the coordinator or supervisor of his or her students' learning. This shared sense of responsibility has fostered a more open atmosphere in the school. Communication has improved among staff, and teachers are spurred to seek advice and share their triumphs with others. (Odden, Archibald, and Tychsen 1999, p. 28)

In essence, overspecialization is just as much a misplaced business/ efficiency model as large schools and classes (deMarrais and LeCompte 1999, pp. 76–77). Moreover, it is yet another Band-Aid remedy for our inability to meet individual needs in those large groupings. Regarding the history of specialization, Perkinson notes that "as early as 1872," after age-grading became prevalent, some began to complain of "mechanical education that geared instruction to average students, thus handicapping the bright and the slow learners" (1995, pp. 69–70). Once the specialization spiral had begun, it fed on itself:

The obvious answer to such criticism, as they pointed out, was more specialization. Thus we find certain teachers with classes composed only of superior students while others taught only slow learners. In some urban schools, teachers became specialists in one subject. This departmentalization usually took place in the high schools, but a number of cities, beginning with San Francisco in 1887, tried it in elementary schools. (p. 70)

In other words, tracking by ability was the "logical" fix to the drawbacks of age grouping.

But teachers also became grouped and tracked. Ever-increasing teacher specialization became the norm after the late nineteenth century as urbanization, the growth of high school enrollment, and school consolidation made it possible; since then, the test-score craze has made it seem all the more necessary. For example, the seventh and eighth grades were once included in one-teacher-all-day schools that now operate mostly for grades K–6, or sometimes only K–5.[1] That changed with the advent of junior high schools in the 1910s and 1920s (Hunt 2002, p. 87), many of which were reborn as "middle schools" in the 1960s. "The eight-year elementary school remained the standard until the junior high school was developed in the early twentieth century" (Spring 1997, p. 153). That change, together with the explosion of high school enrollment after the turn of the century, led to an enormous increase in the percentage of teaching positions designed for specialists rather than generalists (Fraser 2007, p. 147). Add to this the fact that the once-prevalent one-room schoolhouse, where one teacher taught all grades *simultaneously*, all but disappeared over the same period. This growth in school size is a major factor in our increased faith in specialization—because teachers now *can* specialize, we believe they *have* to. We need a new type of specialist, *a teacher who specializes in a particular—and small—group of children* rather than a category filled and refilled with interchangeable children.

Moreover, even test-score-crisis folks tend to assert that what's wrong is not a lack of teacher expertise in the upper reaches of their subject matter but that not every student learns "the basics" (which seem to get less basic every year).[2] From the perspective of the real nurturance crisis, expertise concerns are clearly secondary to child development concerns. The problems with the teacher quality argument (detailed in Chapter 7) apply here also. In particular, class size reduction will significantly reduce the difficulty of the task of teaching, rendering teacher quality concerns a weak argument for not reducing relationship load.

One telling example of the specialization philosophy is the jaw-dropping prevalence of auxiliary teachers. As Appendix A details, close to one third of our teaching force is not necessary to achieve our current mainstream classes that average twenty-four students. As Appendix B shows, mainstream classes serve 93.5 percent of students at any one time. If one divides the total number nonmainstreamed students at any one time (6.5 percent of them) by the total number of nonmainstream teachers (31 percent of them), it yields *a pupil/ teacher ratio of three to one.* These other teachers are not just special education teachers running self-contained classrooms for the 6.5 percent of student time spent there; they are also the "pull-out" teachers, the reading specialists, the full-time staff developers. No one doubts the hard work and positive effects of the nearly 1 million auxiliary teachers in our schools. The issue is whether their "auxiliaryness" is the best way to meet the adult attention needs of our children, and the only way to get the same level of academic results. These nonmainstream programs for special populations "absorbed 58 percent of the new dollars devoted to education from 1967 to 1991" (Miles and Darling-Hammond 1998), leaving us firmly in the age of specialization.

Small classes could allow all teachers to use their *general* expertise to meet the needs of the twelve students before them by *consulting* with specialists outside of class time rather than by *relying* upon them during class time. I argue that those of us who disagree with that statement have subscribed to a philosophy rather than a fact. One reason many have done so, of course, is that they've never had an opportunity to observe how smaller classes could allow general expertise to function for kids with specialized needs. The status quo has a way of making itself appear natural and necessary. There is no doubt that some of our kids need extra help. There *is* doubt that extra help means *outside* help. Only large class size makes that true.

Another aspect of the separation philosophy is tracking. According to Jeannie Oakes (2005), whose scholarship has focused on the inequities of tracking, the common justification for it is that "individual differences are better accommodated" (p. 58). In other words, it is a Band-Aid—large relationship load's poor substitute for personalization. Oakes found a stark difference in how teachers and students felt about their experiences in high versus low tracks, despite few outward signs during classroom observations. "Relationships between teachers and students were definitely more positive in high-track classes; relationships were clearly more negative in low" (p. 124). Oakes argues further that tracking reinforces class and race disparities in U.S. society.

I believe schools should reduce tracking and ability grouping as they become smaller. Once they have classes of twelve, they should consider eliminating the practice entirely. Some detracking will be forced on educators by the fact of a smaller number of classes on the schedule, but we should embrace rather than bemoan the reduction in ability grouping. Many argue that tracking does not benefit the "top" students enough to justify the harm it does to the others. Elizabeth Cohen summarizes the research by stating, "Students in lower-ability groups and tracks do not do as well as those with similar early achievement scores who are in more heterogeneous settings" (1997, p. 6). Since most minorities are underrepresented in higher tracks, tracking also involves either direct racism or indirect because poverty and achievement are not equally distributed across races (Hallinan 2004). Maureen Hallinan observes that nearly all students "benefit from assignment to a higher ability group" (p. 138). The only problem with this is that in order to have a higher group, you also have to have a lower. Someone has to lose. Relationship load reduction will make zero-sum games like this less necessary. Small schools make ability grouping less practical and therefore less likely; meanwhile, class size reduction and teacher continuity allow mixed-ability grouping to be successful.

Let me clarify for potential critics that by calling for a retreat from tracking I'm not advocating that everyone learn the same thing or the same amount—I'm advocating that students learn different things and amounts in the same classroom, and that it be based on their abilities as individuals rather than their class, race, or ethnicity. Random (or purposefully diverse) grouping—rather than long-term ability grouping—will do the least damage to the self-image of our kids and have the greatest benefit for their tolerance of others. Small schools and classes with long-lasting teacher-student relationships will create a climate where tracking is unnecessary to achieve a personalized level of challenge for each student. Wagner writes of an exemplary small school, "Teachers can tailor assignments to individual student learning levels to a great extent—without having to create separate academic tracks for students" (2002, p. 89). Ultimately, since small schools make tracking far less practical, and since detracking makes smaller schools and classes more affordable, this in itself may force it to disappear and thereby end the debate over its value or harm.

Small Classes Fix the Snags of Teacher Continuity

In a small number of schools, teachers follow their students to the next grade until that cohort leaves the school. This ought to become the norm whenever possible, especially in elementary where it presents the fewest pragmatic challenges. So why isn't it? Minimal continuity of teacher-student relationships and large school size are symptoms of the same disease: an antidevelopmental belief in the need for teacher specialization. Unlike with school size, however, one cannot even make the dubious argument of cost-savings to defend the specialization of teachers by grade, the main impediment to relationship continuity, because keeping teachers and students together longer would cost nothing.

Why does a fifth grade teacher "need" to teach fifth grade year after year without instead staying with the same cohort as they progress through the grades? Why does one high school teacher "have" to teach tenth grade history again the next year instead of eleventh grade history to the same group of kids? There are three possible arguments for age or grade specialization, but only the last argument holds much water, and class size reduction will counterbalance any true drawbacks of increasing continuity.

The first argument is that age specialization minimizes how much a teacher needs to know, reducing expertise limitations. As discussed earlier, even from a fake-academic-crisis perspective, this is dubious. This is a fundamental assumption of a belief in specialization rather than a fact of human ability. There is nothing to know about any one year of human development between ages five and eighteen that is different enough from the previous or following year to offer support for this contention.

The second argument is that age specialization allows a teacher to predict what students will need, minimizing time spent on needs-assessment. This is spurious because such time would be negligible in a continuous teacher-student relationship. Small class size would further increase the amount of ongoing needs-assessment teachers could do. This argument is also indicative of the mentality that what or how teachers should teach is independent of which particular kids are in their classes. Chapter 6 will outline how class size in particular will allow personalization to eclipse the one-size-fits-all mentality.

The third argument is that age specialization minimizes teacher preparation time by allowing teachers to repeat as much curriculum as possible. This is a valid drawback: Increased continuity will have the net result of adding complexity and time to the preparation side of teaching unless it is offset by the simplification inherent in class size reduction. Neither school size reduction nor continuity (nor both together) should be asked to replace class size reduction (in the name of lower short-term cost) precisely because class size reduction is the intervention that both (a) has the most impact on the real crisis and (b) offsets the added complexity of the other two aspects.

Small Classes Fix the Snags
of Small Schools

Of the four aspects of relationship load, small schools have by far gotten the most attention as a way of helping solve the nurturance crisis. There is an irony to this fact. If one were to start from the perspective of the real nurturance crisis but could only pick three of the four parts of relationship load, and cost were no object, it would almost certainly be school size that should go. For example, school size reduction is conspicuously absent from the recommendations made by Fredriksen and Rhodes on how to enhance student-teacher relationships (2004, p. 41). I'm not denying that school size has a large effect on the amount (and quality) of interaction, but relative to the other aspects its effect is clearly not *larger*. In sum, the best proof of the need to link small schools and small classes is to see that small classes are the best way to minimize the drawbacks to small schools. Jehlen and Kopkowski (2006) list four downsides to smaller schools that I will address one by one.

First, teachers wear many hats, carrying out functions beyond teaching, and many feel overloaded. This could help explain the 2 percent higher turnover rate Ingersoll found in small rather than large public schools (2003, p. 15). For reasons cited throughout, smaller classes could clearly make teachers feel less overloaded and compensate for any increased duties involved in running a smaller school. Rosetta Cohen and Samuel Scheer, for example, advocate for a lighter workload for teachers, and it is no accident that they place reducing class size and pupil load ahead of reducing the number of preps (secondary) and non–class-time supervision (2003, p. 38). Despite added teacher duties, however, Cohen and Scheer still see small schools as a key improvement to teacher working conditions, calling it "the most meaningful environmental change that would impact teacher morale and efficiency" (2003, p. 52) and citing research that found "dramatic" morale increases (p. 53). The drawback of extra duties appears overblown considering the other advantages teachers gain in small schools.

Second, there is less variety of courses and extras such as sports teams. Harber argues that the course variety squeeze is overdrawn (1996, p. 14). Miles and Darling-Hammond agree, arguing the research shows that "beyond about 400 students, there are few if any gains in curriculum quality" (1998). Small-school pioneer Deborah Meier (1995) has two responses to the reduced curriculum argument: (a) "the average high school student in many large cities never makes it to the grades in which such choices become available," because of the alienatingly large schools they are in, and (b) from the beginning small schools have shared resources to offer what they can't offer alone. To the extent that course variety limitations are a reality of smaller schools, smaller classes would increase the number of teachers per student in a small school, and with it the potential for course variety. For example, a school that was divided in half to form two schools and whose classes were made half the size would experience no reduction in course variety.

The other consideration is that when "course variety" is code for tracking, then this drawback may be no drawback at all. What many perceive as beneficial "variety" may "amplify initial differences in socioeconomic status and achievements that students bring with them to school" (deMarrais and LeCompte 1999, p. 242). These authors argue that there is an unconsidered benefit to structural limitations on course variety: "The more constrained the curriculum, the greater is the academic rigor for all students" (p. 242). They cite research that connects the more equal achievement in Catholic schools to their decreased use of ability tracking compared with public schools (p. 241).

Third, some warn of self-segregation: When students choose their small schools, they may sort themselves out by ethnic group, social class, motivation, and academic ability. This concern is important, but it's tangential to grouping size. It's a result of *how* not *whether* schools are made smaller. There is no need to match small schools with students any differently from how large schools are currently matched with students.

Fourth, many argue that the economies of scale of big schools are lost, driving up cost. We'll take up this issue in detail in Chapter 10. For now, let me simply state that the specter of "higher" cost is deceptive. The deception lies in accepting the assumption that what we currently spend is enough, that kids don't deserve more, that they aren't hurt by our current neglect, and that their neglect doesn't cost us money elsewhere. Chapter 8 will show in detail that rather than a cost-*saving* strategy, large relationship load is actually a cost-*hiding* strategy.

Now let's go into more detail about a few key issues that revolve around relationship load reduction.

How Big Are Our Classes?

I'll use the conservative figure of twenty-four from the data graphed in Figure 5.1 as the current average class size for public schools in the United States. Other sources suggest a slightly lower number.[3] By erring conservatively on the high side, I'll guarantee that my cost estimates—if off the mark—are too high rather than too low.

As averages often do, this average vastly understates the experience of a large portion of our children. California is the only state to top thirty as its average secondary class size (Digest 2006, table 64); unfortunately, California comprises over 10 percent of the U.S. population. Clearly there are a lot of kids in significantly larger classes than the average would suggest. Large classes affect urban and minority children in particular. In New York City, for example, traditional high schools appear to have an average class size of thirty-three ("Top of their class" 2001). Middle schools in Los Angeles Unified and Dade County (Miami), the country's second and fifth largest districts, have a pupil/teacher ratio of 23.9, yielding a likely class size of at least 30; Long Beach Unified, adjacent to Los Angeles, has a high school pupil/teacher ratio of 27.8, which suggests a class size larger than New York City's traditional high schools (NCES 2001, table 7). To a large degree, large schools and classes are more of an urban phenomenon. Luckily, this should make implementation easier, since the problems are more concentrated in these areas that have the most resources (if the suburbs can be compelled to share) and potential for teacher recruitment.

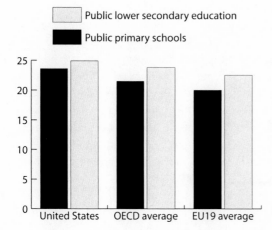

□ Public lower secondary education

■ Public primary schools

Figure 5.1 *Average public school class sizes in the United States, the OECD member nations, and the European Union, 2004.*

Source: Organisation for Economic Co-operation and Development 2006a, table D2.1.

A Brief History of Class Size

As mentioned earlier, Spring reports that nineteenth-century urban schools often put students in groups of up to 300 students, but with the advent of the age-graded school after 1848, class size seldom exceeded sixty (1997, pp. 151–152). Data on true class size from the late nineteenth and early twentieth centuries is scant. Henry Otto (1954) points out that overall pupil/teacher ratio was deceptive then as it is now (p. 2). The pupil/teacher ratio started at about thirty-six in 1900 and descended steadily to about twenty-six in 1964, when it began to drop faster than class size (Lewit and Baker 1997). The main thing that makes the gap larger now is the averaging in of special education and pull-out teachers. These programs came into widespread use in the 1960s, which is partly responsible for the steeper drop in pupil/teacher ratio. Another source of greater pupil/teacher ratio drop than class size drop appears to be an increase in teacher preparation time (National Education Association 2003a, p. 45).

Otto's research points to rural schools having had smaller classes than urban schools. Cuban confirms this, reporting that urban classrooms at the turn of the century were "constructed to house 40 to 60 students" (1984, p. 24), while rural Pennsylvania schools between 1920 and 1940 had an average class size of twenty-six, roughly what we have today in a representative classroom (p. 119). Nationwide, rural class size in 1920 varied anywhere from twenty to sixty (p. 118).

Classes were usually larger at the elementary level than the secondary level. Raymond Callahan writes that during the efficiency or "Scientific Management" movement of the 1910s and 1920s, "elementary classes were so large that even the most economy-minded educators did not suggest increasing their size" (1962, p. 232). "Clearly the way to economize was to get more work out of [secondary] teachers, either by increasing the size of their classes or by increasing the number of classes they taught or both. In this effort the very small classes of ten to fifteen students . . . were doomed" (p. 233). Since there were far fewer secondary students at the beginning of the century, the large elementary classes affected the overall numbers much more heavily. But by the 1930s, Callahan reports, the high schools were doing their part to achieve thirty-three or so in the typical class (p. 239). This was thanks to the growing efficiency movement referred to earlier. But elementaries remained larger. "While classes of 50 or more were common around World War I, class size had been dropping since that time. In 1930, average class size in elementary schools hovered above 38 students" (Cuban 1984, p. 50).

Does this historical drop in average class size mean we're already on our way to class sizes of twelve and needn't worry? No. Average class size declined by *fewer than two pupils per decade* over the twentieth century. We need to accelerate that downward trend for all grades. As I'll detail in Chapter 10, I think we should set a goal of reaching a nationwide class size of twelve in the span of twenty-six years. That would be a drop of about two students per year—*ten times the previous rate*. Inconveniently for adults, children don't judge whether their attention needs are getting met based on charts that show we're gradually getting there—they make their judgments based on their current environment. It isn't good enough yet, and we need to get there as fast as we possibly can.

A Brief History of School Size

The trend in school size has been in precisely the opposite direction. Christopher Berry (2004) writes,

> As late as the 1930s, most American schools employed just one teacher. Over the ensuing decades, however, the number of schools declined rapidly, from a peak of 271,000 in 1920 to a low of around 83,000 schools in the late 1980s (since then, about 10,000 schools have been added nationwide). Meanwhile, public school attendance roughly doubled between 1929 and 1969, the period of most rapid consolidation. The combination of consolidation and rising attendance produced a five-fold increase in school size during this short time, with average daily attendance per school rising from 87 to 440 students. . . . Schools employing just one teacher all but disappeared from the landscape; just 400 one-teacher schools remained as of 2000.

I wish it could be said the upsizing had stopped since its peak. Figure 5.2 suggests that consolidation is still in motion.

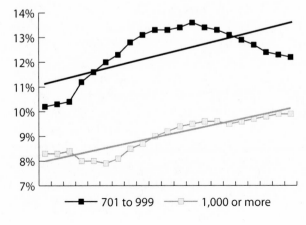

Figure 5.2 *Percentage of U.S. public schools in largest size categories, 1982 to 2004.*

Source: Digest 2006, table 92.

Thankfully, the last decade of the twentieth century saw a movement back to smaller schools:

> It started as an experiment led by a group of dedicated innovators. Their early successes grew into a reform movement. Now, the effort to transform large urban high schools into small schools has turned into a virtual stampede, driven by a giant carrot (Bill Gates' money) and an even bigger stick (No Child Left Behind). Thousands of new schools, generally with 400 or fewer students, have been launched in the last few years. (Jehlen and Kopkowski 2006, p. 24)

We need to intensify that trend.

Why Twelve as the Ideal Class Size?

I propose we have one target class size that will apply to K–12 education regardless of grade.[4] That said, I will acknowledge that students would not be harmed by being in larger groups in subject areas that are more like play, such as gym and art. Research suggests that academic outcomes won't be harmed either. Miles writes,

> . . . effective use of resources does not necessarily require smaller class or group sizes for every subject and lesson. Some elementary schools have found ways to create small reading groups for part of the day by forming larger group sizes at other times of the day. (2000)

At the secondary level, a similarly effective strategy is "shifting teachers from nonacademic subjects toward academic subjects" (2000). As covered earlier, attention needs are much lower during play than work. In Appendix B, I show that having mainstreamed students spend one sixth of the school day in larger classes will counterbalance the costs of smaller classes for high-need populations. That means that when all students are included in the calculation, schools could achieve a median and mode class size of twelve, and a mean that's even smaller.

But why twelve? Common sense and research suggest that there is an optimal grouping size range where peer and adult interaction mutually benefit one another. Let's start by establishing a minimum number below which schools should not venture. Recall that Clarke-Stewart and colleagues studied the proper balance of peers and adults in daycare and arrived at four or five to one (1994, p. 240). Considering that this proposal of the number five applies to mixed-age daycares that are often populated by mostly non-school-age children, it can be seen as a reasonable minimum for school classes, which will often have much older and more independent children in them.

To determine a maximum, let's start by pretending that the real crisis doesn't exist and that we're only seeking improved academic performance from schools. In this case, the research points to the number fifteen. Cahen, Filby, McCutcheon, and Kyle (1983) argue, "Achievement improves dramatically only when class size is reduced below 15 pupils" (p. 207). Indeed, both major teachers' unions (the NEA and the AFT) call for class sizes of fifteen on their platforms.

Now let's unbracket the real crisis and consider that schools need to do much more than just foster academic success. To inform our decision of just how far below fifteen would be worth our money, let's review what sort of groups people do naturally gather in. After all, if a class is to make children feel comfortable, shouldn't it in some way approximate the size of group in which they'd naturally associate? As covered in the first chapter, the answer seems to be from four to ten for adolescents (Clark 2004, p. 79) and two to seven for adults (Hare 1976, p. 217). Sociologists tend to agree that the optimum size for a discussion group is five (Hare 1976, p. 229). But with troubled teenager support groups in particular, some have suggested a higher number—nine—to keep discussion productive (Vorrath and Brendtro 1974, pp. 58–59). Recall that the National Resource Center for Health and Safety in Child Care and Early Education recommends between eight and twelve elementary-age children per adult (Fiene 2002). Those who recommend shifting to advisory groups in secondary schools usually advocate no more than twenty and preferably twelve to seventeen students (National Research Council 2004, p. 160); Goldberg specifies fourteen (1998, p. 2). A dozen makes for a nice round number that's lower than fifteen but plenty bigger than the minimum of five. Moreover, teachers will find twelve conveniently divisible into two, three, four, or six equal groups.

Should communities where children are more at risk for school failure and lack of adult attention get even smaller classes? I believe so, though not so small as to exceed the minimum size recommended by research. Poverty, racism, and other sources of social "disadvantage" are highly correlated with insecure attachment and insufficient positive adult attention (Garbarino 1995, p. 144). Indeed, under our present educational funding system based on local property taxes, poor families that are concentrated in one area in effect can't afford quality schools either, as if the system weren't a public one at all. In other words, stigmatized kids, communities, and districts need equity—rather than mere equality—if they're ever to have anything but preparatory schools for second-class citizenship. The long-term solution to reducing the effects of poverty may be not allowing it to concentrate in particular areas, or better still, living wages for all workers.

For reasons discussed earlier, the number of nonmainstream classes should be brought to an absolute minimum. Students with special needs (including those who excessively disrupt) should be mainstreamed with others to the greatest extent possible. For the extremely disabled (particularly those with severe behavioral disorders) a few special education classrooms will need to remain. Small relationship load and the additional full-service-school recommendations made in Chapter 1 will reduce the number of students who create excessive disruptions. Unfortunately, some severely troubled children will remain. As with extremely disabled students, these disruptors may have to be removed from mainstream classes and dealt with in even smaller groupings and perhaps in separate buildings. But only in extreme cases—where the disadvantages of inclusion outweigh the advantages—should any child be isolated from the rest. The next chapter will go into more detail on how smaller groupings will facilitate a school's ability to help these kids with special needs.

With all this in mind, I propose the following, which I also illustrate in Figure 5.3:

Class Size Recommendations

- Students from most schools should be in classes of a dozen.
- Students in communities of concentrated poverty and racism should be in classes of no bigger than nine.
  A lower size of six is needed for nonmainstreamable special education students and extremely troubled and disruptive students who are unable to function in mainstream classes.
- There should be a certain number of double-sized classes in disciplines more akin to play (such as PE and art) that can counterbalance the resource use of the previous two categories (see Appendix B).

Increasing Teacher-Student-Guardian Continuity

Returning students to the same teachers for two or more years ("looping") is used in 23 percent of public elementary schools and 15 percent of secondary (Strizek et al. 2007). This way of increasing continuity in most elementary schools (those where teachers stay with one group all day) is the easiest piece

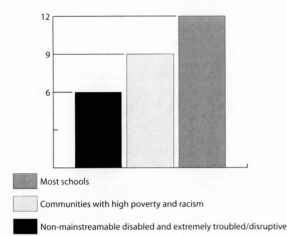

Most schools

Communities with high poverty and racism

Non-mainstreamable disabled and extremely troubled/disruptive

Figure 5.3 *Recommended class sizes.*

of grouping size reduction to implement—it will cost nothing since it affects only the assignment of pupils rather than classroom space or hiring. It should be implemented as soon as possible in all elementary schools by having students remain with the same teacher for as many years as possible. At the secondary level—in both small and yet-to-be subdivided schools—administrators should rethink course assignments to find ways to maximize the extent to which students keep the same teachers as they move through the school.

Some may object that this proposal may force elementary teachers and students who don't get along to spend counterproductive time together. I have several responses to this concern. First, I will try to show in Chapter 6 that on average there will be fewer such poor relationships after relationship load reduction. Second, in extreme cases students could switch teachers. Third, schools could strike a compromise: Either students could have the same teacher all day long for half (or a third of) their time at the school, or they could have the same two or three teachers every year for even portions of each day. This second option seems a better balance of variety and continuity.

Others may object that this proposal asks elementary teachers to be experts in too many skill levels. Here again a group of two or three teachers offers a solution: Elementary teachers could begin to specialize in content rather than age. They could then teach repeated lessons to rotating classes, as secondary teachers are allowed to do, thus reducing prep time. As I argued earlier, we should rethink our expertise priorities: Expertise in particular kids will be more beneficial than expertise in particular ages. The transition could be eased if teachers spent some professional development time (and/or some of summer break) collaborating with the colleague who last taught the next grade up to swap ideas and materials.

Eliminating the Intermediate Level

Intermediate schools serve no nurturance purpose. They are a development of the specialization/efficiency movement (Noddings 1984, p. 190). Their main negative impact is to limit the continuity of guardian-teacher-student relationships. They also force an additional anxiety-producing transition that Alexander and colleagues (2003) argue is more psychologically harmful than being held back a grade (p. 250). They argue that marginally successful kids tend to take a turn for worse after the move to intermediate school (p. 255), and that student attitudes toward school in general take a dip at this time (p. 256). As possible reasons they offer the following ingredients that tend to go with the move to middle or junior high school:

- A new building
- Starting over on the bottom of the grade hierarchy
- A larger school enrollment
- Several teachers rather than one
- More competitive atmosphere
- More distant and controlling teaching style
- More public evaluation
- More formalized and permanent ability grouping (p. 256)

A survey focused on the transition to secondary school corroborates this, finding,

> Secondary school students are less likely to feel safe at their current school than their previous school (29% strongly agree vs. 43% strongly agree). Secondary school students are less likely to say that their teachers care about them at their current school than their previous school (28% strongly agree vs. 37% strongly agree). (MetLife 2005, p. 5)

Only inasmuch as schools might have been much larger had intermediate schools not existed could they be argued to have had some nurturance value. But once all secondary schools are small, there is simply no defense of a separate intermediate level. As discussed earlier, intermediate, middle, or junior high school is an "efficiency" development of the early twentieth century. Prior to intermediate schools becoming the norm, eighth grade was the end of primary schools, but many rural schools offered all twelve (and later thirteen) grades (Hunt 2002, p. 87; Spring 1997, p. 153).

Local communities would most likely choose one of the following options for dividing up the grades into available buildings: K–8 and 9–12, K–7 and 8–12, or K–6 and 7–12. Let's consider the most difficult situation an elementary school might face: It is attempting to conform to the maximum school size but includes the most grades districts would most likely attempt to put together, K–8. That means that it would need to fit nine grades in one school of 300. Fortunately, of course, the classes have only twelve students. Such a school could have three teachers in each grade with exactly twelve students per class and only exceed the maximum by twenty-four students.

The main tension in making this choice is that the later the students make the transition to secondary schools, the more stress there is to curriculum variety while still seeking to remain under 300 in total enrollment. As long as the critical ingredient of class size reduction is not left out, any damage to curriculum variety or teacher expertise will be counterbalanced by increased numbers of teachers per small school and increased ease of teaching. Again, *class size is the lynchpin of relationship load reduction.*

The ideal would perhaps be to have schools that served students for all thirteen years of their school careers—or at least to have the elementary be adjacent to the secondary. That would clearly maximize the continuity and impact of relationships between parents and teachers, and teachers and children. Once students reached a certain grade, they could still begin to have multiple teachers but remain in the same building with the elementary teacher with whom they remained attached for many years. This teacher could be available as a resource for the student or for later teachers of that student.

Though far less simple than elementary continuity issues, eliminating intermediate schools would nonetheless dovetail smoothly as a subset of a district's school size reduction plan. The elimination of intermediate schools won't exactly be free if done in isolation, but its costs will be negligible when combined with school size reduction. Obviously, buildings currently used as intermediate schools could be redeployed to house one or more small primary, secondary, or K–12 schools.

What's the Right School Size?

Meier's definition is, "Small enough so that children belong to the same community as adults, not abandoned in adultless subcultures. Small enough to both feel and be safe" (2000b, p. 185), though elsewhere she tacks that down to 300 for elementary and 400 for high schools (1995, p. 102). Because the costs of reducing school size are less dramatic than for class size, the political stakes are much lower. Perhaps for that reason there is greater willingness for researchers to offer solid numbers, allowing for much more consensus. Clearly we want to stay well below a thousand. "The bleak immensity of these schools designed to hold from 1,000 to 2,000 students not only condemns students to loneliness and isolates teachers but also intimidates parents" (Johnson 2004, p. 80). DeMarrais and LeCompte recommend 300 for elementary and 600 for secondary (1999, p. 88). Five hundred gets mentioned frequently: "A number of studies have demonstrated that students in smaller high schools participate more in extracurricular activities. . . . The relationship holds true, at any rate, for high schools with fewer than 500 students total" (Steuer 1994, pp. 642–643). Five hundred has also been seen by many researchers as a significant number in two other regards: (a) It appears to be the maximum number of names an average person can remember, and (b) it tends to be the maximum tribe size in most tribal cultures (Scott 1981, p. 221). As a last point in favor of 500, a recent report found that although "high schools with less than 500 pupils have higher expenditures for operation on a per pupil basis than" high schools over 1,500, they had "lower expenditures per pupil than schools in the 500 to 999 range" (Commission on Business Efficiency of the Public Schools 2003, p. xi).

Others have recommended fewer than 500, including the academic widely blamed for having begun the trend toward larger high schools. Littky observes, "In his 1959 book, *The American High School Today*, Conant argued that high schools could get academically stronger if they got bigger. He did, in fact, say this. But by 'bigger,' Conant meant schools of 400 students, not thousands" (2004, pp. 67–68). Berliner and Biddle write, "Control typically becomes more impersonal in large settings, and for this reason, some researchers have recommended that high schools serve no more than 250 students" (1995, p. 297). John Gatto speaks for the extreme position: "Schools are too big by a factor of ten or twenty. What is needed are hundreds of thousands of intimate, *ad hoc* facilities—park benches, rooftops, river banks, living rooms, places of business" (2001, p. 45). In my judgment, schools of such small proportions should be an alternative to rather than a replacement for mainstream schools. A last disturbing piece of evidence for a number lower than 500 comes from deindividuation research: Mann's 1981 study of "baiting" crowds (crowds that urge a potential suicide to endanger him or herself) "found that large crowds (more than 300 members) baited more than small crowds" (Forsyth 1999, pp. 461–462). In other words, people can be mesmerized into a sadistic state in groups over 300. Every teacher (and student) knows at least a taste of that crowd-borne sadism.

Besides being first on the list to receive small schools, should high-risk communities have schools that are *extra*-small? I believe so. One study observes, "Schools of 300 to 900 students performed better than both larger and smaller schools" but acknowledges "an interaction effect of socioeconomic status and school size, in which larger sizes are particularly harmful in low-income communities" (National Research Council 2004, pp. 114–115). The study cites the example of how New York City schools were reorganized into "houses" averaging 250 students (pp. 115–116). Robert Hagerty (1995) writes,

> Vulnerable and neglected youth desperately need small schools which provide meaningful personal relationships. Such schools could become the focal point for regenerating communities and *encouraging more parental support*. This judgment and proposal is grounded on thirty-five years of experience in public education, most of it in poor, working-class communities, and for the past three years researching exemplars of school success. (pp. 97–98, emphasis mine)

Note the acknowledgment of the parent aspect of relationship load.

There is also evidence that elementary-age children should be in smaller schools; thankfully, common practice already dictates this on the whole (Howley 2002, pp. 52–53). Since there tends to be little to no subject specialization in elementary schools, the drawback of curriculum restriction is less of a concern. In other words, we *can* make elementaries smaller so we might as well. Hagerty writes, "Once an elementary school has more than about 200 to 350 students and middle or high school 400 to 500 or more, a host of potentially unhealthy effects become noticeable, especially for vulnerable kids" (1995, p. 99). According to Williams, "Research indicates that the effective size for an elementary school is in the range of 300–400 students and that 400–800 students is appropriate for a secondary school" (1990). Craig Howley's review of the class size literature defines high schools of 400 or fewer and K–6 or K–8 schools of 200 or fewer as "small," but he cites recommendations ranging from 300 to 1,000 as an upper ethical limit (2002, pp. 51–52).

I recommend schools of 300 in all cases but secondary schools for low-risk communities, which could safely be as large as 500, as illustrated in Figure 5.4.

Again, these are maximum sizes meant for comprehensive schools. Charter and magnet alternatives to comprehensive schools may be smaller if founders so desire. Some communities may even want their mainstream schools to be smaller. Even academically, becoming "too small" appears to be unlikely. In one study where the connection between school size and test scores appears insignificant in either direction, the authors nonetheless note, "Many (18.4 percent) of the most successful schools are tiny, enrolling fewer than 100 students, while none of the least successful schools is so small"

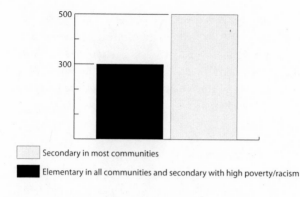

Secondary in most communities

Elementary in all communities and secondary with high poverty/racism

Figure 5.4 *Recom-mended school sizes.*

(Chubb and Moe 1990, p. 105). An example of a very small school approach (forty-four students) is the Urban Little Schools (ULS) proposal of Robert Newman:

> ULS elementary children have as long as it takes to learn to use the basic skills independently. That is because of the school's individualized learning system guided by teachers who work one to one with their groups of twelve children from five-to-twelve years of age. . . . These parent-choice schools are just a few doors down the block or around the corner from where the forty-four children live. (2000, pp. 9–10)

The secondary schools are even smaller—one-teacher sites of twelve kids (p. 10). This may appear extreme, but many have praised the nation's few remaining one-room schoolhouses, and some have proposed an increase in them.

6

The Core of the Relationship Load Effect

Here I want to highlight the reasons teachers cannot be as caring or effective in large groups as they can in small, nor can students feel as cared for or as capable. More evidence could be marshaled to support what I say here, and many more effects of relationship reduction could be similarly supported, and I hope to do just that in a later volume.

The evidence presented here counters common assertions that changing relationship load has no effect on its own and therefore should not be pursued on its own. For example, Ancess writes, "When only structural change occurs, as when schools are 'broken down' into smaller versions of their bigger selves, assumptions about students remain unchanged" (2003, p. 140). Similarly, Miles and Darling-Hammond write, "There is little rationale for restructuring resources without an underlying educational design" even if the rationale is simply reducing class size (1998). As another example, Meier argues that we should not "downsize all schools by fiat" but allow them to propagate slowly of their own accord because we are "aiming at change that sticks, not another fad" (2000b, p. 187).

I respectfully disagree for several reasons. First, research contradicts these assertions. Smallness has an independent effect on the amount and quality of attention students receive. Teacher behavior in smaller versus larger classes suggests they intuitively agree with the philosophical basis of this book—that this extra attention is in and of itself more important than (though not in competition with) changes to methods or improvement of academic outcomes. One study reads, "The largest effects we found were that a reduction in class size induces teachers to devote less time to group instruction and more time to individual instruction" (Betts and Shkolnik 1999). Simply put, quickly downsized schools and classes get these effects just as quickly as they are downsized, whereas slowly downsized schools and classes get them slowly.

Second, these calls for caution are beholden to the fake academic crisis. As detailed in Chapter 7, achievement *gains* do not necessarily accompany quick downsizing, but *worse* academic results have not been documented in either school or class size reduction. Third, philosophical or curricular change is not mutually exclusive of size change—both enhance and facilitate one another. The one qualifier is that such changes can enhance but not replace the effects of relationship load reduction, except in exceptional schools. Fourth, assertions like the above have a bothersome subtext: They imply that children whose educators are not creative enough to forge unique, extraordinary, or built-to-last smallness do not deserve smallness at all.

Students

School is for now, not just for later. Children deserve to feel good at school, to like it. One study found that students assigned for multiple years to the same teacher "were less likely than those in traditional school to report a dislike for schoolwork or to say that they found school boring" (Flinders and Noddings 2001). Similar findings occur in studies of the other aspects of relationship load reduction. Children also deserve to be influenced to behave well. If subjected to an environment that makes them tend to behave in a less-than-ideal way (which could arguably include thinking shallowly rather than deeply), they are in effect practicing and honing that behavior, making a habit of it. As well, in an environment with very little adult attention to go around, negative behavior will tend to be undesirably reinforced with *negative* adult attention. How a child feels, how she is allowed to act, how much attention she gets, and what kind of attention it is all make a difference in her development and socialization. School is not a magical place where an exception is made to these principles.

Because, in my estimation, too many people mistakenly prioritize academics over nurturance, I try not to overplay the academic aspects of the grouping size effect, but they are significant. Again, this is because they are put in their proper place, secondary but simultaneous. As Bernstein-Yamashiro observes, students use good work, good scores, and good behavior "to communicate their respect and hold up their sides of the friendships" with teachers; she argues, "They are deliberate in their decisions to work or withhold academic effort, to participate or misbehave" (2004, p. 61). And her study confirms that one of the core connections between emotion and learning is that students do not "take intellectual risks in uncomfortable settings" (p. 58). Only by dethroning achievement can we see how it is intertwined with relationships.

Teachers

Though I am generally referring to classroom teachers here, many of the effects I mention could easily apply to other educators who would form relationships with happier kids and teachers in a small school with small classes. Teachers are human beings whose feelings and behaviors are just as influenced by their environment as anyone's are. They are also grown-up children who are influenced by their childhood experiences; Fredriksen and Rhodes write, "Researchers have linked teachers' attachment histories with their primary caregiver with the quality of student-teacher relationships" (2004, p. 27). One example that many are beginning to recognize the similarity of teacher and student needs is a MetLife (2005) study that looked at the effect of analogous transitions on both teachers and students, one into the profession, the other into secondary school:

> For both students and the important adults in their lives, transitional periods can often be a time of flux or stress. These periods of stress bring to the forefront what is working in the educational system and also where there are areas of weakness. (p. 3)

Though we may find it convenient or guilt-softening to call teachers "bad" just as we do kids, it doesn't help us any. Take this negative assessment by Clark, who overflows with empathy for young people:

> (1) Most teachers believe that learning for its own sake should be enough to motivate students. (2) Far too many teachers pigeonhole students to the detriment of their developmental health and progress. (3) Teachers feel overburdened and overwhelmed, and the consequences of this spill over into their teaching. (2004, p. 90)

A likely explanation for numbers (1) and (2) is contained in number (3).

Adults are clearly limited in how many children they can be caring toward at one time; in other words, they have an insurmountable limit to what relationship load they can effectively handle. As Garbarino puts it, it isn't that educators are intentionally "more inclusive in small schools while those in large schools are elitist. It is a function of the situation itself, a socially toxic situation versus a socially healthy situation" (1995, p. 97). We waste our teachers when we make them teach so many. We squander the chance to harness their potential to treat our kids the way we want them treated.

In sum, there is a close relationship between the grouping size effect and the kinds of behaviors we use to distinguish between "good" and "bad" teachers. By reducing grouping size, we would suddenly find ourselves blessed by more good teachers than we thought we had, simply by altering their working conditions. Let me spend some time substantiating a few key effects as examples of how relationship load has a direct impact on teachers' treating our kids the way we want them to.

Style of Relation and Control

As I hinted in the Introduction, perhaps the most pernicious effect of large grouping size on schooling is its tendency to increase the need for coercion (and the resulting resistance) in the teacher-student relationship. As early as 1899, Dewey acknowledged the connection between large class size and "external forms of 'keeping order'" (1990, p. 176). Not only is this demoralizing for both parties, it also narrows the pool of interested and potentially effective educators, as well as tending to burn out those who are effective. Noddings (1984) argues that the structure of schools has already severely limited the number of teachers we can come to see as "good" by creating the "need" for unnatural crowd control skills. "Many of the skills we associate with teaching are, if they are skills at all, skills whose need is induced by the peculiar structure of modern schooling. . . . Many so-called 'management' or 'disciplinary' skills would be unnecessary in schools organized for caring" (p. 198).

Excessive coercion and control are a predominant means of coping with the unnecessary chaos created by an unhealthy grouping size. DeMarrais and LeCompte note an irony: "One need only watch the behavior of adult teachers in faculty meetings to question whether adults can be as quiet, sit as still, and listen as well as children are expected to do" (1999, p. 246). This reflects the understanding that teachers are not that dissimilar from their students, and being so, their social situation (e.g., relationship load) largely determines their perceptions. Sizer writes,

The very existence of schools this large sends a confusing message to their faculties and the children's parents. Bigness all too readily signals a need for order—crowd control, some call it—and order all too usually implies standardized routines and rule-driven, impersonal school culture. (1996, p. 30)

Reasonable commentators do admit that coercion is sometimes unavoidable, but they force us to admit that only by using it sparingly can we hope to overcome its negative effects with our otherwise nurturing behavior (Noddings 2003, p. 247). In my experience, it is often necessary to suppress undesirable student behavior coercively, but until I address its roots with listening and concern, a student will continue to harbor something he or she needs to "act out."

In their daycare research, Clarke-Stewart and colleagues found that more important to development "than the amount of one-to-one attention from caregivers was their disciplinary style" (1994, pp. 237–238). They note elsewhere, however, that grouping size and discipline style can maximize (or minimize) each other's effects:

> A nonauthoritarian style of teaching that included relatively few demands and directions and more choices was also related to children's advanced cognitive ability, *especially in small classes* . . . and to greater gains in social cognitive development. (p. 135, italics mine)

In other words, grouping size appears to increase the likelihood of both amount of attention and noncoercive discipline style. Because larger groupings by nature are less need-satisfying, they make it increasingly difficult to avoid using a coercive style. Conversely, smaller groupings make it easier for a teacher to use such noncoercive methods to keep things peaceful and productive (Finn 2002, p. xii).

Some amount of student resistance to schooling is probably inevitable, but smallness does not force educators into the simplistic choice of either punishing or ignoring it. Ancess observed a more subtle solution in operation at three successful small schools:

> The schools do not make the resolution or elimination of students' resistance or ambivalence a precondition for learning or support. Instead, the schools facilitate students' development of intense relationships and strong attachments to their teachers, who can negotiate and renegotiate students' ambivalence and build the students' affiliation with their school's values and goals that is necessary for students to meet their learning demands. (2003, p. 128)

Smallness facilitates the welcoming of students into learning not by making it a condition of receiving positive attention but by allowing students to express their feelings about school in the same way that any child should be allowed to express his or her feelings about caregiver decisions, whether or not those decisions ultimately change.

Equity of Attention to All Students

Many have observed that the distribution of attention in large classrooms is often unequal. You could call these teachers who "play favorites" petty, or you could call them human. Fredriksen and Rhodes write, "Elementary teachers' levels of stress and negative affect predicted the number of students with whom teachers had negative relationships" (2004, p. 47). It will clearly be impossible to find 3 million teachers immune to human nature. Finn and colleagues find that class size reduction research has good news in this department, writing, "When the class is smaller, teachers are compelled to attend to all students regardless of their abilities, motivation, or classroom demeanor" (2001, p. 174). Achilles powerfully compares large classes to triage—the non-ideal medical care situation where doctors can only pick a few patients to save (1999, p. 114). Why do we insist on forcing—or at least tempting—teachers to pick and choose?

Cultural Inclusiveness, Response to Diversity

Unfortunately, race, ethnicity, and class are often the variables by which teachers choose the portion of their large classes they truly commit to meeting the needs of. Racism and other forms of discrimination are age-old problems that will probably never disappear completely, but they are intensified by context. Just as smaller groupings will allow teachers to categorize students less according to their attitudes toward school, they will also help them to see past such things as their students' fashion choices, skin color, dialect, accent, social class, or lack of conformity with traditional gender and sexual orientation norms.

Again, though, this change will be facilitated more than caused by relationship load reduction. Clearly educators still need to take responsibility for responding to the people in their care as authentic and unique, rather than in terms of a prefabricated category that excludes a large portion of children. Educators need to take a good share of the responsibility for overcoming the lack of correspondence between the social characteristics of teachers and students. Public school children are obviously about equally divided into males and females and were 58 percent white in 2005 (NCES 2007a, indicator 5). But according to an NEA survey,

> More than three-quarters (79%) of teachers surveyed are female. The vast majority of teachers (about 90%) are White; about 5 percent are Black/African American; and the remainder are other races. Across

racial categories, 5 percent of all teachers reported being of Hispanic origin. (National Education Association 2003b)

Based on the more balanced racial composition of alternate recruitment, the addition of new teachers that would result from relationship load reduction could help equalize these numbers (Feistritzer 2008, p. 3).

Mutual Respect, Trust, Loyalty, and Obligation

Imagine a teacher on day one in front of a new class. The teacher has learned from experience and common sense that the larger the group is, the more it needs to be controlled rather than simply taught. Day one, therefore, is critical to establishing authority. The stakes are high if a student challenges that authority. This teacher is afraid of a lack of control in and of itself, as well as the shame he will feel if his supervisors and colleagues consider him to be inadequate because of it. If that class is located in a large school, the emotional stakes are even higher. Teacher and students are more anxious because of the number of strangers around them, many of whose names they will never learn. There will be a constant supply of strangers who will consistently rekindle that anxiety, whose behavior they will not be able to predict except by stereotyping. In such an environment, even a wise teacher can get tricked by his emotions into demanding respect before he'll give it.

Small grouping size, on the other hand, will counteract the tendency of any teacher to fall prey to this trap. The anxiety is lower; the number of strangers is minimized; the teacher is more likely to already know many of his students on day one; the students are less nervous and less likely to act out; the teacher perceives that the small group will not need to be controlled so much as simply taught, meaning that he doesn't have to "establish" his authority by any other means than by being confident, kind, and generous with help. Grouping size reduction can turn a climate of intractable distrust and disrespect into a breeding ground for mutual loyalty and obligation (Toch 1991, p. 266). Students develop a sense of loyalty to their teachers in small groups, which makes them complete sometimes-unappealing work as part of an overall demonstration of respect for them (Bernstein-Yamashiro 2004, p. 61). Likewise, teachers will be loyal to their students in small groups by not allowing them to fail or "slip through the cracks." What is that phrase but a euphemism for the unavoidable results of large grouping size?

Judgmental or Accepting

Again, large groupings tend to trick teachers into selecting some students to work hard for and some not to work hard for. They rationalize this to themselves by judging students, that is, making it appear to themselves that because of this or that trait or behavior, certain students are more deserving and certain students are less deserving. In the context of small groupings, teachers will not tend to fall for these self-protective tricks. Because they will be able to (even compelled to) develop a deeper relationship with each student, they will be more likely to accept all students nonjudgmentally (Finn et al. 2001, p. 174). Students will thrive on this sense of unconditional acceptance. Again, being accepting does not mean being permissive—it means accepting a child "as is" while still setting high standards for accomplishment and behavior. Without the unconditional acceptance, the high standards will backfire, and vice versa. Large classes are a breeding ground for both types of imbalanced climate: rejecting and permissive. Both have the effect of reinforcing underachievement or undesirable behavior. In short, the striking of this balance between acceptance and expectations becomes increasingly difficult as grouping size increases, making "teacher quality" appear all the more essential to educational success.

Clark points to a tendency among teachers to reject students who reject their curriculum (2004, p. 92); it's a simple emotional defense mechanism. Small groupings facilitate relationships that allow teachers to accept students for who they are as opposed to the extent to which they appreciate the curriculum. Again, teachers are human—they need to feel that their work is successful and worthwhile. In the absence of strong relationships with students, they will seek to fill this need by fishing for assurance from students that their lessons are valuable. On the other hand, if allowed to pursue deeper relationships with students that transcend the subject matter they are teaching, more will be able to find this deeper meaning to their jobs. If and when a student rejects the importance of a particular lesson (which, incidentally, will occur less frequently in the context of better relationships), teachers won't feel as personally rejected because they will be less emotionally invested in that aspect of the job. If teachers are allowed to stay in touch with the primary goal of education as a subset of childrearing—creating prosocial adults—they will also keep the lesser importance (though not low importance) of their subject area in its proper perspective. If more teachers can finally keep in mind that, say, diagramming sentences is not as important as a sense of belonging, it will be because they were given the opportunity to develop fewer relationships better.

Others have noted that large grouping size (and its tendency to keep traditional teaching practices in place) also serves to keep the wedge of "teacher as judge" in place between students and teachers:

> Instead of helping teachers to establish these supportive relationships, the system in failing urban schools places the teacher in the role of judge who hands out the grades, as the authority separated from the children who is hired to control groups of children, who is expected to make children work or feel the results of school failure. (R. E. Newman 2000, p. 5)

Gnezda (2005) also points to the fact that this judge role of teachers takes time away from teacher as helper and attention provider (pp. 32–33).

Reactions to Differing Styles and Paces of Learning

Before we leave the subject of tolerance and acceptance, let's consider the diversity of intellectual skills teachers are asked to deal with in the course of teaching. Grouping size directly affects how teachers tolerate learning differences as well. In the Introduction I related how I came to observe my own patience with less-prepared learners decrease in larger classes. I also observed that in small classes my sense of what the objectives should be is more responsive to individual need. Without even really considering that I'm doing something different than I would in a larger class, the class (in the sense of "course") as an idea can become closer to what the students in the room need or want rather than a mere reflection of the core curriculum standards. In a large class, on the other hand, I tend to think of the curriculum as more fixed and more independent from the needs of the students. These experiences, together with corroborating research, have convinced me that it is a reduction in this tendency to teach beyond a student's abilities (through grouping size reduction)—and not an increase in "accountability"—that will keep students from missing out on basic skills. And yet most discussions of school improvement continue to treat class size reduction as either negligible in effect or mere fantasy as a goal.

My experience is not unique. Research has shown that large groupings tend to prevent teachers from being able to individualize their teaching as a means of responding to differing styles and paces of learning among their students (Zahorik 1999). We've already discussed the tendency for teachers in larger groupings to provide unequal attention to the sharper students (i.e., students whose learning is least inhibited by large groups). There is an unfortunate tendency in *all* teachers to see these kids as allies and the slower or less motivated students as opponents. Again, smaller groupings would allow teachers to overcome this stress- and threat-induced mode of thought.

Allow me to deepen what I said earlier about personalization as an automatic effect of grouping size reduction. I like to think of two types of personalization, design and delivery. Personalization that occurs in the curriculum-design process would include allowing for more student choice, discovery, and individual direction. Personalization that occurs at the point of delivery entails helping an individual student get the otherwise uniform material in a way that's customized for that student's particular needs. Delivery personalization can be seen as an automatic result of class size reduction. Although design personalization is made easier by small classes, according to the research it is not an automatic effect. John Zahorik treats the issue with precision; allow me to quote at length:

> Small class size has three main effects that lead to increased individualization: fewer discipline problems and more instruction, more knowledge of students, and more teacher enthusiasm for teaching. In small-size classes, there is less misbehavior. When misbehavior does occur, it is more noticeable, and teachers can treat it immediately before it becomes a major problem. This reduced, if not totally eliminated, time spent on discipline leads to more time available for instruction. More knowledge of individual students is an important result of smaller class size. Teachers come to know students personally, and they have a much greater understanding of each student's place in the learning cycle. A caring, family-like atmosphere develops in the classroom. When classes are small, teachers experience less stress from disciplining, correcting papers, and not having time to do what needs to be done. As stress is reduced, enthusiasm and satisfaction increase, and educators begin to implement teaching procedures that they know will benefit students. The main result of more instructional time, knowledge of students, and teacher enthusiasm is individualization. (1999)

Not wanting to promise miraculous method transformations, Zahorik is careful to define the precise nature of the individualization that arises automatically: "The individualization that occurs in small-size classes is more procedural than substantive. Teachers generally do not alter the curriculum for individual students; they expect each student to acquire the same content" (1999). This description coincides precisely with what I've called delivery personalization. If administrators desire to see more design personalization, then training will be required, but again, delivery personalization is enough to achieve large nurturance-crisis benefits, as well as academic benefits.

Again, quality and responsiveness of instruction are compromised by the need to control a large group:

> Teachers become conservative when it comes to trying ways to diversify their teaching to meet the needs of each child because individualization might threaten the teacher's tenuous hold on control of the classroom. On the other hand, uniformity promises order. And order is the number one goal. (Newman 2000, p. 5)

In Blatchford's research,

> class size affected the amount of individual attention, the immediacy and responsiveness of teachers to children, the sustained and purposeful nature of interaction between teachers and children, the depth of a teacher's knowledge of children in her class, and sensitivity to individual children's particular needs. (2003, p. 66)

Again, differentiated, personalized instruction through relationship load reduction is the more ethical alternative to separate tracks and other means of marking winners and losers.

Reactions to Difficult Kids, Misbehavior, and Neediness

Many argue the best response to difficult children is dialog and understanding rather than punishment.[1] Unfortunately, large groupings make the better response less likely. Let's examine why that is. First, it's a question of time. For example, how much of what Gnezda recommends in her book *Teaching Difficult Students* is realistically going to happen in large classes?

> What we can do is be truly present with our [difficult students], sit down next to them, and treat them like they are worth a million bucks. We can listen to whatever they have to say, suspending judgment and hearing the clues about who they really are. Then we will know what they need and how to reach them, and they will begin to trust us enough to reach back. (2005, p. 53)

Second, it goes beyond just time. Similar to the dynamic described in the Introduction, if a student is acting out home problems in a large class, the teacher tends to fear that (a) he or she won't succeed with that student and/or

(b) the problematic student will sabotage the teacher's success with the others. As a subconscious, self-protective reaction, the teacher often declares the kid hopeless, unreachable by anyone. By locating the problem within the kid (and not the lack of time to give adequate attention), the teacher avoids feelings of failure (Gnezda 2005, pp. 24–25). It's also about avoiding feelings of irremediable pity. To admit the truth about what makes difficult kids the way they are (neediness) is hard if you can't do much to help. Admitting a child needs more love than one can give leads to feelings of powerlessness in the face of tragedy. Rather than feel a seemingly pointless pity (since very little can be done to help such a kid in a large class) a teacher unconsciously replaces that empathy with callousness and labels the kid "bad," reassured by the false impression that the kid has rejected an adequate offer of help.

This returns us to the heart of the recognition that teachers are just grown-up kids. Though not as acutely, teachers—like difficult kids—are influenced by emotions (Gnezda 2005, p. 67), including a lack of positive attention they may have experienced in their own childhoods. By creating conditions that allow teachers to operate well below their emotional breaking points, we can ensure that they'll treat our kids the best they can, and further, that they'll be more receptive to our entreaties to treat them even better, for example, by becoming conscious of and reducing their prejudices. But when we push teachers to their emotional limits, they can't help but focus on their own needs first—it's instinctual. If we want them to be able to put their needs equal or second to their students' needs, they need to work in conditions that keep them well below relationship overload.

Academic Expectations

As a last highlighted effect of relationship load on teaching, let's look at what (nearly) everyone agrees is important about school: making students think. Even if we accept the real nurturance crisis and reject the fake academic crisis, there is certainly still room for improvement in academic expectations. Many have pointed to unchallenging or uninteresting work being assigned in schools, but few have connected it to class size. The key to connecting it to grouping size is to link it to the increased need for order or compliance in larger groups. Sizer does this when he writes,

> Horace painfully knows that one cannot teach a student well if one does not know that student well. If the task is the mere memorization of simple lists, maybe, or the development of a routine skill. Serious understanding of an important and complex issue, the stuff of good secondary education? Rarely, if ever. (1996, p. xiii)

The next step in his logic is that only smaller groups will promote that knowing of one another that allows for complex learning. Plenty of others have spoken to the connection between low expectations and order-keeping. Mary Kennedy writes,

> Teachers need student cooperation in order to do anything in their classrooms, and they often obtain that cooperation through tacit bargaining. These bargains usually take the form of offering a more predictable and routine curriculum or a curriculum with fewer serious intellectual challenges in exchange for a more docile and pliant student body. (2005, p. 16)

By offering this compromise to students (as a mass), the teacher gets cooperation from a group that is too large to get cooperation from on challenging work (and too large to deal with as unique individuals). Thomas Toch writes, "In many classrooms, nothing more is expected of students than that they aren't disruptive. Keeping their classrooms free of hassles, rather than educating students, seems to be the first priority of many teachers" (1991, p. 242). So long as a critic avoids the issue of class size, such statements participate in the national sport of teacher-bashing as an easy way out of addressing alienating conditions (deMarrais and LeCompte 1999, p. 91). If a critic of schoolwork admits that a group of students does need to be managed as well as taught, then the question of whether a particular group size is manageable rears its long-suppressed head. If we want the average teacher to be effective, we need to create conditions that make management more possible *by means of* appropriately challenging activities rather than *at their expense*.

In sum, quality schoolwork is personalized. Its quality arises from three sources: (a) being precisely challenging enough for the individual student, (b) involving student decision-making and choice, and (c) including the motivating individual attention from the well-known teacher who personalizes it.

7
The Counterarguments

O f the major arguments used against grouping size (and particularly class size) reduction, these are the two I have dealt with so far:

1. It doesn't make any difference without retraining.
2. It doesn't always raise test scores.

I addressed the first in Chapter 1 and the second in Chapter 2. Here are the others:

3. Class sizes came down over the history of public schooling and it hasn't helped.
4. It dilutes the overall quality of teachers (and/or the integrity of the profession).
5. Its effects can be reproduced by increased teacher effort, training, or quality.
6. It's too expensive.

These are mainly arguments against class size reduction in particular. In Chapter 5, I dealt with the arguments against smaller schools and teacher continuity, showing that class size reduction would solve all the legitimate ones. As argued there, if people can be convinced to invest in class size reduction, then adding on school size and teacher continuity would be a minor additional commitment. As usual, that brings us to back to the issue of cost, which turns out to be no less overstated than the rest. Because of its importance, I'll give the issue of money its own chapter, where I'll show that large relationship load doesn't lower costs, it simply hides them: Pay now or pay later.

To complete the picture, let's add the structural alternatives that recognize the consequences of relationship load but offer a more limited fix; I'll classify them as cost arguments since they're usually offered because they're "cheaper" (in the short term only):

- Reduce class size for early grades only, where it most matters to test scores.
- Reserve smallness for the neediest kids (medicine rather than diet).
- Reduce school size and/or increase teacher continuity without reducing class size.

The last option has already been shown in Chapter 5 to be a good step but a small and problematic step toward solving the nurturance crisis.

Counterargument 3
"Class Size Reduction over the Course of Time Has Made No Difference"

When a critic tries to argue that the class size reduction in the twentieth century did not lead to either learning gains or a reduction in social problems, the response is that it might have if it had been less gradual and other nurturance effects of school had remained constant. I detailed earlier that during the twentieth century, the average class size has dropped about fifteen students. That's about one seventh of a student per year. Any effects of this gradual drop in class sizes thus far would be hard to measure considering all the other intervening variables. In terms of the erosion of nurturance overall, four measurements of the extent to which kids were exposed to dehumanizing groupings—the number of students enrolling in school, the number of years they stayed in school, the length of the school year, and school size—all increased over the period in question, partially if not wholly nullifying the real-crisis effects of reducing class size at a snail's pace. So school relationship load taken as a whole has almost certainly resulted in net losses in the realm of adult attention, though clearly those losses are smaller than they would have been had class sizes remained as they were.

Counterargument 4
"Class Size Reduction Dilutes the Overall Quality of Teachers (and/or the Integrity of the Profession)"

The teacher-quality-over-smallness argument sets up a false dichotomy. Class size and teacher quality are far from mutually exclusive—they are in fact connected. I'm all for continuing to raise the prestige and academic effectiveness of teachers, but not at the expense of children here and now and our society's mental health later on. Again, the satisfaction to be gained from meeting students' needs for attention will be of far greater value—to both teachers and students—than a nobility gained through suffering or hollow reverence. Professional pride in teaching can sometimes function as a defense mechanism that undermines the most important aspect of teaching, nurturance. Since society at large devalues the childrearing part of the job, teachers can sometimes overcompensate by focusing too heavily on the expertise/knowledge part (Fibkins 2003). This phenomenon is yet another Band-Aid (this time for the teacher's self-worth) on the unacknowledged problem of large grouping size.

The National Academy of Education (2005) states, "It would be naïve to suggest that merely producing more highly skilled teachers can, by itself, dramatically change the outcomes of education." As evidence presented throughout has suggested, a large part of what determines teaching's level of difficulty is relationship load:

> It is not enough to prepare individual good teachers and send them out to dysfunctional schools. If teachers are to be effective, they must work in settings in which they can use what they know—where they can come to know their students and their families well. (p. 68)

Certainly grouping size reduction will open up the profession to new teachers, many of whom will be less qualified *in the short term*.[1] But even a critic of class size reduction like Robert Franciosi argues, "The link between certification and student performance was weak. There was a much stronger effect due to experience" (2004, p. 192). Linda Darling-Hammond, perhaps the best-known advocate of improving teacher training, claims that such findings are the exception rather than the rule, citing research that controls for experience and finds that in-field teachers outperform out-of-field teachers (2006, p. 20). Even so, lesser effectiveness at teaching is clearly *partly* due to inexperience, which is inherently temporary, and partly due to lack of training, which never needs to be permanent. Mainly high attrition—which I showed in Chapter 1 to be linked to relationship load—creates the situation where neither can be resolved. Experience and training are not mutually exclusive or in conflict. Christopher Jepsen and Steven Rivkin write that effects of increased inexperience during class size reduction "should disappear as these new teachers acquire experience and full certification" (2002, p. x).

Moreover, since grouping size reduction makes teaching easier for all teachers, including novices, we don't need to fear any net drop in amount of learning no matter what temporary drop in average experience or training shows up in the growing ranks of teachers. Indeed, no such achievement drops appear in the research on smaller-scale projects. For example, many point to the hurried implementation of California's early grades class size reduction as an example of what happens when you let too many underqualified teachers in too quickly (e.g., Franciosi 2004, p. 191). Admittedly, that program had less dramatic academic results than other class size reduction programs, such as STAR in Tennessee. Jepsen and Rivkin report in their study of the California project that overall math percentages went up 4 percent and reading 3 percent; urban areas showed the big gains while rural areas held steady; the one significant drop was in majority African American schools, primarily in Los Angeles (2002, p. xi). They speculate this had to do with the flight of experienced teachers to schools popularly regarded as easier to teach in, an avoidable effect of race-blind and wealth-blind planning (which we'll return to in Chapter 10). Apart from that one exception, these are not the shabby results many have made them out to be. But even those who cast California's class size reduction as a failure never try to claim that students learned *less* on average. In other words, less qualified teachers got the same results or better (except when overly concentrated in racially stigmatized schools) because the smaller classes made those qualifications less necessary. Thus, the fastest way to increase a teacher's quality is to give her a smaller class.

If we look at the big picture of teacher quality, the training and induction of teachers is clearly important. Darling-Hammond characterizes these systems as in a state of gradual improvement in the United States (2006, p. 275). There is no reason to argue that class size reduction would disrupt or slow this improvement. Indeed, conditions that research has shown to be effective for teacher training and induction can be facilitated by smallness despite increasing the number of inductees. For example, Chapter 10 will outline how placing yet-to-be-certified and first-year teachers in "proto-internships" with a mentor teacher who shares a class of twenty-four will offer a more effective induction environment irrespective of any qualitative change to the process. And smallness will not impede such qualitative change but in fact facilitate it.

A related argument is that class size reduction wouldn't work because the new positions wouldn't get enough applicants. For example, Franciosi writes of California's class size reduction, "The initiative ran straight into an unanticipated resource constraint: the lack of qualified teachers" (2004, p. 193). It's

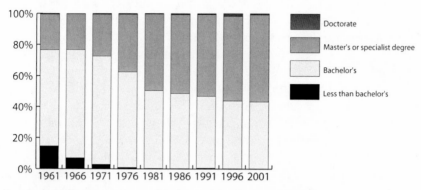

Figure 7.1 *Highest degrees earned by U.S. public school teachers.*
Source: Digest 2005, table 68.

as if to say that all we owe our children is to *advertise* more teaching positions, not to make sure they get filled. At its core, the argument is tautological: "The reason we can't put more adults back into kids' lives is that we've taken them away." The finding of teachers is a challenge, but not a roadblock. Chapter 10 will discuss the practicalities in more detail, including the fact that we already have a highly functional system in place to make up for the limitations of the traditional way of training teachers: "Alternate routes" are now bringing in a third of new teachers, and the data show they're more diverse, possibly more committed, and often better at getting academic results.

Let me conclude with the following fact: During the baby boom we doubled our teaching force in a mere twenty years. By 1970 the *percentage* of the workforce made up by teachers—not just the raw number—was double what it was just twenty years earlier (Wyatt and Hecker 2006). Those who make the teacher quality dilution argument would be hard pressed to explain away the combination of these data and the data in Chapter 2 that show academic achievement did not go down over this period; on top of that, the teacher quality argument must overcome the fact that teachers became increasingly well educated over this period. Figure 7.1 shows the trend since midcentury.

The trend is a continuation of a steady increase since public schooling began. As a further example, during the 1917–1918 school year in New Mexico, 55.5 percent of teachers did not have a high school diploma (Gribble 1948, p. 12).

Counterargument 5
"Better, Better-Trained, or Harder-Working Teachers Can Be Just as Nurturing in Large Classes"

This is another version of the false dichotomy of smallness and teacher quality. To believe that increased teacher effort, training, or innate quality can simulate the nurturance effects of grouping size reduction on a wide scale is fanciful, to say the least. In essence it is the "simple" plan of turning all teachers into above-average teachers. Sidorkin (2002) attacks this assumption "that we all can do what the best can," adding,

> There is something sinister in all schemas that count on extraordinary personality, enthusiasm, and sacrifice. . . . The schools should be able to make the economy of relations work in such a way that an average teacher can enjoy respect from students, feel good about herself, and be an effective instructor. (pp. 111–112)

This longing for an all-above-average teaching force—not the increasing of the size (and innate effectiveness) of the teaching force—is the truly pie-in-the-sky thinking we need to be wary of. Any solution to the real nurturance crisis, which is primarily a quantity problem, needs a solution that is primarily a quantity solution. Quality will follow from increased ease of the task.

The teacher quality argument's view of teacher training is beholden to the fake academic crisis. As discussed, it may be true that improved teacher preparation would have an effect on academic outcomes, but society's best interests do not lie in improving test scores while ignoring the nurturance crisis. Training is largely tangential to the issue of nurturance. As a perplexing example, Leach remarks, "If we are determined that teachers should" help with childrearing "schools do not just need more teachers, but many more and *infinitely better-trained* teachers than any country currently provides" (1994, p. 164, emphasis mine). If adults in general require no training to become parents and be primarily responsible for the emotional health of children, why should teachers require special training merely to be an assistant in the process?

The teacher quality argument appears to be the favorite way to avoid discussing how difficult we've made the job of K–12 teaching. Blatchford (2003) writes,

> It has been argued by both researchers and politicians that it is not size of the class that is the problem, or the solution, but the quality of teaching and teacher training. This argument is, of course, convenient for policy makers because responsibility is then attached to the

teacher. . . . Teachers will vary in their effectiveness, but the size of the class and the size of the groups in the class necessarily affect what a teacher has to deal with, and can present her with choices and the need for compromises. (2003, p. 160)

Despite research like Blatchford's, the situation remains largely unchanged with respect to class size research and policy. With the focus on its impact on test scores, the teacher quality argument still seems to offer the most bang for the buck. But as soon as we draw our eyes away from the test score idol, we can begin to see that instead of simply continuing the wild-goose chase for "better" people to staff hard jobs, we can simply make the jobs easier. In this vein, Wagner (2002) unravels what he calls the "higher salary" and "teacher preparation" myths regarding teacher effectiveness. Allow me to quote him at length as he draws on a study by Public Agenda:

The vast majority of new teachers—71 percent—felt generally well prepared for their new careers, but not for the working conditions they experienced. Almost 60 percent of the teachers surveyed said that upon entering the profession, they did not know how to best help the lowest achieving students. However, the majority did not blame their training. Nearly three-quarters (73 percent) of the teachers surveyed agreed that "talented teachers are not enough on their own" to turn around the performance of low-achieving students, prompting the authors of the study to observe that, "The frustration of simply not being able to get through to some kids, to help them progress, takes a calculable—and debilitating—toll on teachers." (p. 98)

It leads one to ask, are we looking for smarter people or stupider people to agree to and stick with this situation? People who are more compassionate or people who are more masochistic? Wagner cites the critical warning from the report: "*Who becomes a teacher seems less of a problem than what happens to them once they enter a classroom.* In the rush to improve education for the nation's youngsters, policymakers may do well to revisit their assumptions of what is wrong" (via Wagner 2002, p. 98, italics mine). Relationship load is what is wrong.

So what would these new teachers change to feel more able to succeed? When the researchers asked them to pick which from a list of suggestions would be "very effective" ways to improve teacher quality, "reducing class size" topped the list at 86 percent, while the next highest response only reached 59 percent (Public Agenda 2000). In other words, they concurred overwhelmingly that class size reduction *is* about teacher quality, rather than in tension with it. Thus the flimsiness of the argument that class size reduction would *lower* teacher quality is apparent when one bends it backward. By making teaching easier, more attractive, and more rewarding we will be allowing the average teacher's skills to have a greater impact; and it's quite possible that we'll be able to bring in and keep a higher percentage of great teachers than we've ever had before.

In sum, "relate rather than restructure" arguments are flawed on their face (e.g., Fibkins 2003). They pretend that we have to make a choice between the two and they obscure the more logical option of "restructure *so that* we can better relate." Yes, we should try our best to be caring under current conditions. No, that does not mean that things can get significantly better without relationship load reduction.

Counterargument 6
"Cheaper Alternatives"

"Small Classes for Early Grades Is Good Enough"
I like to think of this as the "glorified preschool" argument. A large proportion of small-class advocates seek class size reduction for the early grades alone. In fact, when many speak of class size reduction they are actually referring only to K–2 or K–3 reduction. The reason seems to be that few get the crisis right. For example, Blatchford observes "there is no evidence we have seen that small classes introduced later in children's school lives are as effective" at increasing test scores (2003, p. 144). Other research suggests, however, that academic effects of early interventions like grade retention, full-day kindergarten, and Head Start tend to fade by middle school (Alexander et al. 2003, p. 254), providing evidence that "early" is certainly good, but it's no substitute for "throughout."

Far too many studies seem to assume (perhaps rightly) that policy-makers will snicker at discussions of attitude, morale, or emotional well-being. Hence, most research on class size reduction centers unflinchingly on test scores. Nonetheless, Blatchford himself noted, "It may be that a smaller class size allows a teacher to approach children in a more personalized and more humanistic way, but this would be hard to measure and then enter into statistical analysis!" (2003, p. 160). The exclamation point is his. Other researchers have made similar comments as postscripts to their studies, for example:

> It should be noted that these enrichments to the curriculum may not be reflected in evaluations of class-size effects. Typically, achievement tests in reading and mathematics are used to evaluate outcomes. This narrow definition of achievement overlooks learning in other academic areas, areas which may be valued by consumers of education. Also, many of the enrichment areas are intended to promote positive

> attitudes, enthusiasm, and overall learning skills. These factors may have long-term effects not in evidence on short-term achievement tests. Research in education may be misled by its focus on short-term achievement outcomes. (Cahen et al. 1983, p. 206)

Nevertheless, most research continues to be misled in this way and to make only minor acknowledgments of the possibility.

In general, the K–3 camp echoes the thinking that instead of making school easier for kids to succeed at, what we need is preschool that prepares them for school. In other words, class size reduction as purely an early-grades phenomenon is more an expansion of the preschool approach than a fundamental change to the structure of education. "Don't change school so it's easier to handle," the thinking goes, "change people so they learn to handle it." DeMarrais and LeCompte refer to this phenomenon as goal displacement—prioritizing the inertia of the institution over the needs of the client the institution was built to serve (1999, p. 68). Changing only the beginning of schooling would clearly be better than nothing, but it's also clearly a copout. The most it will achieve is to delay the neglect, bring it on more gradually, and bring it to students who are hopefully less sensitive to it.

In terms of attachment needs, there is nothing at all significant about the third or fourth grade, no reason at all to draw an arbitrary line there rather than at age eighteen, where we already draw the line for most things childish. Besides test scores, the obvious explanation for the cutoff is cost. But why should we let cost concerns invade so early in our determinations of what children need? Revealingly, discussion of attachment is visible in the preschool and early elementary literature, but it doesn't reappear to any significant degree until the troubled teen literature. This is not an accident: Our troubled teens are the by-product of our lack of a model of continuous need for attachment. The reason we address attachment when we do, apparently, is that the consequences of insecure attachment are very visible at these two life stages. Out of thrift, we respond with Band-Aid approaches for these groups only.

A chief problem with the early-grades-only proposal is how it fits with the play-work continuum discussed earlier. Yes, younger children have more intense needs for adult availability *when playing*, but when working, every child needs it. And since school gradually (whether naturally or unfortunately) becomes more like work and less like play as children age, the net grouping size needs of children do not diminish. Meier writes, "The more complex the learning, the more children need genuine adult company, and the more trusted the adults must be" (2002, p. 13). Moreover, secondary school children usually have to adapt to having multiple, specialized teachers. Thus they are forced to adapt to even larger groupings, to the larger pupil loads of the teachers, and to being told it's okay because they don't need our attention anymore. Whom are we really trying to convince?

"Use Smallness as Medicine Rather Than Diet"
Part of the evidence for how smallness works is that we already use it for our second-chance schools:[2]

> Ironically, many school systems are attempting to combat their dropout problems by assigning truants and other "borderline" students to "alternative schools" with enrollments of 200 to 300 students that provide intensive remedial instruction and extensive student-teacher contact. If similarly supportive environments were more generally available for students before they reached the point of dropping out, perhaps the need for such schools, which are widely viewed as academic dumping grounds, would not be as great. (Toch 1991, p. 271)

In such schools the ingredient of smallness is not so secret as in other cases. Is "bigness first, then smallness for the failures" the only strategy that will prepare enough people to fill our academic-skilled jobs? Personalization is the more humane and effective way to challenge every student to the best of their ability and ensure that our smartest (no matter what their race or class) fill our most intellectually demanding jobs. As Noddings suggests, if we truly seek equality of opportunity in cutthroat higher education, it is no solution to cut our primary and secondary students' throats in preparation for it (2003, p. 200).

The partner to patch-up schools is catch-up tutoring. Here the logic goes, "If they fall behind the large-class pack, give them smallness in a concentrated dose." Robert Slavin (1989) proposes this as an alternative to the expense of class size reduction and its sometimes meager effects on test scores.[3] This method uses smallness as a medicine to be taken in strong doses by the few but kept from the many as a staple in the daily diet. Whatever its effect on the fake academic crisis, clearly this is not a preventative way to approach the crisis in childrearing. In essence, the debate is a game of definitions: Researchers create a false distinction, defining small classes as far enough from tutoring (say, eighteen) to create a foregone conclusion when their effects on test scores are compared. Thus current-size classes with occasional tutoring win out. Clearly, class size reduction is a continuum whose effects (and costs) increase steadily as class size approaches what we call tutoring, or what Achilles calls "the ultimate class size reduction" (1999, p. ix).

I am no opponent of tutoring per se. After all, its uncontested effectiveness only lends credence to my argument. Philip Jackson writes,

All of the teacher's actions described so far are bound together by a common theme. They are all responsive, in one way or another, to the crowded condition of the classroom. If the teacher dealt with one student at a time (as does happen in tutorial settings) most of the tasks that have been mentioned would be unnecessary. (1990, p. 13)

The problem is that tutoring used as a fake-crisis Band-Aid for low test scores is nowhere close to a substitute for classes of twelve used as social alienation prevention. Admittedly, even with classes of twelve, there still may be a few cases where tutoring is needed to assure adequate academic results for some kids (Achilles 1999, p. ix). But these cases will be greatly reduced once there are not as many cracks for kids to fall through—because, one could say, the teaching will be more similar to tutoring in the first place. Smallness for all will reduce the need for smallness for a few, freeing up resources for its own continuation.

Reading tutoring in the early grades is a common incarnation of the "concentrated doses" reasoning (e.g., Barr and Parrett 2003, p. 323). In a way it's preventative, but in another it suffers from the glorified preschool mentality: "Get them reading early so they can handle reading tasks in big classes that are nothing like tutoring." Again, frontloading education for "disadvantaged" children with a bunch of personal attention in the early grades, including additional personnel who work one-on-one as tutors, is a great idea. The problem is that it's usually proposed under the assumption that kids don't deserve and won't get that level of attention *throughout* their schooling. I propose using smallness as our comprehensive reform of schools, our children's daily diet, not as a medicine too expensive for anyone but those we've most malnourished.

So much for the "cheaper" alternatives.

8

The Costs and Savings

In the German fairy tale, the Pied Piper didn't get paid when he led the rats out of town by playing his inviting music. In retaliation for this, he led away the town's children with the same music, never to be seen again. If we don't want to lose our own kids, then we also need to pay the piper. This chapter examines whether that payment will be all that large in the long run. It challenges the most prevalent counterargument, demonstrating that the proposal is at worst cheap and at best free. I'll start with ongoing costs, then move to up-front costs (new space needed) and savings. Before I delve into tax increases, though, let me address the common complaint that Americans are overtaxed already.

Putting Costs in Perspective

Figure 8.1 compares the U.S. tax burden with that of the rest of the "developed" world.[1]

The United States, with an average class size of twenty-four, taxes one quarter of its wealth (25.5 percent in 2004). As I'll show, dropping to a class size of twelve would add 0.8 percent of gross domestic product (GDP). Only South Korea invests less in government services than we currently do, and we would not pass Japan by instituting classes of twelve. Incidentally, in 1991, South Korea's lower secondary average class size was an astounding forty-nine, and Japan's was thirty-six (NCES 1996, indicator 21). By 2004, they were thirty-six and thirty-four, respectively; but they remain by far the two highest in the OECD—indeed, there is only one other country (Mexico) above twenty-six (OECD 2006b, p. 54). If accurate, this suggests that South Korea succeeded in a thirteen-student class size reduction for middle school students—compared to the twelve-student reduction I am advocating—in a mere thirteen years, which is *half* the time that I am advocating! Despite being the next country up in tax burden, Switzerland has the second lowest class size (lower secondary) of "developed" countries at nineteen (p. 54).

Compared to the United States, the average "developed" country reinvests 11 percent more of its wealth for the public good. Admittedly, not every dime is spent ideally, but it is clear the United States is far less profligate (or generous, depending on your perspective) than countries with comparable economies. Thus, by international consensus, we would hardly be stepping out on an economic limb or risking economic collapse by investing more in childhood. In 1997, only 4 percent of America's GDP was spent on K–12 education (McCrery 1997). For a comparable essential, health care, when public and private expenditures are combined, we spend about four times that much at 16 percent of our GDP (Kaufman and Stein 2006). As you'll see below, my proposal will raise current education spending by 19.6 percent. That would add under 0.8 percent of GDP to our tax burden, putting our expenses for K–12 education at under 4.8 percent, between a third and a fourth of what we spend on health care.[2]

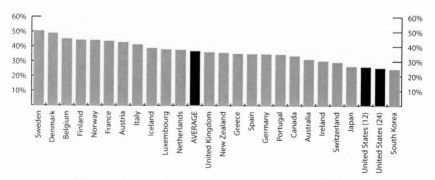

Figure 8.1 *Total 2004 tax revenue (including social security) as a percent of GDP in "developed" countries.*

Source: Swiss Federal Tax Administration 2006.

Ongoing Cost Projections

Ongoing educational spending would increase by 19.6 percent in order to reduce the average class size from its current twenty-four to the ideal twelve.
Remember, this is for cutting classes by nearly half nationwide. This projection puts the lie to the widely shared assumption that class size reduction is
expensive to the point of being off the table. By spending 20 percent more
than we do now, we can give kids what they deserve and what will give society the prosocial adults it needs.

Far from being overly optimistic, the calculations detailed below are conservative for the following reasons: One, I chose to start from the highest average class size number supported by the data, twenty-four. Other sources
suggested an average as low as 21.9 (see Chapter 5). Starting at twenty-two
would make the 19.6 percent increase quoted below drop to 14.3 percent!
Two, I call for the reassignment of *at most* half of non–regular classroom
(auxiliary) teachers. There is ample evidence presented in Chapters 1 and 4
that schools have reassigned many more than half of such teachers and still
been able to serve their special needs children as well or better via small
classes for all. Even in the most radical plan, 25 percent of aides are still in
place to help special needs students, and every fourteenth teacher would remain available as a nonclassroom specialist. Three, I assume a 50 percent increase in space costs. This is higher than what will likely be required considering that classes of twelve or fewer will take up far less space and thus
existing classrooms could be divided and spaces once too small converted to
classrooms (see Chapter 9). This is corroborated by the fact presented below
that the number of teachers needed will only increase by 53 percent. Even
with a modest amount of classroom subdividing, these extra teachers won't
require the full 50 percent more space included in the projections.

Figure 8.2 calculates increases in nationwide spending. It takes into account three sources of savings (in money and new teachers) recommended by
class size researchers. All three curves include the elimination of 75 percent
of classroom aides. Each curve represents a different scenario for reassigning
auxiliary teachers and guidance counselors.

"Auxiliary teachers" refers to those full-time equivalent teaching positions (FTEs) left over when the total number of students (minus those in
separate special education classrooms at any one time, which Appendix B
shows is 6.5 percent) is divided by current class size (twenty-four). I consider
the more radical reductions quite possible but have included the more conservative ones for the skeptical. The upper curve is included for comparison
purposes only. It is based on the faulty assumption that a proportional number of auxiliary teachers would be needed despite classes of twelve and that
the advisory system could not reduce the need for counselors.

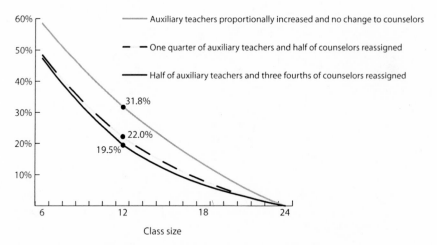

Figure 8.2 *Projected increase in total U.S. K–12 spending. (See Appendix A.)*

I did not include greater administration costs. Any administration cost increases due to more teachers are likely to be offset by the reduced administration costs of small schools. As Cohen and Scheer observe, "Small schools require fewer administrators" (2003, p. 53), which is corroborated by the fact that small school administrators often have enough free time to teach classes, as at Central Park East (Wagner 2002, p. 89), where there are no guidance counselors, no assistant principals, no attendance officers, no security guards, or other similar types of personnel (Miles and Darling-Hammond 1998).[3] In Chapter 9 I show that the current number of principals is sufficient to staff the new schools.

To crosscheck these findings, I have used Robert Reichardt's (2000) simulation of K–3 class size reduction in seven Florida districts. His sample had an average class size of 24.1 and he calculated a reduction to 15 students (p. 50). He included space costs, which he offset by the maximization of current space (p. 62), as well as savings from the elimination of instructional aides (p. 72). He did not include counselor and auxiliary teacher reduction. I have extrapolated his raw cost findings graphically in Figure 8.3 to match the extent of my proposal. Unsurprisingly, the extrapolation fell near my auxiliary-blind projection.

To compare more accurately with my projections, which separate new classroom space as an up-front rather than ongoing cost, I removed the $6,000 Reichardt allotted for this from the $53,000 per new class, which comes to 11 percent (p. 41).[4]

Since Reichardt did not reallocate any auxiliary teachers or counselors, his 30–34 percent is right in line with that version of my projection. Since he

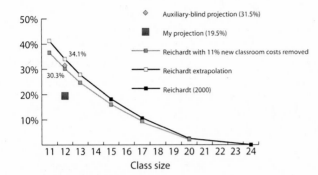

Figure 8.3 *Extrapolation of Reichardt (2000) spending increase estimates.*

is studying elementary-level reduction, counselors are not a significant source of reduction. And although the lowest reduction he considers is only three students less drastic than mine, he does not consider the vast numbers of auxiliary or "pull-out" teachers Achilles (1999) as well as Eugene Lewit and Linda Baker (1997) recommend reassigning to small classes of their own. Again, the difference between pupil/teacher ratio and class size reveals this pool of human resources. Only 69 percent of our teachers would be needed if all classes were exactly the average mainstream class size of twenty-four for the 92 percent of students in mainstream classes at any one time (see Appendices A and B). Miles and Darling-Hammond corroborate this, finding that "In 1991, in Boston, teachers in specialized programs working outside the regular classroom represented over 40 percent of the teaching force" (1998).

Auxiliary Teacher Details

Can auxiliary teachers really be reassigned to the degree I'm assuming? Yes. Case studies of schools that used inclusion on this scale and reassigned special education teachers to regular classrooms in order to achieve class size gains show no reduced attention to special needs students (Achilles 1999, p. 145). For example, one school went from twenty-five to fifteen students per class partly by implementing increased inclusion (Odden and Archibald 2000, p. 6). Elmore and colleagues write about one school that reduced class sizes from thirty to twenty-two using just this method (1996, p. 21). Miles and Darling-Hammond write, "Reducing the use of pull-out programs for special education, language and Title 1 instruction becomes a primary lever for creating smaller groups for all in elementary schools" (1998). Archibald and Odden (2000, p. 8) present yet another example. In short, since much of the overspecialization in schools is a Band-Aid response to the inability to meet all needs via large grouping size, fewer specialists are needed in a school with small classes.

This use of auxiliary teachers will greatly reduce the cost and need for recruitment. Figure 8.4 demonstrates how many teachers will need to be added to implement the proposal. Only a 53 percent increase in teachers will be needed to cut class size in half if reassignments are made. Assuming reduced attrition, recruitment will not have to increase by the same factor. In Chapter 10 I project that reducing attrition by a third would mean we would need only 33 percent more recruitment than we currently conduct to reach 153 percent of our current workforce in twenty-six years.

In order to use the auxiliary teachers to offer nonmainstreamed special education students the classes of six they deserve, I propose to allot one sixth of the mainstream school day (about an hour) for doubled-up, play-like classes. (See Chapter 4 for why this would not be neglectful.) Table 8.1 summarizes such a plan. The overall pupil/teacher ratio of 10.4 matches the total pupil/teacher ratio in the target scenario.

Currently about 40 percent of "disabled" students are mainstreamed at any one time, which makes about 5.5 percent of the student body (Appendix B). Depending on how many more students can be mainstreamed, a complementary proportion of nondisabled but troubled and disruptive students can also be given classes of six. Recall that 25 percent of current classroom aides will remain to help special needs students and teachers. And notice that this plan very generously leaves 7.5 percent of teachers (one out of every fourteen) at the discretion of schools as nonclassroom specialists, who would be particularly useful as trainers of the new teachers added during the implementation period. If the 5 percent allowed for nonmainstreamed students is too large, or fewer nonclassroom specialists are needed, a smaller portion than one sixth of the day could be allocated for doubled-up classes, or these could have fewer students.

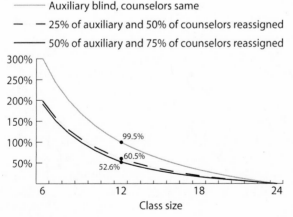

Figure 8.4 *Projected increase in teachers needed. (See Appendix A.)*

TABLE 8.1 PROJECTED DISTRIBUTION OF CLASS SIZES AND TEACHERS

	MAINSTREAM	MAINSTREAM (CONCENTRATED POVERTY)	MOST DISABLED OR TROUBLED	EXTRA TEACHERS
Target class size (5/6 of day)	12	9	6	
Play-like time (1/6 of day)	24	18	6	
Percent of students	64%	31%	5%	
Percent of teachers	50.9%	32.9%	8.7%	7.5%

Note: Calculations driven by target pupil/teacher ratio of 10.4 (see Appendix B).

Ongoing Cost Broken Down

The United States spent $8,310 per student in 2003–2004 (Digest 2006, table 170). Rounding up the funding increase from the above projections to an even 20 percent, the "additional" per-pupil cost would be about $1,662.[5] There were an estimated 48,948,000 public school students in 2006 (Digest 2006, table 33). That gives us just under $81.4 billion in "extra" yearly spending as a nation. There were about 189 million Americans between the ages of eighteen and sixty-five in 2006 (U.S. Census Bureau 2008). Per working-age American, then, the yearly $81.4 billion would cost $430. Not all those people work, of course, nor is all taxable income in the hands of workers. Per-capita income in the United States in 2006 was over $36,000 (U.S. Bureau of Economic Analysis 2007). A little less than half of the population (150 million) is in the workforce at any one time (U.S. Bureau of Labor Statistics 2008). That means that the average amount of taxable income available per worker is about $72,000 per year. The average hourly wage in 2005 was about $19 (U.S. Bureau of Labor Statistics 2007), or about $38,000 per year, very close to the per-capita income. Thus, this average $19-an-hour worker only needs to pay about half the price tag. One hundred fifty million of these average workers paying half the $81.4 billion would yield about $270. For the benefit of the dubious, however, I will use a generous guesstimate of $420 per worker.

At the $19 hourly wage, that's less than twenty-three hours of work per year. That's equivalent to taking just under three days off a year to volunteer at a school. Spread over 180 school days a year, the "extra" $420 would cost this average wage earner $2.33 every day school is in session—thirty-nine cents every hour kids are in class. That's a bit over *half a penny a minute* from each worker for nationwide, humane instruction.

So much for the argument that implementing class size reduction is inordinately expensive. Since this finding directly contradicts the most frequent argument against class size, I assume it's one of the most persuasive in the book. Moreover, we haven't even figured in any savings that will begin to accrue, which we'll return to below.

Up-Front Cost Projections

Because of all its various implementation choices, the up-front costs for the space increases needed by grouping size reduction are more nebulous, but they're also smaller; thankfully, we still spend less on building buildings than on building people. In the long run, of course, the upfront costs will diminish to nil and the ongoing projections above will hold true. If current space is maximized, cutting class sizes in half will likely lead *at most* to the construction, buying, or leasing of 50 percent more space than we currently maintain. (Again, I've included 50 percent more space-related expenses in the ongoing costs.) By way of a rough estimate, U.S. public schools spent $47.6 billion in facilities acquisition and construction in 2005 (NCES 2007b, table 8). If we spent an additional 50 percent of that amount—again, a generously high estimate—for the implementation period, the "extra" ongoing cost of $81.4 billion would go up by $23.8 billion.

To check this estimate, let's find a per-student price. According to one report, in 2008, elementaries cost $19,685 to build per student, middle schools $23,529, and high schools $29,289 (Abramson 2008). According to another, in 2004 they cost $16,396, $16,206, and $21,785, respectively (Agron 2005). A rough average of those numbers, considering that fewer high schools are needed, and leaning toward the more recent, yields about $20,000 per student to construct a new school. There were nearly 50 million public school students in 2007 (Digest 2007, table 33). Adding 50 percent more space would be equivalent to increasing the number of students by 50 percent. That yields $500 billion over twenty-six years, or $19.2 billion a year.

If we average those two results we get $21.5 billion. The 19.6 percent increase would become a 24.7 percent increase during the twenty-six-year implementation period I propose in Chapter 10. At just over one fourth the ongoing cost, the up-front cost raises the average taxpayer's yearly share of $420 by $110. Not a bank-breaker by any means. Now let's turn our attention to what savings we'd start to see from our investment.

Is Bigness as Cheap as We Think It Is?

Many have doubted that big schools have even produced their assumed savings. A report on New Jersey public schools concludes, "Small schools have significantly higher value per dollar spent than large schools" (Commission on Business Efficiency of the Public Schools 2003). This is on the basis of test scores and dropout rates alone. Harber summarizes the research as "inconclusive one way or the other" (1996, p. 6). Williams writes, "Research also indicates that larger schools with enrollments in excess of 1,200 have not produced expected economies of scale and that sufficient numbers of students do not enroll in enhanced curricular offerings to justify availability" (1990). In studies where large schools do appear to reap savings from economies of scale, the return is often a diminishing one. One study, for example, found that Wyoming schools save only 2 percent in cost per student from being 10 percent bigger (Bowles and Bosworth 2002). Again, none of these studies attempt to include the social costs of poor school relationships:

> Setting aside the proportionately greater administrative, security, discipline, and busing costs, large schools' long-term educational, psychic, and social costs have never been estimated. What community has determined even crudely how much its large schools may have contributed to its miseducated and disenfranchised students' drug, unemployment, welfare and prison costs five, ten, and fifteen years after dropping out, if not physically, then mentally and emotionally? (Hagerty 1995, p. 98)

As discussed in Chapter 1, the secret ingredient of class size is often one of the sources of "savings" in large schools. Contrary to popular assumption, Miles and Darling-Hammond argue that large schools also tend to increasingly specialize their staff and create more bureaucracy per student:

> Research suggests that high schools have created more internal specialization and departmentalization than can be scientifically justified. Most studies have found that, all else being equal, above about 800 students, larger schools produce . . . larger numbers of administrative staff, thereby deflecting resources from classroom instruction. (1998)

On the other hand, smallness offers several *ethical* sources of savings. Let's explore whether better taken care of, happier kids could save American taxpayers at least $81.4 billion a year, the price of twice as much teacher attention. What follow are a few areas of savings that could become possible after grouping size reduction.

Savings 1
Grade Retention

One automatic savings that will result from grouping size reduction is the ability to end the practice of grade retention or *literally* "holding students back." Not only is grade retention ethically hard to swallow—being the ultimate (very sticky) label of failure—it's also incredibly expensive. Claire Xia and Elizabeth Glennie (2005) report "this common practice of retention costs taxpayers over 18 billion dollars every year." The 2.4 million students it affects are about 5 percent of all public school students. At $50,000 of compensation, that $18 billion could pay 200,000 new teachers to serve those same 2.4 million students in classes of twelve where they could become sure successes. (Recall that class size reduction research has shown that test scores rise particularly consistently for the lowest achievers.) And $8 billion would still be left over to pay enough teachers for almost two million more students! Thus, we've already gone from $81.4 billion down to $63.4 billion a year, a 22 percent drop.

Savings 2
Security

We've already discussed how large schools in particular lead to safety issues. What about the costs of increased security?

> The research shows that small schools are safer and easier to secure. Think about this: A large public school system may spend more than 50 million dollars per year on school security. Instead of spending all that money to make their huge schools safer, why don't they just use the money to make smaller schools? (Littky 2004, p. 67)

The figure of $50 million Littky mentions translates into 1,000 teachers at $50,000 a year, who could serve 12,000 kids in classes of twelve in thirty or so small, safe schools. Littky's figure of $50 million would constitute 1.7 percent of the budgets of the five largest districts in the country but a whopping 7.8 percent of the average district in the largest 100 (NCES 2001, table 10). In other words, decreased need for security could conceivably shave the 20 percent increase for relationship load reduction down at least one percentage point.

Savings 3
Teacher Attrition

The three major reasons cited for the high rate of teacher attrition are "inadequate preparation and support in the early years," comparatively low pay, and poor working conditions (National Academy of Education 2005, p. 53). Relationship load reduction would improve the last of these. It would reduce teacher attrition (and its monetary costs) because it would make the job more doable (Achilles 2003; Heller 2004, p. 40). If teachers aren't doomed to a sense of failure (or, at best, frustration), they'll be happier, they'll be more effective, and they'll stay longer. Unlike in much of the for-profit sector, the work of teaching involves a high level of passion. That passion is relationship centered and depends on relationship-fostering conditions. According to a recent report, "New teachers who are likely to leave the profession in the next five years are less satisfied than others with their school relationships" (MetLife 2005, p. 5). Relationship load reduction clearly harnesses and fertilizes educators' passion for their work. In addition, increased continuity of teacher-student relationships will tend to counteract attrition because quitting would constitute opting out of ongoing relationships rather than simply opting out of forming a new set of relationships with the next year's kids. With regard to quality, more of the best and the brightest (and passionate) will be attracted to and remain in the field. With twelve students, it will be hard to fail at or get jaded about teaching, and it will be very easy to spy who truly doesn't belong.

The costs are staggering. One study found,

> Using the most conservative turnover cost estimation method, Texas is losing approximately $329 million each year due to teacher turnover, with alternate estimations for these costs reaching as high as $2.1 billion per year. . . . 19 percent of beginning teachers leave at the end of their first year of teaching, costing upwards of $216 million per year. . . . After three years, as many as 43 percent of new Texas teachers have left the profession, resulting in a three-year turnover cost for new teachers as much as $480 million. (Texas Center for Educational Research 2000, p. 16)

Barnes, Crowe, and Schaefer (2007) write, "In a very large district like Chicago, the average cost was $17,872 per leaver. The total cost of turnover in the Chicago Public Schools is estimated to be over $86 million per year." Another study found, "A conservative national estimate of the cost of replacing public school teachers who have dropped out of the profession is $2.2 billion a year" (Alliance for Excellent Education 2005). That figure is nearly 3 percent of the "extra" cost.

Savings 4
The Improvement Industry

Many have claimed the existence of a "reform industry" that gets its livelihood from recommending changes that never seem to improve things all that much. Gatto writes, "Surely it is an immense irony that if our children were doing well, the people who make a living from their trouble would not be"

(2001, p. 86). Tye agrees that there must be *someone* who benefits from a constant turnover of educational tactics and materials (2000, p. 91). If these accusations are true, they constitute another hidden cost of large grouping size: constant miracle seeking. Achilles argues that class size reduction is not simply another vial of snake oil:

> Experts, developers, consultants, peddlers, project pushers, publishers, staff developers, evaluators, and others are first in line with their hands out for education-improvement funds. Class-size change presents an entirely different matter. Small classes are a sure-fire shot for education improvement, and the class-size benefits go *directly* to the pupil. (1999, p. 118)

Imagine the savings of simply putting trust in our teachers to help every student in their small classes succeed—without feeling compelled to invest resources in the latest hyped-up, prefab curriculum fad. Small groupings are not a fad; as argued earlier, they are the norm in human interaction throughout human history. It is large grouping size that is a recent fad, an experiment that has failed and needs to be brought to an end. Moreover, those currently employed in the school improvement industry are prime candidates to fill new teaching positions. After all, they already claim to have the secrets to good teaching!

Savings 5
Fat Cutting

Although several researchers have argued that education is relatively un-top-heavy when compared to private industry (Berliner and Biddle 1995; Robinson and Brandon 1992), there may indeed be areas to trim in order to find money or potential teachers for smaller schools and classes. After all, "Employment in public school has doubled since 1964. As a result, the student-to-employee ratio fell from 13.3 in 1964 to 6.4 in 1990" (Morisi 1994). My cost projections already reallocate some of the funding for instructional aides and counselors. The Digest of Education Statistics, after enumerating school personnel in ten categories, still left just under 20 percent of school employees with a nebulous "other support services staff" designation (2005, table 80).[6] Small, manageable schools and classes would surely present opportunities for absorbing some of these duties into core positions, perhaps freeing up potential teachers or teacher trainees. Miles and Darling-Hammond (1998) cite research showing that only 43 percent of U.S. school staff is engaged in classroom teaching, compared with 60 percent to 80 percent in most other European countries.

One area many would like to see cut is the enormous amount of money and energy put into preparing standardized tests. Berliner and Biddle cite research suggesting that standardized testing consumes each year between $700 million and $900 million of education money and some 20 million school days' worth of student time (1995, p. 197).[7] If we average that number to $800 million, that's 16,000 teachers at $50,000 a year—enough to serve 192,000 kids at twelve per teacher.

The excessive need to revitalize teachers is another hidden cost of large relationship load. There are many dynamic (and well-paid) speakers available at conferences to get our blood pumping again, remind us why we're doing it—for kids—and send us back to our classrooms and schools reenergized. Of course, the energy soon wears off and we must return to another conference for refueling. There is nothing wrong with conferences and their revitalizing effect, of course, but large grouping size causes an excessive need for them, creating yet another hidden cost of time and money inherent in a supposedly cost-saving grouping strategy.

Savings 6
Private Tutoring

As mentioned earlier, the fact that private tutoring exists is nearly proof enough on its own that class size is too large. This is another case of how we're already spending the "extra" money we ought to spend *preventatively*: Parents who can afford tutoring for their kids to make up for what they're missing in personalized instruction in large classes are spending money that could otherwise go to taxes to help schools reduce class size—that is, to make teaching more like tutoring in the first place. Any private tutors who are put out of business would be an excellent source of the extra teachers needed in schools. It is estimated that America's parents spend $2.5 billion per year on private tutoring (Reid 2006). Let's figure all tutoring won't go away and round down to a mere *billion and a half*; that unspent billion brings our subtotal of $63.4 billion down to $62.4 billion.

Savings 7
Transportation

To the extent that new small secondary schools are created, the average student will live closer to school—this is assuming we choose not to go with theme-based schools that draw students from far away. Such a situation would logically lower the cost (and time) of parent-funded travel and publicly funded busing (Harber 1996, p. 6). Reducing busing may be a savings we don't want to exercise, though. As mentioned elsewhere, integrating poor and nonpoor citizens reduces the negative impacts of poverty—on both groups. To the dismay of many, the U.S. Supreme Court has gradually dismantled the racial integration busing that came out of the *Brown v. Board* decision. But busing students for the purpose of integration by parental income is alive and well ("Mixing wealth" 2006).

Savings 8
Community Commitment

Harber makes the point that "For a number of reasons small schools might find it easier to raise community resources. This is because . . . it is easier to identify with them and . . . individual contributions are more likely to be noticed and appreciated" (1996, p. 7). Whether this takes the form of volunteering or donations, there is certainly a savings to be had from the effect smallness has on community involvement.

Subtract the Savings

Recall that the total "extra" yearly cost of grouping size reduction would be about $81.4 billion and that there are a few savings we can easily calculate:

- $18 billion per year from phasing out the practice of grade retention
- $1 billion per year from not needing private tutoring

That eliminates over 23 percent and leaves us at $62.4 billion. The potential savings from cutting security costs, test-making budgets, and miracle-promising programs could be phenomenal. Those are just education budget savings; add in social services, law-enforcement, and justice system savings and you've got a bundle. Let's look at those now.

Let's estimate the savings from the perspective of how a hypothetical, average kid would have to change to pay, in effect, his or her own way. Each kid would constitute an "extra" investment of $1,662 a year to get through the thirteen grades to high school or about $21,600. Coincidentally, at the average wage of $19 an hour cited above, this will be slightly more than the average kid will go on to earn every six months. In other words, in terms of the value of human labor, it's as if we're investing half a worker-year more into each citizen's future. Would such an investment pay off with a combination of increased earning power and decreased social encumbrance? In order to pay his or her own $21,600 "debt," each worker-to-be would need either (a) to earn about $720 more per year (and work at least thirty years) to spend on the increased taxes incurred by his education, (b) cost society $21,600 less in services by the end of his life, or (c) do some combination of the two.

The first option, more earning power, is not so silly a notion. Berry's research

> found that smaller schools had a significant positive effect on students' wages as adults. That is, students from states with smaller schools fared better in the labor market. . . . My findings suggest that increasing a state's average school size by 100 students . . . would amount to a 3.7 percent decline in earnings for a high-school graduate. (2004)

At the average wage quoted earlier of $18.62, which is about $37,000 a year, that's $1,370 extra for simply going to a school that's 100 students smaller! This effect alone could more than pay for the "extra" cost.

Might similar findings apply to class size reduction and increased teacher continuity also? Yes. Alan Krueger (2003) subjected the *test score results alone* of the STAR class size reduction study to a similar economic analysis of future earnings increases. He writes, "The cost-benefit calculations . . . suggest that the internal real rate of return from a 7-student reduction in class size in the first four years of primary school is about 6%. At a 4% discount rate, every dollar invested in smaller classes yields about $2 in benefits." Again, this is only for a seven-student reduction for grades K–3. In other words, class size reduction (down to fifteen) for grades K–3 could pay for those grades and four other grades. Presumably a bigger decrease (to twelve per class) could pay even more generously. Krueger's calculations are based only on the connection between test scores and earnings; he mentions a few other benefits but without quantifying them:

> Class size probably influences other outcomes with economic consequences, such as crime and welfare dependence, and there may be externalities from human capital, so *the economic benefits could be understated*. In addition, improved school quality probably has non-economic private and social benefits, such as improved citizenship and self enlightenment. (2003, emphasis mine)

And he touches on the ethical issue of leveling the socioeconomic playing field:

> The cost-benefit calculations do not take into account distributional effects. Because smaller class sizes appear to generate greater benefits

for economically disadvantaged students, an argument could be made that they generate positive welfare gains apart from efficiency considerations. (2003)

The findings of Berry and Krueger are echoed by another study that focused on the social costs of the high school dropout rate. Henry Levin reports that the average high school dropout pays $60,000 less in taxes over his or her lifetime than a graduate does (2005, p. 16). That's almost three times what is needed to cover one's own "extra" cost of relationship load reduction. The link between relationship load and the dropout rate is hard to dispute. Toch cites several studies showing higher dropout rates in larger schools (1991, p. 269; see also Lee and Burkam 2003). Relationship load reduction's potential to eliminate grade retention links it doubly to the dropout rate. Xia and Glennie (2005) report that retained students are "two to eleven times more likely to drop out." Dropping out in and of itself is not the end of the world, of course—it's more an effect than a cause of an unhappy life. Those who drop out are generally the least nurtured inside and outside of the school system, the ones who fall farthest through the cracks of large grouping size. Alexander and colleagues note that, perhaps counterintuitively, "most dropouts are *not* failing at the time they drop out. Rather, dropout risk is elevated by problems of social and personal adjustment" (2003, p. 257).

For the sake of caution, let's remain skeptical that wage effects could be sustained on a nationwide scale—after all, at least a few of us have to end up at the bottom of the pay scale. What about potential savings from less government dependence and other socially shared costs such as insurance premiums? Levin reports that the average person who finishes no more than the eleventh grade incurs $83,000 more in health care costs over his or her lifetime than the average graduate (2005, p. 16). He also adds the finding that if one third of all Americans without diplomas "went on to get more than a high school education, the savings would range from $3.8 billion to $6.7 billion for [Temporary Assistance for Needy Families], $3.7 billion for Food Stamps and $0.4 billion for housing assistance" (2005, p.17). Certainly not all the liabilities of these most vulnerable students could disappear simply because they stayed in school, but these data demonstrate how much cost is out there waiting to be at least trimmed by prevention.

So how much could well-nurtured children really save society as adults? The average lifespan in the United States is about seventy-seven years (American Psychological Association 2001). That's fifty-nine years of post–high school life. The per-student cost of my proposal, $21,600, spread over that time is about $366 a year. Could being well nurtured make you need that much less in public help each year, a dollar less per day? Just like above, it could be spread out: Either (a) every person could cost society $92 less a year in four of the following ten areas, or (b) every tenth person could save society $920 in four of them:

1. Crime fighting
2. Welfare payments
3. Unemployment payments
4. Physical health care
5. Mental health care
6. Homeless services
7. Child protection services
8. High incarceration rate (the loss of tax revenue from potential workers)
9. Unemployment and absence from work (additional losses in tax revenue beyond lower wages)
10. Social security need (lack of own savings)

Any number of combinations could cover the "extra" cost of smaller relationship load.

Let's take the first area as an example. Crime fighting cost the United States $204 billion in 2005 (U.S. Bureau of Justice Statistics 2007). Using our workforce figure from earlier of about 150 million, that's $1,360 per taxpayer (over three times the "extra" cost of the proposal). On June 30, 2005, there were almost 2.2 million people incarcerated in the United States, two thirds in prison and one third in jail (Harrison and Beck 2006). According to the Sentencing Project (2006), that's 0.737 percent of the population, which is far ahead of our next competitor in incarceration, Russia, at 0.611 percent, but they are even farther ahead of South Africa at 0.335 percent. There's a whole lot of room for improvement there. Considering that the next country, the similarly wealthy and even more ethnically contentious Israel, has a rate that's "only" 0.209 percent, there's no reason to suspect we're bumping up against the natural limits of human behavior. This and other evidence suggest that both our criminality and our punitiveness are effects of a nurturance crisis (combined with good-old-American racism).

Levin summarizes another researcher's findings on the connections between crime, money, and the dropout rate:

> Increasing the high school completion rate by one percent for all men ages 20 to 60 could save the U.S. up to $1.4 billion a year in reduced costs from crime, according to Moretti. He also finds that a one-year increase in average years of schooling reduces murder and assault by almost 30 percent, motor vehicle theft by 20 percent, arson by 13 percent, and burglary and larceny by about 6 percent. (2005, p. 17)

A whopping one in thirty-seven Americans has spent time in prison (Chaddock 2003). That's a large number of (probably) troubled folks who could be helped by a strong attachment to a teacher during childhood. The money we invest in that teacher's salary now will come back to us soon.

Lastly, let's assume happier people will waste less of their income on luxury items. Should my proposal fail to prove fully self-funding and require some tax increase to remain permanent, the reduced "need" for luxury items would provide the income to pay those taxes without affecting any spending on real needs. Conservatively, let's say grouping size reduction could only achieve 50 percent of the savings needed to cover its own costs to the public purse. That makes for a tax increase of only $210 a year, a figure comparable to the price of upgrading every year to the latest electronic gadget we're urged to buy—an urge any well-nurtured person could surely manage to resist. Clearly many of the nonessentials parents buy for their kids are, whether we admit it or not, intended to make up for the lack of attention they get. For instance, Americans spent an average of $220 per child on toys in 2001 (Hong Kong Trade Development Council 2002). A kid who got more adult attention could entertain himself or herself a lot more creatively with many fewer things.

In closing, the monetary costs of relationship load reduction, considering that it's an ethical imperative, are reasonable regardless of possible savings. Only the belief that adults are more important than kids could defend the "too expensive" argument. This is ethically wrong for obvious reasons, but it is also logically wrong by virtue of the fact that children and adults are the same group of people just seen at different times. If we do not care about kids, then we do not indeed care about adults either. Thus the only belief left to underlie the "too expensive" argument is that *no one* matters, or at least no one who can't both afford private schooling and afford to insulate themselves from all the social costs of the nurturance crisis. That makes for very few of us indeed.

9

Implementation at the School and District Levels

The role school and district administrators can play in helping to solve the real crisis is to increase teacher continuity, bring down school size, and facilitate parent-school relationships. As well, they can reduce class size significantly within the current budget constraints by reducing separation of programs and specialization of teachers. The major barriers to helping kids at this level will be the following:

- Racial and class-based equity challenges without coordination from above
- The limitations placed on teachers by classes that remain too large in some areas because of budgets that cannot be increased without changes from above
- Recruitment and certification challenges that may need coordination from above

Local Empowerment

Within broad guidelines that assure equity, local educators should be empowered to make their own implementation decisions to the greatest extent possible. That will help changes match local needs as closely as possible as well as reduce the dehumanizing effects of excessive bureaucracy. For those same reasons, school personnel below the level of principals should be invited to participate in decision-making as much as possible. Recall that there is a direct benefit to the nurturance crisis here: The more empowered school employees are at every level, the more powerful (and happy) they seem in the eyes of students (deMarrais and LeCompte 1999, p. 180). This gives them greater psychological value as attachment figures. At the end of the chapter, however, I do offer an appeal to national coordination. There seems to be no other way to guarantee that the downsizing of schools and classes is targeted to the most "disadvantaged" areas first.

Because of the need for this local decision-making, the suggestions I make here are just that, suggestions. Though I am confident in my understanding of the on-target aims of schooling, I don't claim to have all the answers to implementation. Local officials will certainly come up with even more creative ways of making small grouping size work for the least money, headache, and political resistance. The main purpose of these considerations is to demonstrate that the proposal *can* be done, not to give the final word on exactly how.

School Size and Continuity Changes

The primary task of school and district-level administrators in ensuring psychologically healthy schools would be to meet the teacher continuity and school size proposals detailed in Chapter 5. Here are the major changes again:

- Keeping elementary students and teachers together year after year
- Eliminating intermediate schools while simultaneously meeting school size limits of either 300 or 500, depending on the age and social challenges of the students

Recall that the first change is probably best implemented by also having students learn from more than one teacher per day. The second change is more complex, but there are many resources available to administrators in hammering out the details of how best to reduce the size of their schools. Two wonderful resources are Feldman, Lopez, and Simon's *Choosing Small: The Essential Guide to Successful High School Conversion* (2006), and Ancess (2003), who describes how to make sure a smaller high school is not *just* smaller but truly a "community of commitment" that smallness makes possible. Here I'll just mention a few basic guiding principles.

First, remember that a large school can be subdivided into many schools that occupy and share the same facilities and resources. According to Meier, "if there's a bunch of small schools in the same building, they can combine to offer things. The Julia Richmond [sic] Complex in New York City has a shared basketball team, a shared pottery studio, and a shared drama club" (via Jehlen and Kopkowski 2006, p. 31). This not only lowers physical plant cost (not to mention new construction cost) but also reduces the impact on curriculum and extracurricular breadth, a drawback of smaller schools noted earlier. The sharing of resources would also benefit students in particularly small social minorities, such as a minimally represented ethnic group or queer community, who may feel themselves to be an even smaller minority in a downsized school. The creation of multi-school student organizations that maximized a sense of community for students in this situation would likely be a great help to them. In many instances they may understandably request to be enrolled together in one of the several schools in a building.

Second, autonomous small schools appear to last longer. Many draw a distinction between truly autonomous schools that share a building and "small learning communities" within a large school, sometimes called "schools-within-schools." Feldman and colleagues caution,

> Although small learning communities have been found to be effective to the extent that they have the conditions that are critical to small autonomous school success, . . . it is common for small learning communities to revert to big-school strategies and lose much of the autonomy that makes them successful. (2006, p. 11)

Mary Anne Raywid and Gil Schmerler concur that schools-within-schools often "exist at the pleasure of the principal" and often disappear as soon as a new one arrives (2003, p. 6). Howley's review of the research concludes that the benefits of small schools cannot be generalized to schools-within-schools without more study (2002, p. 49).

Third, if administrators don't make sure that stakeholders correctly understand the benefits of small schools, there may be a disappointed backlash. The trend toward smaller schools appears to be slowing. Why? Because it was sold by many as a solution to the fake academic crisis rather than the real nurturance crisis. For example,

> But recently, Gates Foundation leaders have sounded less enthusiastic about the virtues of smallness. A Gates-commissioned study revealed that test scores in a sample of Gates-funded schools were slightly lower than for comparable students in regular public schools. (Jehlen and Kopkowski 2006, p. 25)

School administrators need to justify and promote small schools with higher goals in mind than test scores.

Fourth, large classes will remain the thorn in the side of small schools until funding is increased at the state and national levels. In similar fashion, if stakeholders are allowed to ignore this fact, they may develop expectations that are far too lofty. Thus far, the small school movement has been sold as a solution that doesn't need to be paired with small classes (e.g., McCluskey 2002). Increased workloads seem to be the other factor slowing the progress of the small schools movement.

> Small school teachers told the [Gates Foundation] researchers they were struggling with heavy workloads.... "We still believe in small schools," says James Shelton, the foundation's education program director, but adds that they now put more emphasis on improving the quality of instruction because downsizing is not enough. (Jehlen and Kopkowski 2006, p. 25)

As discussed earlier, workloads in small schools could be reduced by having classes of twelve. Again, the "teacher quality" issue is a diversion from admitting that class size reduction, though more expensive, should go hand in hand with school size reduction. Only class size reduction will remove the "need" for a superhumanly skilled and energetic faculty.

Fifth, there is danger in forcing small schools to compete with each other for students. Small-school pioneer Meier speaks of small schools in New York City being made to compete for the best students and some becoming known as "loser schools" (Jehlen and Kopkowski 2006). Choice is unhealthy if it leads to segregation by ability, becoming a new form of the tracking that now exists within large schools. This tracking by school is likely to have the same racist effects that within-school tracking has currently.

Sixth, a related assumption that drives self-segregation among small schools is the belief that they should be theme based or unique in their curricular focus. I don't doubt there is a place for *some* such schools, but, in light of the nurturance crisis, I think there is a larger need for schools whose identity is simply the neighborhood where they sit. I believe schools that have the goal of serving their communities and feel no need for thematic gimmicks are more likely to strengthen rather than undermine or ignore those communities and their ability to raise healthy kids. Most of the time, of course, the reason small schools are forced to be thematic is that they won't be allowed to exist under current rules if they don't do anything unique. Those rules should be changed. Neighborhood schools do not need unique visions to help their communities. They can have the very run-of-the-mill vision of being small solely for the purposes of harnessing the power of human relationships. It's in those relationships that true uniqueness is to be found.

Certainly there is a lot to be said for choice, but oftentimes I think the idea of school choice is a way to sidestep the issue of neighborhood choice.

School choice advocates argue that inner-city kids are offered failing schools and should be allowed to commute to a successful school across town. All kids have a right to go to a good school, but that shouldn't cover up the fact that they also have a right to live in a safe, nurturing neighborhood. In that sense, school choice can be abused as another way to abdicate our responsibility for having ghettoized our citizens (Noguera 2003, p. 97). Berliner calls this "attempting to fix inner-city schools without fixing the city" (2006). This is why I advocate full-service schools as an empowerment tool for economically and racially marginalized communities.

As a last point, until classes of twelve arrive, districts should feel entitled to some forgiveness on the school size limits in the proposal, since strict adherence may create challenges only smaller classes can solve. Plowing ahead with school size reduction will be better than waiting, however, because it may put just the right pressure on policy-makers to provide the simplifying effects of classes of twelve. The large schools that have been downsized in the past few decades have proven that it can be done to a large degree on its own, partly because it does involve some degree of class size reduction.

How Many of Our Schools Are Too Big?

In 2004 there were about 96,500 public schools in the United States; 72 percent of elementary schools were larger than 300 and 49 percent of secondary schools were larger than 500 students. (There were also 1,000 K–12 schools that were over 500, which we'll lump with secondary.) That's 47,750 elementary schools and 12,500 secondary schools that definitely don't meet the recommendations (Digest 2006, table 91). (Some of those secondary schools are in communities with concentrated, racism-imbued poverty and should be no more than 300 in size, but let's bracket that for a moment.) That's 62 percent of our schools that need to be subdivided. Fortunately, there is a "more bang for your buck" aspect to the school size situation. Big schools by definition serve more kids. Those 72 percent of our elementary schools larger than 300 taught almost 90 percent of elementary students. More lopsided still, those 49 percent of secondary schools that were over 500 taught over 86 percent of our secondary students (table 91).

As I will show in a timeline in the next chapter, my suggestion is to focus on school size in two phases, downsizing 25 percent of our schools (24,125) immediately, starting with the biggest and continuing down the list, with special emphasis on high-poverty communities. Later on in the implementation process, after class size reduction is more than half complete, the next largest 25 percent of schools could then be divided. Though more than 50 percent of our schools violate the recommendations made at the end of Chapter 5, it is realistic to agree to leave some schools alone—particularly those that are getting good academic results and are located in well-off neighborhoods where nurturance crisis effects are smaller. Creating an exception for affluent area schools may also prove politically strategic; community members around large schools that are getting good results and whose communities perceive fewer problems are likely to resist changes to the school's identity. Schools in rural areas that have lower indicators of real crisis problems might also be excepted. Leaving these approximately 12 percent of large schools alone would leave more resources to be spent on reducing secondary schools in areas of concentrated poverty in line with the recommendations at 300.

In order to avoid public resistance and the need to make too many exceptions, the breakup of large schools should be carried out with sensitivity to community identity. Allowing alumni to retain a sense of identification with their alma mater would be a logical strategy. As I argued earlier, there is no need to give schools themes or specialties. If a high school with the prototypical president's name is broken into three parts, for example, they could be referred to as Lincoln A, Lincoln B, and Lincoln C. As suggested earlier, they could share certain resources. Not least among those would be pooling resources and students to preserve traditions such as the football team. Although many have argued there are negative aspects to traditions such as competitive sports, small schools and classes may be enough in themselves to counteract the negatives. The adoration of the football players, for example, may be less harmful to the school climate if there is ample opportunity for adult attention and recognition in all areas. Traditions like the Friday football game should not be ignored as opportunities to make schools gathering places for their communities and to enhance cooperation between school and community. Once the money is procured, class size reduction is much less likely to experience the resistance school size reduction may encounter.

At some point after classes of twelve have been fully implemented, there may be a new climate that is more amenable to finishing the job on school size reduction so that all schools meet the recommended limits.

The Implications of Urbanness

Large schools and classes affect cities more than towns. Table 9.1 makes the difference clear.

The implications of this for implementation are quite positive. In terms of teacher recruitment, cities offer a larger pool of potential teachers. In terms of teacher training, cities nearly guarantee the presence of a college or university with which to partner. In terms of increased funding, cities offer a wealthier tax base (so long as suburbs can be obligated to share).

TABLE 9.1   URBAN VERSUS RURAL GROUPING SIZE
            IN U.S. PUBLIC SCHOOLS, 2004

CHARACTERISTIC	CITY AND SUBURBAN	TOWN AND RURAL
Enrollment	33,755,000	14,826,000
	(69.5%)	(30.5%)
Schools	54,712	41,583
	(56.8%)	(43.2%)
Average school size	605	386
Pupil/teacher ratio	16.7	15.1

Source: Digest 2006, table 86.

Will We Need More Administrators?

If we divide the number of students in schools above the threshold by the maximum school size I've recommended, the number of schools would go from 96,500 to 158,650–113,000 elementary and "other" schools (which are predominantly similar in size) and 45,650 secondary and K–12—an increase of 64 percent (Digest 2006, table 91). The number of principals and assistant principals employed in 2004 was 165,693 (Digest 2006, table 77). That leaves enough trained principals to staff all added schools immediately. If each elementary or "other" school of 300 got one principal, that would leave each secondary or K–12 school with 1.15 principals. The extra principals could either be shared assistants or go full-time to schools in communities with more social challenges. These schools will have classes of nine rather than twelve, meaning more staff per child to manage.

Policy Changes Needed to Facilitate Small Schools

Raywid and Schmerler (2003) highlight several current policies that stand in the way of the spread of the small schools movement. First, the customary method of creating case-by-case exemptions for small schools leaves them in a vulnerable position. "It is almost inevitable that they come out to be perceived within the system as 'precious' institutions that, a bit like spoiled children, are constantly demanding special attention and consideration" (p. 88). They argue that "policy by exception" is a poor substitute for "positive support" and clearly leaves the big school mentality as the norm (pp. 88–89).

Second, Raywid and Schmerler argue that the most problematic rule for small schools is the seniority preference in filling teaching vacancies. They argue that this debilitates schools' abilities to gather like-minded faculty with a shared vision (p. 89). Third, they argue for a less autocratic, "zero-sum conception of power" in the principalship to better create a climate of teacher empowerment in small schools (pp. 96–99). This would increase job satisfaction and retention for teachers and nurturance effects for students.

Ancess (2003) emphasizes the tolerance of difference. She writes, "When a district can support flexibility, risk-taking, and site-based autonomy and accountability, it can produce schools that are communities of commitment" (p. 134). She adds,

> The practice of differentiation allows schools to be responsive to the concerns of their local population and to the learning needs of their students. . . . Mandates for uniformity can undermine local innovation and coerce compliance with practices and policies that conflict with site-based educator's values, knowledge, experience, and judgments about what achieves the standards they set. (p. 136)

To make the downsizing of schools successful, districts will have to outgrow the one-way-serves-all mentality. Accordingly, Ancess argues that making smallness successful on a larger scale will involve replicating conditions of increased autonomy rather than exact copies of successful small schools (p. 138). "Replication of results requires schools to have the capacity and agency to invent, reinvent, and change themselves" (p. 140). This challenges a passive attitude toward the assumption that what "school" means has already been agreed upon and set in stone by our culture. But universal schooling is still young, still in its experimental stages, if you will.

Class Size Considerations

First of all, much of the work of class size reduction can be done without increased numbers of teachers. Research suggests that elementary schools on their own can reach class sizes of about fifteen students without increasing budgets:

> To create class sizes of 15 students at Clifton school, the district eliminated all instructional aides and converted the allocated dollars to hire more teachers. In addition, a guidance counselor and 1.5 social workers were eliminated to pay for additional teachers. The school partnered with social service agencies to provide some of the lost social services. Teachers, who then had smaller class sizes, were able to take on more personal, advisory roles with students. All Title I funds were used for classroom teachers, and one of two special education resource teachers became a classroom teacher of both regular and special-needs students. (North Central Regional Educational Laboratory 2002)

Nor is this school a solitary miracle.[1] Secondary strategies are similar. Archibald writes, "Reducing the size of academic classes almost always means that the high school has to shift resources away from nonacademic subjects and pupil support toward academic teachers" (2001, p. 9). Recently downsized high schools have often been able to reach classes of eighteen without money for additional staff (Miles and Darling-Hammond 1998). Wagner explains the strategy one famous school used:

> The class sizes and student load of teachers is further reduced by the fact that almost everyone teaches at Central Park East—even the principal. There are no nonteaching administrators or "specialists" who, in a typical school district, can consume as much as half of the total personnel budget. The final result: teachers see an average of only forty students per day—much closer to a typical elementary school than a high school. And this is accomplished at virtually the same per student cost as large comprehensive schools. (2002, p. 89)

These same accomplishments may not be possible in areas with a higher pupil/teacher ratio, as western states tend to have. In general, though, it appears a drop in class size of five to ten students is possible through despecialization alone.

Second of all, the best way to implement class size reduction appears to be to add one grade a year as the first cohort moves through any one school (Achilles 1999, p. 29). This allows for fine-tuning of the process (p. 151).

Class Size Equity Caveat

The one caveat is that if wealthier districts continue past this point and begin to recruit more teachers simply because they can, experienced teachers will be drawn away from poorer and racially stigmatized districts and inequitable staffing will result. In the case of California's early grades class size reduction program, African American test scores actually declined for this reason (Jepsen and Rivkin 2002, p. xi). Schools and districts should stop short of hiring additional teachers on their own. Instead, they should participate in statewide planning that will guarantee race and class equity for the state's kids. Multistate plans may be preferable in some areas.

Single-Adult Classrooms

Some have suggested that adult/child ratio reduction can be a substitute for true class size reduction and avoid space and cost issues. The options include team teaching and the use of teacher aides or assistants. Research suggests that one teacher with one small class per room is the most effective way to achieve better emotional *and* academic results. There are several reasons.

First, research has found that group size tends to be a more significant variable than adult/child ratio for promoting healthy child development. Because of this research, state childcare regulations have been shifting from strictly limiting ratio to limiting group size as well. "Staff : child ratio ... is somewhat less important, making the greatest difference for children under the age of 3" (Steuer 1994, pp. 624–625).

Second, multiadult classrooms do not minimize the number of relationships teachers and students need to navigate. This likely explains why group size is statistically more important. As groups grow larger, the number of relationships each member has to sustain escalates exponentially (Napier and Gershenfeld 1985, p. 45). This is frequently offered as the principal reason that members become less satisfied with group experiences as the size of the group grows.

Third, multiadult classrooms (when they have more kids) make community building more difficult (Blatchford 2003, p. 148). Smaller groups are less likely to divide either physically or psychologically (Douglas 1995, p. 41). Because of the increased number of relationships, the smallest possible group (above the minimum we discussed earlier) is the most likely not to subdivide into "popular" and "losers" or school-enjoyers and school-haters. Harris writes, "The kids are less likely to divide up into contrasting groups with contrasting attitudes toward schoolwork if there aren't very many of them" (1998, p. 249).

Fourth, experimental studies of early elementary class size reduction found that extra adults had no positive impact on academic achievement. Blatchford finds "there is no apparent 'compensation' effect of having extra adults in the class" (2003, p. 141). To some extent, academic results do help to measure more important real-crisis factors. For example, loyalty to (and desire to please) the teacher by learning what the teacher wants to teach is a sign of secure attachment.

Fifth, a second adult presents an unnecessary complication. Research has shown that not all teachers could use assistants effectively even if they did have potential advantages. Blatchford's research showed "the presence of classroom support did not have a consistent or clear effect on teaching and curriculum time and none on the time a teacher had to hear children read individually" (2003, p. 118). In other words, teachers were not consistently able to save time or get more done by having an assistant. And since the effects of assistants are dubious all around, there is no reason to suspect it is worth time and money training teachers to use them better.

Sixth, children don't attach strongly to the lower-status adult. In my experience, children tend to value the affection and approval of the teacher more than the aide. This is simply because children tend to seek a sense of safety from the most powerful adults available. According to Meier,

> You need a community of adults with authority to make important decisions. . . . And kids like powerful adults. It gave us a lot of advantages to be seen very rarely having to say, "We're doing this because we're told we have to." Most of the time we could say, "We're doing this because we think it's the best decision." (via Jehlen and Kopkowski 2006, p. 30)

Cohen and Scheer agree: "When schools are small, teachers necessarily have more discretionary power; their voices are heard, their decisions are more likely to be heeded, and they are happier" because they are more "known and appreciated" in the same way their students are (2003, p. 52). When children challenge an adult's authority, what they're often expressing is their need for that adult to be powerful enough to handle it, to keep them safe from themselves, in essence. Oftentimes they haven't learned self-control because their attachment figures lacked the appearance of being in control of their own lives. This could be why, in my experience, troubled male teens often respond better to large male teachers—it may satisfy a need for someone more powerful than themselves. Meier asks, "What kid, after all, wants to be seen emulating people he's been told are too dumb to exercise power, and are simply implementing the commands of the real experts?" (2000c, p. 15).

Seventh, teachers tend to prefer one-adult autonomy. Tye suggests that teachers tend to want to work with kids, not adults; they therefore tend to resist team-teaching arrangements (2000, p. 133). That said, teachers who seek more collaboration should clearly not be prevented from collaborating in ways that do not adversely affect the amount of attention students receive.

Eighth, there probably won't be twice as much teaching going on. Students provide the principal accountability for teachers' being prepared, positive, and interactive. The presence of other adults, on the other hand, offers teachers the temptation to "escape" either mentally or physically from that accountability. One study found that in the SAGE class size reduction experiment in Wisconsin, teachers who were teamed with thirty students rather than each having their own class of fifteen tended to do just this:

> Responding to the ever-increasing intensification of their work, teachers placed in teaching teams overwhelmingly resorted to tag-team teaching. This model had one teacher managing instruction while the other teacher did administrative work. This strategy resulted in an effective increase in class size for the students involved. (Graue, Hatch, Rao, and Oen 2007)

This is not to suggest that teachers are any less responsible than anyone else. Teaching is a challenging activity, and as in all other challenging activities, people tend to minimize the challenge as much as possible without sacrificing satisfactory, perceptible results. Said another way, it is illogical for a person to make a task more difficult than it has to be. By having only one adult in the room, there is a clearer sense of how difficult the job *has to be* and there is less temptation to "take a break."

I recommend, therefore, that extra adults be used only when their labor is free. Though there may be some advantage in giving children a chance to watch adults interact, it is outweighed by the need for the smallest group possible. Yes, volunteers will be a more inconsistent presence than an aide, but in a small group that inconsistency is less likely to be problematic. Because of a stronger attachment to the teacher, other adults do not need to be as reliable.

There is one possible exception to the superiority of single-adult classrooms. New teachers would be better inducted by coteaching with an experienced teacher in one class of twice the size, that is, twenty-four. This would be a short-term concession to the long-term good of training and retaining able, confident teachers. In sum, aides are not inherently unhelpful to nurturing schools; they are simply worth less to kids per dollar than teachers are. A teacher-in-training, who functions as an aide but becomes a teacher within a few years, is a more valuable investment. I will return to issues surrounding training in the next chapter.

Multigrade Flexibility

Reichardt's study of class size reduction costs suggests that a choice must be made between capping class size at an absolute number and allowing for flexibility; his simulation uses a flexible "target" method where a new teacher is not added to a grade until the number of excess students for that grade is 51 percent above the target size (2000, p. 43). Thus, a new teacher would not be added in order to bring classes back down to (or below) twelve until the number of excess students reached seven. Clearly this reduces the cost of implementation,[2] but it also allows the average class size to creep above the targeted size. Theoretically, since the new class formed is nearly half as small as the target size, the average remains nearly on target in the big picture. The size of the creep is proportional to the number of teachers available to students in that grade. Reduced school size, therefore, creates tension with class size here. Under this method, the smaller the school, the larger the classes are allowed to become before a new teacher is hired, as demonstrated in Table 9.2.

Thus, although the overall average will be affected only slightly, schools farther below the 300 recommendation will be more likely to have classes near the edges (and especially the top) of the seven-to-eighteen range than

TABLE 9.2 CLASS SIZE "CREEP" UNDER FLEXIBLE TARGET METHOD

TEACHERS PER GRADE	TARGET ENROLLMENT (12 STUDENTS PER TEACHER)			MAXIMUM CLASS SIZE CREEP
	K-6	K-7	K-8	
1	84	96	108	18
2	168	192	216	15
3	252	288	324	14
4	336	384	432	14
5	420	480	540	14

Note: Shaded enrollments exceed school size recommendations by more than fifty students.

larger schools would have. As enrollment begins to exceed the 300 recommendation, however, the benefit of reduced class size creep disappears.

For schools that have only one or two teachers per grade, I recommend exploring a modified option that offers flexibility with less variation from the target: Allow multigrade combinations. Needing a new teacher for, say, second grade would result in larger classes while waiting for the cutoff to arrive, and a new class far below the target after hiring a teacher, making it relatively quite expensive. Both problems could be minimized if the new teacher taught the extra students from two or more grades. This practice is far from unheard of in elementaries for fixing precisely this resource efficiency problem. But again, smaller classes increase a teacher's ability to individualize the curriculum, counteracting the central challenge of multigrade grouping. As implied in Table 9.2, this cost issue mainly applies to elementary. Most small secondary schools already recognize the need (and have more capacity) to combine grades when necessary and adjust offerings to balance class sizes.

Miles and Darling-Hammond (1998) point to precisely this sort of flexibility as a key source of resource maximization. The standard procedure is "to assign students to classrooms in a regularized fashion by age, subject and program. These practices are costly, because the uneven allocation of teachers over grades, small programs and undersubscribed subjects contributes to unplanned differences in class size." They recommend "assigning students to groups based on educational strategies rather than standard classifications."

Centralized Enrollment

The class balancing issue reveals, also, a certain tension between class size and teacher continuity. If students are being moved to new teachers for the sake of adhering to a class size target, the attachment gains may not be worth the costs in many cases. If, on the other hand, it is mainly new enrollees that are assigned to the new teacher, then the damage to continuity will be minimized. New students in a district could be directed strategically to the school most able to accommodate them at the current time. Such a central database would also allow for strategic prediction of where increases are likely to happen midyear. In cases where a new teacher has to be added with seven or so students, the new teacher could be placed in an area most likely to see an increase. Rural schools will be more limited in this capacity for planning than urban schools, but the option of multigrade accommodation still remains a more flexible and efficient way of handling enrollment fluctuation. Furthermore, districts that border one another might make mutually beneficial agreements to refer students who live near the borders to the bordering district depending on space availability.

Funding and Staffing Formula Changes

Miles and Darling-Hammond (1998) write, "District student and teacher assignment policies can frustrate attempts to use teachers differently." They found a catch-22 where schools that mainstreamed more students into small classes by incorporating special education teachers "faced a potential loss of teachers because special education staff were allocated based upon the number of students requiring separate education." To solve precisely this conundrum, Boston "has adjusted its staffing formula to allow schools to use the resources for special needs students in inclusive settings." Miles, Ware, and Roza (2003) suggest that a move toward student-based over staff-based budgeting could resolve these glitches and allow the flexibility necessary to achieve small classes with a minimum of cost and extra teachers—as well as a maximum of inclusiveness and attention for students.

Finding the Space for More Classes

To begin with, I admit it's a pain to teach in a nonideal space. But the benefits of a smaller class would far outweigh the headaches of a smaller or less convenient space. There are three ways to find the space to teach the increased number of classes. First, large rooms could be divided (Lewit and Baker 1997). At best, they could be retrofitted with sound-resistant, collapsible walls to become two rooms. At worst, less sound-resistant partitions could be used at least temporarily. In one elementary case study, the six largest classrooms could each fit two newly reduced classes of fifteen, and two of those rooms already had optional partitions in place (Odden, Archibald, and Tychsen 1999, p. 30).

Second, schools could maximize their use of space. Most schools do not use every classroom every period. In addition, some schools have spaces that are too small to serve as classrooms currently but could make viable classrooms once class sizes were reduced to twelve, nine, or six. Reichardt found that over a third of the schools in his sample had more classrooms than teachers (2000, p. 72).

Third, more schools can simply be created from unused or underused space in the community, including formerly closed schools or vacant office buildings (Toch 2003, p. 118). Achilles suggests partnering with local groups that could use school space on weekends (1999, p. 143). Such public-private partnerships would be one way the private sector could help take more responsibility for the healthy development of the community's children. When the above options run out, new space will have to be built. But often school districts find it politically easier to obtain money for new buildings than for other significant changes.

From Nonteaching Counselors to Teacher-Advisors

As discussed earlier, despite the hard work of this nation's high school counselors, the counselor system is inadequate for meeting the needs of our kids. However, increasing the number of counselors would not be the best use of extra funding. Most of what kids need does not require anything but the most generalized training in psychology, class scheduling, and career planning. According to the National Research Council,

> the traditional model of counseling has failed to ensure that all students, particularly those at risk, receive the adult attention and guidance they need. Systemic change, rather than merely an increase in the number of counselors, is a more promising avenue for improving student achievement. (2004, pp. 156–157)

We need more preventers, not more patchers.

I recommend that the current counselor system be replaced by a combination of the advisory system and true psychological counseling by the counselors. One case-studied high school that reduced class size from twenty-five to eighteen and divided itself into five schools-within-schools did just that: "It made sense to reallocate 2.0 FTE [full-time equivalent] guidance staff positions to hire two more academic teachers who could now perform the functions of a guidance counselor with their smaller groups of students" (Archibald 2001, p. 8). My cost projections included a 75 percent reduction in counseling positions and shifted those human resources to classrooms. To pick up where the power of teacher attention can't reach, the 25 percent remaining counseling positions could be redefined as authentic mental health positions free of scheduling and career-advising duties. Counselors could follow one of two paths: In schools with more mental health needs, they could spend 100 percent of their time on mental health sessions with troubled students. These counselors would preferably be working with families and not just kids. Ideally, they would work in tandem with cooperating agencies that can give comprehensive services beyond just mental health. Especially in full-service schools, non–school-specialized mental health workers could be employed through the local public mental health system,[3] providing additional services and perhaps freeing up even more school-employed counselor time for the classroom, which leads to option two: They could become part-time teachers and part-time counselors in schools that had fewer mental health needs because of small size. If there were emotional crises regular teachers couldn't handle, the counselor could step in while administrators or others covered his or her classes. As part-time teachers, counselors will also have more buy-in from the students as opposed to being a virtual stranger tucked away in an office somewhere.

The advisory model could take over the scheduling and career advising counselors have been relieved of. Although Goldberg (1998) is careful to stress that the advisory model was not conceived as a way of reassigning or reducing the number of counselors (p. 54), I think he would agree it *could* be used for that purpose. Goldberg proposes that advisors do the scheduling for their fourteen advisees after having been trained by counselors, and some portion of the career and college planning (p. 55). He also argues they should refer emotional issues to counselors only when they exceed the skills of an average adult or teacher (p. 54). Again, I do not mean to argue that counselors do not do important work or do it well, merely that a different structure might allow them to serve students better.

In the advisory model, each teacher becomes the mentor for a small group of students that stays as stable as possible. Though different schools set aside various amounts of time, the most generous is to dedicate an entire (or nearly entire) class period focused on the needs of the students, as is the case in my own school. Goldberg allots only ten minutes per day (p. 2). In essence, the advisory system is a class size reduction intervention for a short period of the day. After comprehensive class size reduction, however, advisories could be even more intimate, thus requiring a smaller share of the school day to be equally effective. The best models keep the students together and with the same advisor as long as they stay at the school. Most often, the other certificated personnel in the school must join the classroom teachers to become advisors in order to make groups small enough, and Goldberg prescribes this (p. 20). The small schools movement has tended to follow the advisory model (Jehlen and Kopkowski 2006, p. 29).

Advisories have many advantages. First, they maximize child-centered time with a primary attachment figure at a school, providing the best chance at teacher continuity in secondary school. Johnson, Poliner, and Bonaiuto (2005) write, "Although some students easily find mentors in their teachers, coaches, and club advisors, a dedicated [advisory] facilitates that sense of connection for students who might otherwise fall through the cracks." Second, they give students (and advisors) a psychological "home team." Third, they provide a catch-all time period for announcements, paperwork, and life-skills-style curricular items that get neglected in the other disciplines. Fourth, the advisor becomes the point-person for the student's school issues and gives the school a "face" for the family to relate to, thus reducing the relationship load of the parent or guardian and promoting more depth of communication and collaboration. Fifth, as discussed, the lower ratio can be just as effective for quality counseling on scheduling and students' career paths as the "expertise" model, if not more effective. After all, the national average ratio of students to counselor FTE in 2002–2003 was *315 to one* (NCES 2003c).

Reduce Grade Retention

Grade retention, or "holding students back," as it's accurately dubbed, should be reduced and eventually eliminated as classes and schools become small. It is philosophically difficult to defend, but research hasn't quite proven it to be ineffective at minimizing the school failure of some children. In Chapter 1 I offered reasons for why its apparent effectiveness depends on its use as a Band-Aid for the neglect inherent in large relationship load. As its ethics are questionable and its results mixed, its expense should settle the argument. Earlier I discussed the $18 billion in annual savings that could be gained from abolishing it, fully 22 percent of the cost of this proposal.

Move Away from Tracking

Tracking naturally is—and should be—reduced in small schools. This process can accelerate once classes of twelve arrive. For reasons cited in Chapter 1, small classes will make it such that the "need" for tracking will truly show itself to be imaginary. If a small school with small classes truly can't provide the equivalent of an AP course through diversified study in a multiability classroom, then perhaps a highly skilled student who isn't getting his or her needs met could be allowed to attend college part of the day or move on from high school entirely. Local colleges could become more active partners in offering some students early part-time or full-time entrance. Part-time college during the later years is part of the plan of several intentionally small high schools, including Central Park East (Miles and Darling-Hammond 1998).

Reduce Expulsion

For similar reasons to those just outlined, once we have small classes we will have the ability to truly help the troubled kids we currently expel or allow to drop out. When the original school doesn't do the repair work, some other institution will have to. Every time a child is rejected, passed along as "too difficult," the possibility for remediation gets that more and more remote. The cost projections reserved space for about 1 percent of students to get classes of only six students where extremely challenging kids (who don't qualify for special education) can get the attention they need. Schools should partner with local mental health services to help these kids (Williams and Pritchard 2006).

10

Implementation at the State and Federal Levels

T he key contribution of state and federal decision-makers would be to coordinate and fund the critical piece of grouping size reduction: classes of twelve. They can also be critical players in ensuring more funding equality across local school districts and that the largest schools, and those with the most poverty and racial stigmatization, get priority in school and class size reduction. Again, what follows is not a binding prescription. I want to show that the proposal *can* be done, not to give the final word on *exactly* how.

Funding Inequality

It is widely known and discussed that local tax collection based on property values creates severe disparities in the funding of schools. This should be remedied. As we figure out how to fund an increase in the number of teachers and schools, we should simultaneously plan how to equalize funding overall. Funding equality is not integral to the proposal, but an implementation of the proposal would present a political opportunity to put it on the agenda. Some argue for compensatory equity rather than mere equality. Berliner and Biddle write, "Instead of merely demanding strict equality in funding, Americans should spend *more* money on schools located in communities where the needs are greatest" (1995, p. 292). Two implementation strategies would help turn grouping size reduction into a prime opportunity for funding equalization as well: (1) central planning from a state and national level, and (2) beginning in the most "disadvantaged" areas. In the worst case, should grouping size reduction not spread to all schools, those it will have helped will at least have been the most in need.

Poor and Racially Stigmatized Areas First

There is wide agreement that poor and racially stigmatized areas ought to receive the benefits of relationship load reduction first. Jepsen and Rivkin find in their study of the early grade class size reduction program in California in the late 1990s that its major implementation mistake was the failure to start with schools already difficult to staff, which led to a drop in African American test scores. "A better approach to class size reduction would have been to reduce class sizes in a subset of schools each year, starting with low-performing schools serving high-poverty populations" (2002, p. xii). The drawback of not doing so was the flight of experienced teachers from the harder-to-teach-in to the easier-to-teach-in schools (Rice 2002, p. 92). Again, by giving the "disadvantaged" schools smaller classes first, the incentive to work there will be drastically increased. Apart from being strategic, of course, the idea is also simply ethically self-evident. This expands the call for closing the racial achievement gap to include closing the racial adult attention gap. Rather than simply calling for no excuses for lower minority test scores, let's call for no excuses for *structures* that doom the nonwhite and nonrich to lower *everything*.

A coordinated federal and state grouping size reduction plan could guarantee that implementation happens where it's most needed first rather than simply in districts with the most resources (Ward and Laine 2000). We've already provided small classes to the most deserving students first in that we've given them to students with special needs. The next most deserving group that deserves them is students in areas of concentrated poverty, which often correlates with race. After that, we should give them to all students.

One Grade at a Time

There is wide agreement that the best way to implement class size reduction is to add one grade a year as the first cohort moves through any one school (Achilles 1999, p. 29). "Incremental phasing in of small classes provides time and experience to guide future decisions" (p. 151). What should *not* be the implementation plan is a gradual, nontargeted reduction of all class sizes nationwide. The effects would be diluted, and the gains would not reach the new teachers in particular as incentive to come and to stay. Classes should drop directly to twelve, one grade at a time, starting at the schools in the poorest urban areas and proceeding up the socioeconomic ladder until all kids get the attention they need at school. Again, by starting in schools that are currently least likely to recruit and retain teachers, the incentives will be reversed from the get-go.

Example Timeline

Table 10.1 is an example framework of various levels of commitment to making schools attentive to kids. The minimum level represents what should be acted on immediately, the others coming later as society sees the benefits in action. I propose meeting the first two levels of commitment within twenty-six years—I've chosen twenty-six because it encompasses two 13-year (kindergarten to twelfth grade) phase-in periods.

Again, this timeline is simply a rough sketch offered with the intention to show that it can be done; it is not meant to imply there is any one best plan. An even speedier and/or more complete implementation may be possible.

Has Any Comparable Teacher Recruitment Been Done Before?

Recall from Chapter 8 that South Korea appears to have accomplished a thirteen-student class size reduction in the mere thirteen years between 1991 and 2004. Could something similar be done in the United States? First, we should acknowledge that we have long been humanizing our schools by

TABLE 10.1   PROPOSED 26-YEAR IMPLEMENTATION

	COMMITMENT		
	MINIMAL (13 YEARS)	PARTIAL (13 YEARS)	FULL
School size	Subdivide the largest 25% of schools with special attention to poor and racially stigmatized areas	Subdivide the next largest 25% of schools, including all high-poverty areas	All schools small
Class size	Poorest 40% of schools meeting recommendations K–12; all schools meeting recommendations K–3	All schools meeting recommendations	
Continuity	Teacher continuity at all elementary schools	Teacher continuity maximized in all unchanged secondary schools	

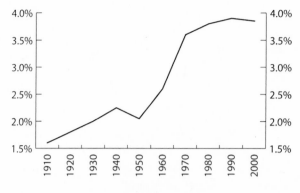

Figure 10.1 *Noncollege teachers as a percentage of the U.S. labor force.*

Source: Wyatt and Hecker 2006. Public domain.

increasing the number of teachers per capita, albeit slowly. This increase has been the product of two trends: (1) a gradually decreasing pupil/teacher ratio and class size and (2) increasing numbers of students completing all thirteen years of schooling. Significantly, there is one glaring exception to the gradualness of the trend that says nay to the naysayers.

As Figure 10.1 demonstrates, between 1950 and 1970 teachers essentially doubled as a percentage of the workforce. "The increases in 1960 and 1970 reflect higher enrollments as the baby-boom generation, born between 1946 and 1964, moved through the system" (Wyatt and Hecker 2006). My proposal seeks to increase the teaching force by roughly half the percentage it increased during the baby boom, allowing twenty-six years rather than a mere twenty. In other words, we've already accomplished a feat twice as great in less time.

Has anyone ever successfully argued that the 1950–1970 teacher influx damaged our schools academically? That it diluted the quality of our faculties? No. Recall from Chapter 2 that the only score that has come down significantly is the SAT, and it came down for one of the same reasons that the number of teachers per capita went up: A higher percentage of kids were finishing high school and taking college entrance exams. In fact, the baby-boom doubling of the teacher workforce occurred simultaneous with a trend during the postwar period to make teaching credentials more rigorous.

How Much Does Recruitment Really Have to Go Up?

Figure 10.2 projects how many teachers we will need to recruit each year under three different scenarios of how much the proposal could reduce teacher attrition. It assumes a twenty-six-year implementation and 53 percent more teachers needed (see Chapter 8), and it decreases the attrition only by the same factor that the proposal has been implemented.

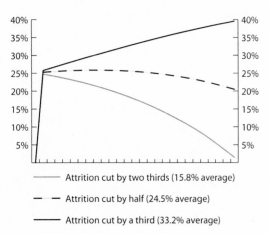

Figure 10.2 *Projected increase over number of new teachers needed in 2004 (using 1999–2000 turnover rates).*

Sources: Digest 2006, table 61; NCES, 2005, figure 6.

As the averages clearly demonstrate, even the most conservative estimate is reasonable considering that average class size will be cut in half.

Finding Teachers Part 1
Reorganizing Staff

As described in Chapter 9, there is strong evidence that schools that reassign specialized staff to classrooms through increased inclusion of special needs students can reduce class size by five to ten students without increased funding. Far from being the ones to pay the price, formerly nonincluded students arguably enjoy a much greater quality of experience and a better education in this scenario.

Finding Teachers Part 2
Alternate Routes

For the 53 percent more teachers needed, we will not need to create a new recruitment system—we already have two in place: traditional and alternate. All states now offer programs referred to as "alternate routes" to certify individuals with bachelor's degrees who hadn't planned to become teachers the first time through college, up from eight states in 1983 (Feistritzer 2008, p. 1). Alternate recruitment of teachers is no longer small time. Many may be surprised to learn that in 2006 "approximately a third of the 147,000 new-to-the-profession teachers hired by school districts came through alternative routes to teacher certification" and that the system expanded another 18 percent to produce 60,000 new teachers in 2007 (p. 1). That's 2 percent of the approximately 3 million public school teachers in the United States, and it's precisely the percentage of teachers who *retired* from teaching after the 1999–2000 school year; the arguments presented throughout the book hopefully show that relationship load reduction will go a long way toward keeping the 4 percent who leave teaching every year for other jobs, which will minimize recruitment need (NCES 2005, figure 6).

There is also an important demographic difference between traditional and alternate teachers. Alternate routes are a major force in bringing diversity to the teaching force so it can better correspond to the student population. Though the regular teaching force is only 15 percent nonwhite, alternate-route teachers are about a third nonwhite. Moreover, 37 percent of the alternate-route teaching force is male, compared to only 18 percent of teachers as a whole (Feistritzer 2008, p. 3). On the flip side, one study found that alternate-route programs in math and science tended to be more female than the math and science teaching force already in schools (Darling-Hammond, Hudson, and Kirby 1989, p. 103). As well, the nature of alternate routes is that these teachers tend to fill needed slots, "specific subject areas in specific geographic areas where demand for teachers is greatest"—97 percent go to high-poverty schools, 20 percent teach math, and over 50 percent teach special education (Feistritzer 2008, p. 3).

Does the urgency under which they were hired mean that they aren't as committed as the average teacher? According to Feistritzer (2008), it's the inverse: In most states, 85 percent to 95 percent are still teaching five years later, a far cry from the 50 percent of traditionally trained teachers (p. 3). Does their alongside-the-job training mean they aren't as effective at producing academic results as traditionally trained teachers? That depends on how well they are supported in their work and their simultaneous training, of course, but evidence suggests that they equal or exceed the competence of their traditional peers in well-designed programs. For example, The New Teacher Project is a multistate program that is responsible for hiring 16,000 alternate-route teachers since 1997—2,500 in 2005 alone—bringing in about half of New York City's math, science, and special education teachers (Rhee and Keeling 2008, pp. 2, 33). Independent studies of their "fellows" have found that on average they have higher GPAs and higher scores on state certification tests than their traditional peers, which tends to correlate with academic results for students; and by the second or third year in the classroom, these teachers are matching or outperforming their traditional peers in academic outcomes (p. 34).

One example of a successful model of alternate recruitment is Troops to Teachers, which has provided about 10,000 teachers since 1994 (Shea 2007). A group of researchers who studied the effectiveness of the program found that participants exhibit research-based best instructional and classroom management practices linked with increased student achievement and work well within the school environment at a higher rate than do other teachers with similar years of experience. Almost 90% of supervising principals say that their [troops-turned-teachers] have a more positive impact on student achievement than other teachers with similar years of teaching experience. (Owings, Kaplan, Nunnery, Marzano, Myran, and Blackburn 2006)

The authors also noted that this group reflected the two other tendencies mentioned above: higher diversity and higher retention rate.

Cost is another potential advantage of alternate routes. Darling-Hammond observes that when quality training can be guaranteed, alternate routes have the advantage of a guaranteed pipeline from training to work, reducing the waste society bears training the many teachers in traditional routes who never enter teaching at all (2006, p. 330).

States should facilitate the partnering of districts and nearby colleges in creating alternate-route programs that are customized to local needs. Simultaneously, they could also retool the current licensing system. With its firm faith in specialization and mutually exclusive categories, current teacher licensing impedes relationship load reduction. Teacher despecialization is one of the key ways to keep class size reduction within reach in terms of recruitment and cost. Miles and Darling-Hammond (1998) write, "Using teachers across subjects or programs" and interdisciplinary teaching "can require waivers." They are careful not to conflate official recognition with true ability. "Although certification in both fields is one indicator" of the ability to teach two subjects, "it is not the only means for developing expertise in a second field." Some districts that have recognized how traditional certification requirements require too much specialization to make small schools and classes work have created "alternative personnel tracks for specially designated schools." States could facilitate and standardize a broad consensus on the benefits of some despecialization of teacher certification. For instance, states may want to rethink how difficult they make it for teachers to add a secondary license when they only have a primary, and vice versa. This could make the teaching force more flexible.

Finding Teachers Part 3
Traditional Routes

Alternate routes are arguably not the ideal source of new teachers, of course. Darling-Hammond is perhaps the foremost voice in critiquing U.S. reliance on uncertified teachers to fill empty slots. She is a staunch proponent of focusing on intensifying teacher training as a means of decreasing attrition and thus the need for uncertified teachers. She has criticized the minimal preparation and high turnover associated with Teach for America, for example. I agree with Darling-Hammond's preference for traditional routes, but I believe significant class size reduction is worth a temporary increase in alternative recruitment. Class size reduction is a harmonious complement to the goal of improving university training because it lowers the stakes by making the teaching task easier: It would enhance the effect of current teacher training, and it would enhance the effects of any improvements.

Darling-Hammond (2006) suggests that higher education bears some of the responsibility for the relative unattractiveness of the teaching profession. "If teaching is a low-status occupation in the United States, teacher education is an even lower-status enterprise within most universities" (p. 277). It will take the leadership of colleges and universities to increase the number of teacher candidates. They will also need to partner better with districts to take more care of the leaks in the training-to-job pipeline. Darling-Hammond suggests that supply is not the primary problem, arguing that other factors are preventing the trained supply of teachers getting to (and staying) in teaching positions. She writes, "There are actually more than enough newly prepared teachers each year to satisfy demand (more than 150,000 annually for the fewer than 100,000 slots that are filled by beginners)" (pp. 311–312). Only 70 percent of those who complete bachelor-level teacher education programs ever enter teaching at all! (p. 311). She suggests, consonant with the principle of relationship load, that smaller rather than larger (and longer rather than shorter) programs may be better at producing teachers that stick it out and may be more cost efficient for society (p. 310).

Further along I will discuss how government incentives could increase the commitment of trained teachers to the profession by reimbursing them for their training to the extent that they keep teaching.

Finding Teachers Part 4
Training: Proto-Internship with an Apprenticeship Door

The key to making alternate and traditional routes effective, then, is to ensure quality training. The National Academy of Education writes, "The preparation of excellent teachers is the central commitment without which other reforms are unlikely to succeed" (2005, p. 69). They argue the key challenge to alternate routes is the time needed to both teach and take coursework at the same time and that this puts a negative incentive on depth and quality (p. 64). Their report, *A Good Teacher in Every Classroom*, makes several recommendations relevant to how quality of training could be ensured under this proposal:

- National coordination of licensing
- Quality coursework
- A lengthy, well-supervised internship experience
- A path to entry for paraprofessionals and members of underserved communities

National Coordination

The National Academy of Education argues there should be standardization and/or increased mutual recognition of licenses among states. "Many teachers who move between states leave the profession for other careers" because of current red tape resulting from discrepancies in licensing procedures among states (p. 61). This aggravates recruitment problems because "many states have surpluses of teachers while others have shortages," suggesting the need for "policies that can get teachers more effectively from where they are trained to where they are needed" (p. 62).

Coursework

Quality coursework will depend on the cooperation of higher ed. As suggested above, local colleges could collaborate in school district recruitment plans by offering coursework that works around the school schedule to allow teachers-to-be to be interning in the classroom from the start. Few fail to acknowledge that this start-before-certification situation is unavoidable to a large extent. First of all, traditional recruitment through undergraduate colleges can no longer meet teacher demand because of high turnover. Second of all, there are not enough people around who don't have bills to pay.

> Many candidates do not get access to adequate preparation because they cannot afford either the tuition or the opportunity costs of being without employment for a period of time. And these costs are harder to bear when a recruit is entering a profession that does not promise large salaries later to compensate for loans taken earlier. (p. 64)

Third, experience suggests that policy-makers will be unwilling to invest sufficient money in training *potential* classroom adults—rather than *actual* classroom adults—to make the prospect sufficiently attractive for a sufficient number of people. Fourth, even if policy-makers did cough up enough money, kids would still be waiting that many years more for the adult attention they deserve right now.

Proto-Internship

Though I believe large grouping size accounts for much of the attrition in teaching, training programs (and administrators) that ignore a teacher's need for induction are clearly no help. Darling-Hammond writes that newly trained teachers are "squandered when they land in an unsupportive system that treats them as utterly dispensable" (2006, p. 331). Grouping size reduction would create a situation nearly ideal for implementing any of several promising induction models that have yet to make strong inroads into schools beset with large relationship load. For example, Darling-Hammond, Wise, and Klein (1999) propose an internship model that would mirror those used in other professions such as psychology and medicine. The training scenario that I propose could function as a precursor to such a model. Once the implementation period for relationship load reduction is finished, a more tightly controlled internship system could evolve that could operate with a more select and well-trained force of mentors. Again, relationship load reduction is valuable enough to put before even the laudable goal of a thorough teacher induction. Moreover, such a system is far more likely to evolve after smallness rather than before. In order to meet hiring demands for the implementation period, a longer and better internship system will have to exist in a kind of semifinished state until recruitment levels off. There is no reason to suspect, however, that the quality of induction will decline in such a scenario relative to its current state, which many admit is parsimonious.

This proto-internship would in essence be some variation of having a first-year and/or yet-to-be-certified teacher coteach with a mentor in a class of twice the recommended size rather than alone in a recommended-size class. The long-term benefit of recruitment and solid training justifies the short-term sacrifice of larger group size (the adult/child ratio remains as recommended). To ensure that this experience is beneficial to students and teachers alike, it should conform to research on effective teacher induction. A survey of principals and new teachers found that their top two ingredients would be an experienced mentor and a year-long internship (MetLife 2005, p. 5), which clearly fit this proto-internship. The National Academy of Education has four basic recommendations for a quality induction program:

1. A mentor is regularly available to coach and model good instruction.
2. The new teacher has a reduced teaching load.
3. The program lasts at least a year.
4. The program has a thorough assessment component. (2005, p. 66)

Clearly a coteaching situation would create ample opportunity for the first recommendation. This would be the greatest strength of the small class situation, since "relatively few programs . . . ensure that expert mentors in the same teaching field are made available for in-classroom support, the component of induction with the greatest effect on teacher retention and learning" (p. 67). In addition, recall that the proposal allows for up to 7.5 percent of teachers to remain classroom free in order to provide additional support. This means one for every 13.3, to be precise, which is below the average supervisor/employee ratio in education (Berliner and Biddle 1995, p. 80). During the implementation period, a good use of these human resources would be to free up the most talented teachers, for example, National Board certified, as trainers and mentors for new teachers.

In terms of the second recommendation, new teachers clearly should get an easier assignment than veterans. Very often new teachers—the most likely to leave at the end of the year if overwhelmed—are given the "largest classes, most difficult students, and most preparations and duties" in an effort to reward the seniority of others (National Academy of Education 2005, p. 66). This strategy may be a tolerable tradition in a more financially rewarding profession, but it is shooting oneself in the foot in the running of schools. I propose a certified first-year teacher would have a lighter load by virtue of being able to piggyback on the curriculum of the mentor teacher and being able to leave the whole group with the mentor teacher in order to attend trainings when necessary. A yet-to-be-certified teacher would most benefit by having the mentor teacher be the one to plan curriculum and prepare materials, freeing the inductee to have the entire afternoon to work on coursework toward certification. Naturally, the mentor teacher should be compensated extra for his or her role.

The third recommendation, a full year, is inherent in the proto-internship. Inductees who take longer to become certified would get more than a year of internship. The fourth recommendation, the assessment piece, would be a matter of following a model such as that outlined by the National Academy of Education (2005).

An Apprenticeship Door
The National Academy of Education recommends that high-need communities should be targeted for programs tailored to their needs and committed to recruiting their residents, such as current school paraprofessionals "already knowledgeable about and committed to their communities" (2005, p. 60). Darling-Hammond calls this a "grow-your-own strategy" (2006, p. 330). This community commitment increases the promise for teacher retention in high-turnover schools. It could also help lead to parity of teacher-student race and ethnicity, since high-turnover communities also tend to be communities of color. (Again, increased diversity is already a feature of our current alternate recruitment pool.) One school (which reduced its class sizes in the process) latched on to this apprenticeship style of recruitment, finding

an untapped resource from which to draw new teachers in its pool of support-staff workers already employed in schools. "If we have someone who wants to go through a program and pick up their bachelor's degree, we're working directly through the universities to have that happen. We've found that the people who have worked in our schools before seem to be more committed to stay in our schools." (Legler 2000)

Currently, aide positions seldom function as a stepping-stone to becoming a full-fledged teacher. To become a teacher, an aide often has to quit, finish college, and then come back to work in a school years later—nearly always a different school.

A shift toward an "apprenticeship door" would mean an important change to transition into the profession: Ongoing contact with the school and the people in it could become the focus of training and of one's motivation to become a teacher. As it currently stands, one most often has to want to become a teacher while in college and prepare for entering a school as a full-fledged teacher. Even most alternate-route teachers often have to have hatched the idea of a career change while in a job isolated from schools, clearly making for fewer of them. This means that we optimistically rely on a large number of people to maintain a very abstract desire to help an abstract group of kids in order to staff the teaching profession. And very often these people discover they lack the true ability or desire to help kids in the face of the challenges of the job as currently defined, principally large grouping size. It is likely that the reverse is a more motivating scenario: The chance to discover a concrete, tangible calling by working with the adults and children in a school before pursuing an undergraduate major, postbaccalaureate or master's in education—often with the hopes of working in that same school. This is what happened to me—I showed up as an uncertified sub one day and simply never left. Teaching didn't interest me until I'd tried my hand at it—and found I couldn't let it go.

For those skeptical of my proto-internship proposal, recall from Chapter 7 that no academic setbacks have been documented from less qualified people teaching smaller groups—with the exception of their overconcentration in certain schools; barring that, the only academic risk being taken is equal rather than improved outcomes. In fact, far from increasing the number of uncertified personnel in charge of classrooms, during the implementation of my proposal, it is likely that fewer and fewer uncertified teachers will be teaching without supervision precisely because of this ability to pair them with certified teachers without making a class larger than the current average. This is due largely to the fact that those schools with the most yet-to-be-certified and other out-of-field teachers will be first to undergo the class size reduction that makes a proto-internship possible. According to a 2004 report,

At the high school grade level, students in high-poverty schools were more likely to be taught English, science, and mathematics by an out-of-field teacher than students in low-poverty schools. The same held true for students in high-minority schools compared with students in low-minority schools. (NCES 2004, indicator 24).

Darling-Hammond (2006) finds similar results. In California, for example, over a quarter of teachers in schools with over 90 percent minority students are underqualified, while it's only 5 percent in schools that have fewer than 30 percent students of color; similar but less extreme differences hold true when subsidized lunch is considered (p. 23).

Finding Teachers Part 5
Good-Old-Fashioned Government Incentives

The National Academy of Education (2005) suggests society should invest more heavily in the training of public-school-teachers-to-be (p. 65). This would be one way to increase the influx of both traditionally and alternately trained teachers. Just as the GI Bill rewarded returning soldiers with education, this could reward men and women who perform a comparable service to society in a comparable way. Darling-Hammond notes that other industrialized countries heavily subsidize the training of their teachers, whereas the United States largely individualizes the costs, which increases turnover and contributes to the low status of the profession (2006, p. 331).

Such a program could work like a cross between a loan and a grant. It could be issued as a loan whose repayment is deferred until graduation as normal, but as long as the recipients can prove they hold a public school teaching job, the federal government will cover the monthly payments. Should a recipient ever leave public schools, the recipient would have to take over the remaining payments. Analogously, should the recipient teach only half time, he or she would pay half of each payment. This would be a simple way to make the profession a lot more attractive without opening the Pandora's box of salary. It could also piggyback relatively easily on the current federal participation in the educational loan and grant system. A small-scale version of what I'm suggesting is already in place for forgiving the loans of those who end up teaching in Title I schools or in high-need subject areas (Federal Student Aid 2006). We could expand it and remove some of its limitations. The incentive to teach in Title I schools, for example, could be replaced by implementing classes of twelve there first. Particularly, it should be guaranteed in advance, rather than applied for in arrears, fingers crossed that some technicality doesn't disqualify one.

Some states have programs in place that go down the same road. For example, South Carolina has a program entitled Call Me Mister that is focused on recruiting black male teachers, who are even more underrepresented in that state than they are nationally. It has gotten 20 teachers into schools so far and has 150 in the pipeline (Holsendolph 2007). In other words, if they're not coming to you, go find them.

Finding Teachers Part 6
Hard-to-Fill Areas

As argued earlier, I recommend a rethinking of strategy with respect to teaching areas that are hard to fill, such as math, science, and special education. Given that retention and recruitment of prequalified teachers in these areas have been a chronic problem, perhaps we could simply work on the "prequalified" part by giving math and science training to committed teachers. Such retraining programs appear to have high attrition rates (Darling-Hammond et al. 1989, p. 104); they would be more attractive, therefore, if they offered extra pay or reduced teaching duties. A coteaching internship identical to the one outlined above could be used for this purpose also. A committed, veteran teacher who would like to become endorsed in math or science could coteach a class of twenty-four with an endorsed teacher. The endorsed teacher could take on the planning burden, freeing up the yet-to-be-endorsed teacher's afternoons for coursework.

Finding Teachers Part 7
Out-of-Work Tutors and "School Improvement Industry" Workers

Earlier I mentioned that one of the savings inherent in grouping size reduction would be less need for private tutoring and less need to fund an "industry" of school improvement recommendations and materials. As business shifts away from these markets, educators of this sort would provide an excellent pool of potential teachers.

Finding Teachers Part 8
Good-Old-Fashioned PR

Recruitment needs to be an active process, an outreach campaign. Darling-Hammond and colleagues found that "individuals typically are not aware of the existence of special postgraduate programs or of sources of financial aid that would allow them to prepare for teaching" (1989, p. 104). They argue that, for math and science at least, "recruitment efforts should focus on those individuals for whom teacher salaries will not be a strong disincentive to enter or remain in teaching" (p. 105). Rhee and Keeling write,

> Job postings. Newspaper advertisements. Career fairs. These are all common elements of teacher recruitment campaigns, but all too commonly they are the *only* elements. In the competitive marketplace from which alternate route programs must draw their applicants, such strategies are simply insufficient. (2008, p. 12)

These authors suggest sophisticated marketing campaigns like the ones carried out by The New Teacher Project, which attracted almost 30,000 applicants in 2006 and could be choosy enough to select just 14 percent of them (p. 11). Their District of Columbia campaign had the slogan, "Do SOMETHING about it. TEACH," while their Philadelphia campaign ran the slogan, "Do something better. *Teach*." A public relations campaign that focused on solving the nurturance crisis might create an even larger pool of applicants.

11

Help from the Private Sector

Thus far we've principally talked about how the *public* sector can reorganize to meet the challenges of the real nurturance crisis. The *private* sector also bears responsibility for the problems and the solutions. The most obvious area is the overworking and underpaying of the parents and community members and the subsequent effect on their ability to raise the community's kids.

> A package of policies that includes generous paid parental leaves, reduced work hours for parents, better pay and benefits for part-time workers, and much more investment in high-quality child care is an indispensable foundation for any enduring attack on the stress and social isolation of mainstream families, the critical public infrastructure upon which everything else depends. Having these policies won't guarantee that . . . parents will do a better job of attentive and engaged parenting. Their absence ensures that many will not. (Currie 2005, p. 283)

In general, however, the business community has pressured governments over recent decades to lessen its public responsibility. Many speak of the general retreat of business from the tax burden through lower and lower rates on companies as compared with individuals, particularly the middle class. According to Tye, "In effect, corporate America withdrew its support of public education: By 1987, the overall corporate share of property taxes had declined to 16% from 45% in 1957" (2000, p. 86). This was achieved through tax cuts, exemptions, and credits leveraged by threats of pulling out of either individual communities or the nation itself. "Big business masked its withdrawal from support of the public sector with small concessions and token gestures" (p. 87). For example, companies now offer support to schools in exchange for in-school marketing privileges (Milner 2004, p. 188). And, of course, the business community is one of the primary beneficiaries of the publicly paid training that public education provides. Even the fake test score crisis rhetoric makes no secret of this fact.

Another private-sector contribution would be a willingness to participate with public planners to help communities become as economically integrated as possible—whether the neighborhoods are preexisting or yet to be built. Spreading poverty out geographically—not allowing it to concentrate in any one area—reduces its negative impacts. In an article entitled "Fixing Schools Isn't Everything," Berliner (2006) argues that poverty is being systematically ignored in the education debate in much the same way as is class size. He summarizes the research on the resilience of poor families who live in communities where most people are not poor: "A 'good' zip code can make a bigger difference than good parenting." *No one* deserves to live in a place where good parenting is not good enough. Only cooperation from the private sector, for example, land developers, will bring about the macroscopic changes needed to reduce the geographic concentration of poverty.

Lastly, the private sector could provide the necessary grants to fund full-service schools as outlined in the previous chapter. Full-service schools can be customized by each community to meet needs beyond those currently met by schools, such as daycare, after care, and empowerment of community adults. The one caveat to public-private partnerships in education is that the private sector might abuse them to exert more pressure on schools to match their interests. They should therefore be approached with this caution in mind. Ultimately, higher corporate taxes, higher pay, and paid parental leave would be the private-sector contributions most likely to benefit students and society.

12

Implementation at Kid Level

I will wrap up the book by bringing it back to where the students are—in their homes and classrooms. What follows is a short selection of how teachers and parents can maximize school's potential impact on the nurturance crisis. I keep it short because it's been generously elaborated elsewhere. What's most often overlooked, of course, are the real constraints placed upon teachers by relationship load—decisions almost entirely out of the hands of teachers. Let's begin by addressing parents and guardians.

Parents and Guardians

A common reaction to the ideas in this book is for parents to feel their turf is being invaded. This defensiveness is based on a faulty assumption: the autonomy of the nuclear family. Humans have always been raised by *communities* of adults, not just one or two. Yes, parents are the primary adults in that process, but their efforts have always been most effective when in concert with those of other adults rather than in isolation (Coontz 2000, p. 288). Some parents may find it threatening, but children most often admire and can't get enough of their teachers. This is because they appear to be biologically programmed to do so, to attach to as many safety-inducing adults as they can (Bowlby 1982). Thus, sending children to school but trying to prevent attachment to the teacher is basically swimming upstream.

At the same time, parents are justified in having concerns about how their children are treated at school. Clearly parents and their children both have the right to kindness, fairness, and educational effectiveness, though this last one should never come at the expense of the previous two. The solution to this tension will sound familiar: relationships. Parents who get to know their children's teachers will be far more likely to resolve this potential conflict. The knowing of one another will reduce mistrust on both sides (Christenson and Sheridan 2001, p. 115). Teachers who know a parent well will be much more likely to understand and accommodate parental requests that might seem controlling or mistrusting outside of the context of a good relationship. Teachers will also overwhelmingly appreciate the insight parents offer about how to approach their kids effectively and sensitively. There is a flip side to this relationship: For the many socially isolated parents we have in our society—and arguably *most* of our parents are socially isolated when compared to those in preindustrial societies—this relationship with the teacher offers an invaluable opportunity for connection that can improve their confidence and effectiveness as parents (Epstein and Sanders 2000, p. 293).

There are two research findings in this area that are cause for hope. First, parents who tend to rate the American public school system as ineffective overall nevertheless tend to praise the school and the teachers they've come into contact with. Berliner and Biddle (1995) cite some survey data that illustrate the point with clarity. The sample of American adults, when asked to "grade" the *nation's* schools, gave them slightly fewer A's and B's than D's and F's. But when asked to grade their *local* schools, they gave them just over three times as many A's and B's as D's and F's. And they gave *the schools their children were in* over ten times as many A's and B's as D's and F's (p. 113). In other words, mistrust of the education process thrives in the abstract but withers in concrete relationships. As I have suggested throughout the book, relatedness reduces mistrust in every dimension of education, as well as other realms of human interaction. Second, smaller schools and smaller classes tend to attract parents to the school and to building relationships there (Achilles 1999, p. 145; Cotton 2001, p. 17; Munoz and Portes 2002).

The increased relatedness at the heart of this proposal may threaten some parents, but that relatedness also opens the schools to more oversight by parents and makes that oversight more likely to be cooperative rather than antagonistic. Epstein and Sanders cite research that suggests that parent and teacher stereotyping of one another is reduced, quite logically, by more frequent communication (2000, p. 289). This has positive implications for the cross-race and cross-class relationships typical of our public schools.

On the flip side, of course, teachers should also make efforts to forge relationships with parents. Clearly, smaller classes would facilitate this because the number of contacts to parents would be a less daunting proposition. The advisory model would also help because it creates a core group of families that each teacher is the chief school contact for (Goldberg 1998). This allows teacher effort to be concentrated on a smaller group of parent relationships, promoting depth over breadth. Again, by including parent-teacher relationships as the fourth aspect of the relationship load equation, we are reminded to see schools as embedded in a larger process of childrearing rather than as an intermission that can follow different rules.

Offering Freedom

The research presented in Chapter 4 suggests that by better meeting our students' needs for freedom, their demands on our attention will decrease and be easier to satisfy. Allowing for more student choice and direction will put students in a frame of mind where they won't feel so deprived of teacher attention. The one caveat is that students are more likely to take positive rather than negative risks with freedom if it is granted in a context of a secure attachment relationship.

Using Play

Another implication of the research in Chapter 4 is that children feel less need for adult attention while playing. What a teacher can take from this is that his or her students are less likely to feel emotionally deprived of attention if class activities resemble play more than work. Although this is not always possible, it is certainly less practiced than it could be.

Proving Availability of Attention

Another implication of attachment research is that teachers take responsibility for ensuring that the child perceives the availability of positive attention. In groups of children who are engaged not in play but in adult-designed chores (such as schoolwork), *the adults must be actively circulating and engaging in order to create the perception of availability.* This becomes increasingly true as groups grow larger, where there is a proportional danger of feeling lost in the crowd. In the culture of school as I have observed it, there is often a sense among students that asking for help will burden the teacher or a fear that the teacher will reject one's request for help. There is also a tendency among students to interpret teacher utterances that do not explicitly mean "Would you like help?" to mean "Don't bother me." In my experience, "Let me know if you have questions" often fails to invite any. As I've endeavored to show, however, even for excellent and committed teachers, there is a group size over which an adult's charisma will not spread sufficiently. At a certain point, despite the adult's active involvement, the children (or at least a good number of them) begin to doubt the availability of attention and, hence, their own value.

Teachers' Unions

Feldman and colleagues write, "Many small school practices run counter to a typical collective bargaining agreement" (2006, p. 51). Teachers' unions will probably have to make three compromises to help relationship load reduction work for teachers. First, in exchange for an easier job through grouping size reduction, they will have to be willing to allow schools to ask teachers to teach a greater variety of courses at any one time. This is a necessary compromise for teachers to make for the opportunity to work in smaller, more pleasant schools.

> "The first two years, I had five preps," says math teacher Richard Boettner, who helped found Life Academy [a 260-student school] five years ago. "This is the first year I have just three." (The contract allows teachers to refuse more than two.) (Jehlen and Kopkowski 2006, p. 28)

Instead of making teachers have to agree not to insist on the terms of their contracts in order to work in smaller schools, the unions should ease their restrictions in exchange for smaller classes. The insistence on limiting the number of preps is, after all, a bulwark against the overwhelming demands of large grouping size. Once class size is reduced, small schools will be less squeezed on course variety and teachers will be less squeezed on prep time.

A second compromise would be not insisting that teachers have a duty-free lunch away from kids. This is ideal attachment-building time. Again, the reason for a "duty-free" lunch is a response to the unwieldy demands of teaching in the context of large groupings. Cohen and Scheer write, "Administrators often claim that such ancillary responsibilities allow teachers to get to know kids outside the classroom. This may be true. But too often the policing nature of the duty simply forces kids to resent adults to see them only as punitive and voyeuristic" (2003, p. 38). The flaw in their logic is assuming that children's resentment would change if nonteachers did the supervision or that the lack of supervision would be preferable to such resentment. A better solution is to have fewer kids per adult, reducing the "policing" feel by group dynamics and deeper relationships. Cohen and Scheer all but admit this when they write, "The smaller the school, the less frequently teachers were asked to perform the tasks that most enervate them—monitoring bathrooms and chasing smokers out of the stairwells" (2003, p. 53).

A third compromise called for by some small-school advocates is the elimination of seniority preference in filling teacher vacancies, which is often a stipulation of the union-negotiated contract (Raywid and Schmerler 2003, p. 89). They argue that this ties a small school's hands in its effort to gather like-minded faculty who can work well together in the more interdependent climate of a small school. They cite the example of New York City's United Federation of Teachers, which compromised by allowing that if a majority of the school's teachers agreed to it, the seniority rule could be voided at that school. This kind of provision may also encourage principals to share power with teachers, for example, by involving them in hiring decisions.

Clearly, unions should make these demands contingent on school and class size reduction. Only when the schools meet—or at least approach—the enrollment *and* class size recommendations should they have the right to ask these concessions from teachers. Indeed, unions can offer these conditional concessions as leverage to get policy-makers to cough up the money for smaller classes.

Serving All Students

Ninety percent of U.S. public school teachers are white, while 42 percent of students are not (National Education Association 2003b; NCES 2007a, indicator 5). Part of forming relationships with students involves the inherent challenge of overcoming one's race and gender prejudices, biased cultural ideals, and other preconceived notions that kill caring relationships before they start. Small relationship load can facilitate this task, but it is still up to the teacher to take it on. The teacher's attention is almost always better than nothing, but when that teacher is ignorant of anything but his or her own experience—or an outright bigot—it could in fact be worse.

If and when classes of twelve arrive, teachers can do all that stuff they know they ought to, everything they've wanted to but have been prevented from doing. They can set high standards—both behavioral and academic—though hopefully not the kind that requires some to lose so that others can "win." But most importantly, they can be the positive, attentive, unconditionally accepting, nonpreferential adults children so desperately need them to be. Teachers: Let them see how much you enjoy being with them. Teaching truly is the best job in the world, a privilege. Let them see it on your face.

Conclusion

What kids these days need is a good listening to!

—**Nicole Gnezda** (2005, p. 39)

When I entered high school as a ninth-grader, the school was bursting at the seams. It was the same year a neighboring high school was being closed down, and the other three were accommodating its students. *Accommodated* is not how I felt among the more than two thousand other teenagers. I became overwhelmed and disconnected. I began to skip classes and stop doing homework. By mid-year I'd succumbed to clinical depression. I was more fortunate than I might have been, though. Because I'm white, I did not also have to deal with a standard dose of institutional racism on top of the alienating size of my school. The history textbooks were full of people who looked like me, and my dialect of English was also the language of instruction. And because my parents could afford the private school where I fled the next year, my family had more options than a poorer one would have. But no one should have to go through what I went through—or worse—and no one should have to pay tuition for what I got: a small school with small classes where I could get to know my teachers and they could get to know my parents.

You may be asking, "How much will all this cost again?" Small schools with classes of twelve will cost a mere 20 percent more. That's $420 a year per worker—estimating on the high side. Spread over 365 days of the year, that's $1.15 a day—the price of a vending machine item or two. Break that down by the 1,440 minutes in a day and it takes a quarter of an hour to spend a cent. *Each of us pays a penny every quarter hour of our 30ish-year work life.*

As a fraction of our country's wealth that goes to all tax revenue, this plan for relationship load reduction would raise our total tax burden by only 0.8 percent, from paying 25.5 percent to paying 26.3 percent, leaving the United States still the second cheapest place to earn income in the "developed" world.

You may be thinking, "Remind me why this focus on relationships doesn't direct schools away from *learning*." I've tried to show that learning is best thought of as a fortunate consequence of the primary goal of paying attention to kids. So long as you meet their need for your attention, they tend to absorb what you want them to know. Even if you're not actively trying to teach them, they absorb the example of what you're doing because they want to grow up to be like you. Evidence suggests that students in small classes are more willing to do unappealing schoolwork. That follows from the fact that the *content* is really secondary to the *context* of childrearing. As long as we care about and pay attention to kids, they give us a lot of latitude in what it is we ask them to do. Even though our curricula could very often be a whole lot more challenging, culturally inclusive, meaningful, or engaging, it matters less than whether grouping size is small enough to be able to meet emotional needs *simultaneously but foremost*. This runs contrary to much of current discourse in education whose subtext is that only rarely attained teaching quality is really "good enough." I find this logic far more utopian than achieving grouping size reduction.

The double bonus of meeting needs in their proper order of importance is that it gets easier to improve the content once you've improved the context. Again, students in a small class whose more fundamental needs are better met will engage with work that they might not engage with in a large class simply because of how they feel—even if the work is exactly the same. Of course, teachers don't have to use the same work if they don't want to; they can assign the kind of work in a small class that's more appropriately challenging and personalized. This corroborates one of my most firm convictions of personal experience: *Small-class work can be made more cognitively challenging for every student because it can require and receive more interaction, support, and clarification from the teacher.* It is largely because the teacher can't help a student through something because of lack of time that that something is "too hard" for a student to do. Small groupings make teachers more available. In other words, *smallness* is what will make it possible for more of our teachers to present *precisely the kinds of challenges we wish they all would or could*—and what will make it possible for our kids to meet those challenges.

"But the nurturance crisis you describe seems too difficult to fix," you may be thinking. Again, despite my use of the word "crisis," it is not my intent to spread fear or to create a useless sense of doom and gloom about the lack of adult attention in children's lives. I see this crisis as very fixable. Indeed, there may even be a bright side to the loss of preindustrial communities. As I argued earlier, there is no golden age to return to. We may in fact be in as good a position as any to get better from: We constantly tout the benefits of postindustrial life—now let's work on one of its principal drawbacks: leaving people susceptible to loneliness and alienation. Schools should be our first focus in this work. Grouping size in our schools has been largely ignored in our recent progress toward doing right by ourselves while we're kids. Recall that in Chapter 1 I argued that daycares have lower relationship loads principally because they were instituted at a later date than schools were; that is, they benefited from a more child-centered "spirit of the times" than schools, many of whose conventions fossilized over a century ago. The tradition of large schools, on the other hand, is only a half century old. Contrary to common perception, we are still figuring out schooling—it's a mere moment in history so far, the early stages of an innovation.

There is nothing inherently magical about schools. I have no objection per se to getting rid of them altogether, but I'm not sure it will solve any more childrearing, mental health, or social justice problems than it will cause. Schools were part and parcel of industrialization, and they can be a "good enough" adaptation to postindustrial society as well, but only if we update them—*with more adults per kid.* Nearly every sixth person in the United States is a public school student. Meanwhile, public school teachers comprise almost exactly one hundredth of the U.S. population. No other link in our childrearing chain is that neglectful.

If and when classes of twelve arrive for all children, it will be because we got the crisis right. We will have realized that our fears of declining achievement were misdirected and that our worship of test scores was, well, profane. We will have realized that closing the racial achievement gap without reducing relationship load would have been next to impossible. We will have seen that our schools are a part of our childrearing system and that they should behave as such. We will have seen that attachment to parents *and* other adults is at the heart of successful childrearing. We will have accepted that only by allowing educators, students, and guardians to concentrate on fewer relationships will those relationships improve significantly. We will have seen that school is for now, not just for later. We—former kids and future adults alike—will have gotten our teachers' attention.

Appendix A

Source Data for Cost Projections

The data in Table A.1 were used to calculate the cost projections using the following steps:

1. Calculations of teachers needed to staff classes multiplied by 1.11 to account for prep time.[1] (This set current pupil/teacher ratio to 14.9 and yielded a target pupil/teacher ratio of 10.4.)
2. Mainstream student FTEs calculated by removing the maximum number of student FTEs in special education classrooms (6.61 percent—see Appendix B).
3. Number of mainstream students divided by 24 to find the number of mainstream teachers needed to staff current mainstream classes (68.75 percent).
4. Remaining teachers set aside as auxiliary (31.25 percent).
5. Teacher, aide, and counselor salaries and benefits, as well as space costs, removed from total budget to form base budget.
6. Space costs increased progressively from 100 percent to 150 percent at target class size.
7. Auxiliary teachers, aides, and counselors reduced progressively to target number at target class size and the savings progressively subtracted from the budget.
8. Mainstream teachers needed to meet class size added in proportionally as target approached.
9. Resulting auxiliary and mainstream teachers totaled.
10. Total teachers multiplied by average salary and added to resulting budget (base − savings + space costs).

TABLE A.1   DATA AND SOURCES FOR COST PROJECTIONS

STATISTIC	2001–2002 SCHOOL YEAR UNLESS OTHERWISE INDICATED	SOURCE
Current per-pupil spending	$7,727	Digest 2004, table 165
Average teacher salary (assumed to be counselor also)	$44,604	http://nces.ed.gov/nations-reportcard/mathematics/results2003/schsystchar-c.asp
Teachers	2,999,528	Digest 2004, table 81
Aides	674,741	Digest 2004, table 81
Students	47,671,877	Digest 2004, table 39
Counselors	100,049	Digest 2004, table 81
Educator benefits as percent of salaries	25.82%	http://nces.ed.gov/pubs2004/rev_exp_02/table_06.asp
Space costs (plant operation) as percent of the budget (current expenditures)	9.45%	Digest 2005, table 156
Aide salary as percent of teacher salary	38%	salary.com, retrieved September 2007
Maximum percent of population nonmain-streamed at any one time	6.61%	Maximum percentage of time spent nonmainstreamed multiplied by percent classified as disabled, both from Appendix B

Admittedly, these estimates don't account for a probable increase in average teacher experience and thus pay, considering that fewer teachers are likely to leave a more do-able and rewarding profession. On the other hand, the estimates also don't include a possible drop in average experience during the implementation period due to a constant influx of new teachers. Thus, predicting how these contrary forces would interact is statistically complex. It's likely that average salaries will start to increase only once implementation has ended. But the concern is tangential to the proposal in a basic sense: We are, after all, already willing to pay higher salaries to more experienced teachers and would presumably feel we were getting our money's worth once their numbers increased. It would be difficult to make a defensible argument for saving money on education by reducing teacher experience.

Appendix B

Source Data for Play-Like Class Size and Special Education

By combining two classes during the most play-like sixth of the day, the below-average-size classes can be counterbalanced. If PE offerings cannot fill up one sixth of the school day, art or music classes could also be justifiably larger considering their resemblance to play. Miles and Darling-Hammond (1998) find that elementary schools normally use specialist teachers for these subjects already, offering a simple opportunity to have each such teacher teach a combined class of eighteen or twenty-four. Table B.1 demonstrates the calculations.

Table B.2 calculates the amount of student time currently spent in nonmainstream classrooms. To get a conservative estimate of how much student time is spent nonmainstreamed, I averaged the middle amount of each category the data were lumped into with the maximum possible amount. For example, the data show that 51.9 percent of "disabled" students spent less than 21 percent of their time outside of regular classes. I split the difference between the likely reality that the average student in the category comes in at about 10 percent with the maximum possibility of 20 percent. In this way I arrived at 448,345 teachers (in 2001–2002, the projection year) as a conservative number needed to serve nonmainstreamed students in classes of six without any more inclusion than that currently practiced. The cost projections (Appendix A) allow for at least 503,597 nonregular teachers.

TABLE B.1 PLAY-LIKE CLASS CALCULATIONS

UNMAINSTREAMED DISABLED AND UNDIAGNOSED TROUBLED	REMAINING AUXILIARY	POVERTY OR RACISM COMMUNITY	MAINSTREAM	TOTAL TEACHERS UNWEIGHTED	WEIGHTED OUT OF 6 CLASSES	DESCRIPTION
5.0		31.0	64.0			Representative 100 students
6.0		9.0	12.0			Academic class size
0.83		3.44	5.33	9.61	8.01	Teachers needed for 5 academic classes (out of 6)
6.0		18.0	24.0			Play-like class size
0.83		1.72	2.67	5.22	0.87	Teachers needed for 1 play-like class (out of 6)
0.83	0.72	3.16	4.89			Total teachers weighted by play dimension (sum of distributions matches vertical total)
8.68%	7.50%	32.89%	50.92%	99.99%		Percent of total teachers
					0.72	Auxiliary brought in for vertical sum
					9.60	Teachers needed to teach all 100 kids (approximates 100 students divided by target pupil/teacher ratio of 10.4 from Appendix A)

TABLE B.2 SPECIAL EDUCATION CALCULATIONS

	TOTAL	PARTIAL INCLUSION: PERCENT OF STUDENTS IN EACH CATEGORY (PORTION OF THEIR TIME NONMAINSTREAMED)			
		FEWER THAN 21 PERCENT	21–60 PERCENT	MORE THAN 60 PERCENT	100% NONINCLUSION
Average disinclusion rate (averaged from the category)	100.0	51.9	26.5	17.6	4.0
Maximum disinclusion rate (maximum from the category)		0.1	0.4	0.8	1.0
Percent of disabled student time disincluded (averaged)	33.9	0.2	0.6	1.0	1.0
Percent of disabled student time disincluded (maximum)	47.9	5.187	10.6	14.08	4.02
		10.374	15.9	17.6	4.02
2001–2002 (projection year) students (Appendix A)	47,671,877				
Percentage disabled 2004–2005 (Digest 2007, table 49)	13.8				
Students disincluded at any one time (averaged)	2,229,331				
Above figure as percent of total student population	4.68				
Students disincluded at any one time (maximum)	3,150,812				
Above figure as percent of total student population	6.61				
Teachers needed to teach that student share at class size 6 (average)	371,555				
Teachers needed to teach that student share at class size 6 (maximum)	525,135				
Average of average and maximum (bare minimum special education teaching force with no increased inclusion)	448,345				

Note: 2003–2004 figures unless otherwise noted.
Source: unless otherwise noted, Digest 2006, table 49.

Appendix C

Criticisms of Attachment Theory

Some have tried to oversimplify attachment theory as "early-life determinism" or purely a mother-infant explanation that leaves no room for the inborn personality of the child (e.g., Chess and Thomas 1999, p. 28). The nature-nurture debate has long since been largely resolved under the interactionist model Chess and Thomas describe (e.g., Kendler and Prescott 2006). As a part of the nurture side of the equation, attachment theory fits with that model and does not contradict the influences of good or poor fit of child and caregiver personality. On the issue of determinism, attachment theory has always left open the possibility for remediation of insecure early attachments with healthier attachments later in life. It does not deny, however, that the early relationships are more firmly rooted. Kendler and Prescott trace how disturbed family environment (for women), low parental warmth (for men), and childhood sexual abuse and childhood parental loss (for both men and women) interact with genetic factors in the causation of major depression in Western adults (2006, pp. 324, 335). They do not try to argue that having analogous experiences in adulthood have as strong an impact on mental health. Neuroscience is increasingly supporting this view in finding that early interpersonal experience has an enduring (though plastic) impact on brain development (Cozolino 2006, p. 38). Yes, remediation after poor early relationships is possible, but it must overcome the entrenched vestiges of those poor early relationships.

Another objection is what conclusions can be drawn from the Strange Situation evaluation method Mary Ainsworth devised to measure the security of attachment in toddlers (Chess and Thomas 1999, p. 25). Any complaints about this practice should not apply to my use of attachment theory since it relies little on the measurement of attachment. I also avoid classification of attachment type, which indeed could be argued to have class and cultural bias.

Still others have cast attachment theory as part of a project to scapegoat women for social and psychological problems (Eyer 1996, p. 77). It's certainly true that when the research began in the 1950s, it reflected the level of sexism of the time. But there's nothing about the importance of childhood that makes women inherently more responsible for it than men—that's a cultural inheritance. Notice that Kendler and Prescott say "parental" warmth rather than "maternal." We should not simply ignore the needs of our children in the name of equality for women. Far from being inherently antiwoman, attachment theory shows why mothers, who are still left with the bulk of childrearing duties in our society, need the help of additional adults to be successful.

Notes

CHAPTER 1

1. Kennedy (2005) and Tye (2000) basically ignore grouping size reduction in their analyses. They take current relationship loads as givens, as static elements that make change less likely, rather than areas for potential reform. That omission certainly strengthens their case, since grouping size reduction bucks the general trend of complicating the work of educators.

2. Unpublished data from National Center for Educational Statistics, SASS: 2003-04 Public Teacher File, retrieved March 19, 2008, from http://nces.ed.gov/dasolv2/tables/index.asp.

3. This is not to imply I'm against sweeping changes that would humanize our economic system; it simply reflects the pragmatism of the proposal.

4. Nor do good attachment relationships foster naïveté, as some might claim. Children, though widely regarded as impressionable, are actually quite circumspect (hence stranger anxiety) thanks to their instinctual search for security (Bowlby 1982).

5. Its founding principal was Deborah Meier, whom I cite frequently.

6. Pupil/teacher ratio normally varies in direct correlation to class size.

7. In Illinois, for example, class size limits range from 5 to 20 depending on the disability and age (Illinois State Board of Education 2007). Other states have similar regulations. Nonsectarian, private special education schools had average class sizes between 7.5 and 10 in 1993 (NCES 1997, table 1.7).

CHAPTER 2

1. None of this is meant to imply that people of color are no longer underrepresented in higher education or frequently underprepared for it by their public schools.

2. There were two minor exceptions: Catholic Order schools had a one-point achievement-test advantage, and expensive secular schools had an advantage in college completion and a sixty-point advantage in SAT score, but no achievement-test advantage.

3. The economic component of these conclusions suggests that increasing educational and income equity is more important than raising average achievement. Relationship load reduction can help us toward that goal.

CHAPTER 3

1. The other policy response they suggest is to screen out teachers with weak academic skills. In Chapter 7 I will develop the argument that class size reduction will assist in this aim by "screening in" those teachers with strong academic skills we can neither recruit nor retain.

CHAPTER 4

1. See also Currie 2005, p. 275; Dryfoos 1998, p. 39; Landy 2002, p. 31; Young 1999, pp. 112–113; Zigler and Lang 1991, p. 66.

2. It's likely that in many, if not most, noncoercive schools smallness is a secret ingredient. Indeed, most nontraditional schools are small and shave off as much class size as they can afford. But, of course, they often tout their method or philosophy rather than these less flashy details.

CHAPTER 5

1. Indeed, the very notion of numbering the years was not regularized until the age-grading that spread after 1848 (Spring 1997, p. 152).

2. Research has found equalization of achievement to be one of the effects of grouping size reduction (for example, National Research Council 2004, pp. 114–115).

3. True class size figures—rather than pupil/teacher ratio—do exist, but currently U.S. class size data have only three sources, two of which are surveys that disagree at the secondary level. (For a discussion of how the abuse of the pupil/teacher ratio measure has been used to obscure the benefits of lowered class size, see Achilles [2003].) In 2003–2004, the National Center for Education Statistics' *Schools and Staffing Survey* put the average elementary class size at 20.4 and the average secondary class size at 24.7 (Digest 2006, table 64). An average to those two is 22.6. The National Education Association's survey results reported in *Status of the American Public School Teacher* 2000–2001, found a much higher number for secondary, 28, and a similar 21 for elementary (National Education Association 2003a, p. 35). There 53 percent of teachers designated themselves as elementary (p. 24), making a simple average at 24.5 close to accurate. The third source is the Organisation for Economic Cooperation and Development's *Education at a Glance* reports. They use a strict division method (the total number of students divided by the total number of classes) rather than surveys. These data are a

little less flattering than the survey data. A strict average would be 24.3 (2006a, table D2.1).

4. My rationale for seeking one number rather than an age-based scale can be found in the "Age Differences" section of Chapter 4 and the "Small Classes for Early Grades Is Good Enough" section of Chapter 7.

CHAPTER 6

1. A certain portion of the population may respond best to a predominantly behaviorist punishment-reward system, but that group is far less than half and would almost certainly be smaller having gone through a school system with small grouping sizes. In addition, small relationship load will give teachers the opportunity for a more individualized behavioral strategy as well, responding to differing levels of need for a behaviorist element.

CHAPTER 7

1. The fact that opponents are obsessed with the few years of yet-to-be-qualified teaching these teachers will do, rather than the many years of qualified teaching that will ensue, echoes the short-term thinking that permeates so much of their criticism. I myself came into the profession "underqualified" and earned a certificate within two years. There are oodles of people like me out there who would never have entered teaching if such nontraditional routes were not available. "About half of the teachers who have entered through alternate routes say they would not have become teachers if the alternate route had not existed" (Feistritzer 2008, p. 2). See Chapter 10 for more on this aspect of teacher recruitment. Indeed, Darling-Hammond (2006), whose recommendations on training I will cite there, entered teaching "underqualified." Her sink-or-swim experience seems to have led her to focus her scholarship on teacher training (p. ix). Class size reduction will provide a perfect context for improved, well-supported training.

2. I work at a second-chance school, for lack of a better term, and I consider it quite enlightened and effective, but its classes are often still too big depending on the fluctuating enrollment. A humane regular school will need twelve students per class, and a humane second-chance school will need six. After grouping size reduction, there will be less and less need for second-chance schools, but until then we'll need to pay the piper.

3. Incidentally, Slavin (1989) makes the point that if test scores are not the goal, class size reduction may in fact have great value for our kids.

CHAPTER 8

1. As represented by the Organisation for Economic Co-operation and Development (OECD), leaving off Eastern Europe (including Turkey) and Mexico (the six poorest members). Mexico, which actually taxes less than the United States at 19 percent, has the second lowest GDP per capita in the OECD, while the United States has the second highest. South Korea's GDP is below the average and ninth from the bottom (OECD 2003).

2. Incidentally, Americans are charged more than other developed countries per capita for heath care that serves a much smaller percentage of the population. The European Union spent about half on average at just over 8 percent of GDP in 2001 (United Kingdom Office for National Statistics 2003). Most of these countries have universal care, often free. In 2005, Canada, Australia, and New Zealand, all with universal health care, spent between 9 and 10 percent of GDP (Fox 2007). Moving to a system like that of any of these countries could free up a lot of money to build one of the most attention-rich school systems in the developed world.

3. I also did not address the possibility of teacher salaries rising—see Appendix A for my reasoning. Below I will argue that any increased costs of recruitment will be offset by decreased attrition costs.

4. Reichardt assumes a new classroom is needed for each teacher (p. 42). My proposal cuts classes by just under half, thus allowing for the possibility of dividing classroom space in half as well. This will not be possible in all cases, but in cases where it is, it will bring new space costs to far below Reichardt's figure of 25 to 28 percent (p. 62). In many cases, the entirety of the increased space cost would be merely the cost of putting in a folding wall and a second door. (Chapter 9 addresses the space issue in more detail.)

5. Because the Reichardt data seem to suggest the reasonability of the lower estimate, I will continue to discuss costs based on a 20 percent funding increase. For those who are skeptical of the lower estimate, inflate my figures by 8 percent for the intermediate estimate (21.6 percent spending increase), or by 50 percent to reach the extrapolation from Reichardt minus the classroom costs (30.3 percent spending increase), which does not include savings from less-needed auxiliary teachers or counselors. For the truly incredulous, the highest available estimate is the extrapolation from Reichardt that assumes and includes a new classroom for every teacher (34.1 percent spending increase), which would be 70 percent higher than the calculations that follow—still a pittance for what it buys.

6. Teachers came in at 51 percent (higher than 43 percent that are classroom (non-auxiliary) teachers, quoted shortly), school and library support staff at 4.7 percent, and student support staff at 3.1 percent.

7. This was *before* No Child Left Behind—the number has certainly risen.

CHAPTER 9

1. For another example of an elementary school that reduced class sizes from twenty-five to fifteen using similar strategies, see Odden and Archibald 2000. Several similar studies are at http://www.wcer.wisc.edu/cpre/finance/research/reallocation.php.

2. Reichardt finds it to be about $200 less per student. For a target class size of fifteen students, it's a 16 percent decrease (2000, p. 54).

3. A Cincinnati school that converted counselor positions to classroom teacher positions "partnered with social service agencies to provide some of the lost social services" (North Central Regional Educational Laboratory 2002).

APPENDIX A

1. An NEA survey found that elementary teachers average 3 hours of preparation time per week; junior or middle, 4; and senior high, 3. Respectively, 53 percent, 22 per-

cent, and 25 percent of respondents were in those categories, yielding 3.22 hours (National Education Association 2003a, pp. 24, 45). The same survey found that secondary schools have an average of twenty-nine 59-minute periods per week that were an average of 59 minutes long (p. 44). Elementary class time data are scarcer, but they can be inferred to be roughly similar from the fact that U.S. average school-day length for grades 1 through 12 is about 6.6 hours (Rose, Sonstelie, Reinhard, and Heng 2003, table 3.5). NEA (2003a) found the average lunch to be 32 minutes (p. 48). With some recess thrown in, 29 hours about makes sense for elementary as well, plus the fact that unions would tend to stipulate the same instruction time for both. Out of 29 weekly hours of student class time, 3.22 hours of nonteaching time is 11 percent.

References

Abramson, P. 2008. The 2008 annual school construction report. Supplement to *School Planning and Management*. Retrieved March 1, 2008, from http://www.peterli .com/spm/pdfs/constr_report_2008.pdf.

Achilles, C. 1999. *Let's put kids first, finally: Getting class size right*. Thousand Oaks, CA: Corwin.

———. 2003. *How class size makes a difference: What the research says*. Paper presented at the SERVE Research and Policy Symposium on Class-Size Reduction and Beyond, Raleigh, NC. (ERIC Document Reproduction Service No. ED 475012.) Retrieved December 12, 2007, from the ERIC database.

Agron, J. 2005, May 1. Mixed results: 31st annual official education construction report. *American School and University*. Retrieved March 1, 2008, from http://asumag .com/mag/university_mixed_results/.

Alexander, K. L., D. R. Entwisle, and S. L. Dauber. 2003. *On the success of failure: A reassessment of the effects of retention in the primary grades*. Cambridge, UK: Cambridge University Press.

Allen, J., and C. Lynd. 2000. *Debunking the class size myth: How to really improve teacher effectiveness*. The Center for Education Reform. Retrieved March 16, 2008, from http://www.edreform.com/index.cfm?fuseAction=document&documentID=710.

Alliance for Excellent Education. 2005. *Teacher attrition: A costly loss to the nation and to the states*. Issue Brief. Retrieved March 16, 2008, from http://www.all4ed.org/ files/archive/publications/TeacherAttrition.pdf.

American Psychological Association. 2001. Historical changes affecting end-of-life care. *End-of-life issues and care*. Retrieved February 26, 2008, from http://apa.org/ pi/eol/historical.html.

Ancess, J. 2003. *Beating the odds: High schools as communities of commitment.* New York: Teachers College Press.

Anderson, L. 2002. Balancing breadth and depth of content coverage: Taking advantage of the opportunities provided by smaller classes. In J. Finn and M. Wang, eds., *Taking small classes one step further.* Greenwich, CT: Information Age Publishers.

Archibald, S. 2001. *A case study of dramatic resource reallocation to improve student achievement: Harrison Place High School* (CPRE-UW Working Paper). Consortium for Policy Research in Education, Wisconsin Center for Education Research, University of Wisconsin-Madison. Retrieved February 20, 2008, from wcer.wisc.edu/cpre/papers/Harrison%20SF%205-01.pdf.

Archibald, S., and A. Odden. 2000. *A case study of resource reallocation to implement a whole school reform model and boost student achievement: Parnell Elementary School.* Consortium for Policy Research in Education, Wisconsin Center for Education Research, University of Wisconsin-Madison. Retrieved February 20, 2008, from http://www.wcer.wisc.edu/cpre/papers/Parnell%20SF%203-00.pdf.

Ballou, D. 1997. The condition of urban school finance: Efficient resource allocation in urban schools. In *Selected papers in school finance 1996* (NCES 98-217). Retrieved February 19, 2008, from http://nces.ed.gov/pubs98/finance/98217-4.asp.

Barnes, G., E. Crowe, and B. Schaefer. 2007. *The cost of teacher turnover in five school districts: A pilot study.* National Commission on Teaching and America's Future. Retrieved February 26, 2008, from http://nctaf.org/resources/demonstration_projects/turnover/TeacherTurnoverCostStudy.htm.

Barr, R., and W. Parrett. 2003. *Saving our students, saving our schools.* Thousand Oaks, CA: Corwin.

Benson, P. 1997. *All kids are our kids: What communities must do to raise caring and responsible children and adolescents.* San Francisco: Jossey-Bass.

Berliner, D. 2006. Fixing schools isn't everything. *NEA Today* 24(5): 38.

Berliner, D., and B. Biddle. 1995. *The manufactured crisis: Myths, fraud, and the attack on America's public schools.* Reading, MA: Addison-Wesley.

Bernstein-Yamashiro, B. 2004. Learning relationships: Teacher-student connections, learning, and identity in high school. In G. Noam and N. Fiore, eds., *The transforming power of adult youth relationships.* San Francisco: Jossey-Bass.

Berry, C. 2004. School inflation. *Education Next* 4(4). Retrieved February 20, 2008, from http://www.hoover.org/publications/ednext/3259476.html.

Betts, J. R., and J. L. Shkolnik. 1999. The behavioral effects of variations in class size: The case of math teachers. *Educational Evaluation and Policy Analysis* 21(2): 193–213.

Blatchford, P. 2003. *The class size debate: Is small better?* Philadelphia: Open University Press.

Bohrnstedt, G. W., and B. M. Stecher. 1999. *Class size reduction in California.* Palo Alto, CA: American Institutes for Research.

Bowlby, J. 1982. *Attachment and loss: Volume I: Attachment.* New York: Basic Books.

———. 1988. *A secure base.* New York: Basic Books.

Bowles, T. J., and R. Bosworth. 2002. Scale economies in public education: Evidence from school level data. *Journal of Education Finance* 28(2): 285–300.

Boy Scouts of America. 2004. *Boy Scouts of America youth protection guidelines: Facilitator's guide.* Retrieved February 24, 2008, from http://old.scouting.org/pubs/ypt/pdf/46-221.pdf.

Bracey, G. 2003. *What you should know about the war against America's public schools.* Boston: Allyn and Bacon.

Braun, H., F. Jenkins, and W. Grigg. 2006. *Comparing private schools and public schools using hierarchical linear modeling* (NCES 2006-461). Retrieved February 20, 2008, from http://nces.ed.gov/nationsreportcard//pubs/studies/2006461.asp.

Bryk, A., and B. Scheider. 2002. *Trust in schools: A core resource for improvement.* New York: Russell Sage Foundation.

Cahen, L. S., N. Filby, G. McCutcheon, and D. W. Kyle. 1983. *Class size and instruction.* New York: Longman.

Callahan, R. 1962. *Education and the cult of efficiency.* Chicago: University of Chicago Press.

Camp, S. D., and G. G. Gaes. 2002. Growth and quality of U.S. private prisons: Evidence from a national survey. *Criminology and Public Policy* 1(3): 427.

Center for Effective Discipline. 2008. *Family and childcare laws.* Retrieved February 24, 2008, from http://stophitting.com/laws/stateLegislation.php.

Chaddock, G. 2003, August 18. US notches world's highest incarceration rate. *Christian Science Monitor.* Retrieved February 20, 2008, from www.csmonitor.com/2003/0818/p02s01-usju.html.

Chatman, S. 1996. *Lower division class size at U.S. postsecondary institutions.* Association for Institutional Research 1996 Annual Forum Paper. Retrieved February 20, 2008, from http://www.eric.ed.gov/ERICDocs/data/ericdocs2sql/content_storage_01/0000019b/80/14/9f/fa.pdf.

Chess, S., and A. Thomas. 1999. *Goodness of fit.* Philadelphia: Brunner/Mazel.

Christenson, S. L., and S. M. Sheridan. 2001. *Schools and families: Creating essential connections for learning.* New York: Guilford.

Chubb, J., and T. Moe. 1990. *Politics, markets and America's schools.* Washington, DC: Brookings Institution.

Church, R. 1976. *Education in the United States: An interpretive history.* New York: Free Press.

Clark, C. 2004. *Hurt: Inside the world of today's teenagers.* Grand Rapids, MI: Baker Academic.

Clarke-Stewart, K., C. Gruber, and L. Fitzgerald. 1994. *Children at home and in day care.* Hillsdale, NJ: Lawrence Erlbaum Associates.

Clinchy, E. 2002. *The rights of all our children: A plea for action.* Portsmouth, NH: Heinemann.

Cohen, E. G. 1997. Equity in heterogeneous classrooms. In E. G. Cohen and R. A. Lotan, eds., *Working for equity in heterogeneous classrooms.* New York: Teachers College Press.

Cohen, R. M., and S. Scheer. 2003. *Teacher-centered schools.* Lanham, MD: Scarecrow.

Comer, J. 1997. *Waiting for a miracle: Why schools can't solve our problems—and how we can.* New York: Dutton.

Commission on Business Efficiency of the Public Schools. 2003. *School size, violence, achievement and cost.* Retrieved February 19, 2008, from www.njleg.state.nj.us/legislativepub/reports/buseff_report.pdf.

Coontz, S. 2000. *The way we never were: American families and the nostalgia trap.* New York: Basic Books.

Cotterell, J. 1996. *Social networks and social influences in adolescence.* New York: Routledge.

Cotton, K. 2001. *New small learning communities: Findings from recent literature.* Portland, OR: Northwest Regional Educational Laboratory. Retrieved December 7, 2008, from http://www3.scasd.org/small_schools/nlsc.pdf.

Coulter, C. 2005, April 22. Overtime just one issue likely to be addressed. *Irish Times.* Retrieved February 21, 2008, from http://iprt.ie/ireland/1291.

Cozolino, L. 2006. *The neuroscience of human relationships: Attachment and the developing social brain.* New York: Norton.

Cuban, L. 1984. *How teachers taught: Constancy and change in American classrooms, 1890–1980.* New York: Longman.

Cunningham, H. 1995. *Children and childhood in western society since 1500.* New York: Longman.

Currie, E. 2005. *The road to whatever: Middle-class culture and the crisis of adolescence.* New York: Metropolitan.

Curtin, L. 2003. An integrated analysis of nurse staffing and related variables: Effects on patient outcomes. *Online Journal of Issues in Nursing* 8(3). Retrieved February 20, 2008, from www.nursingworld.org/ojin.

Dallas Indicators. 2007, approximately. *Average class size.* Retrieved March 19, 2008, from http://www.dallasindicators.org/Education/TeachersReadytoTeach/Average-classsize/tabid/559/language/en-US/Default.aspx.

Daniel, B., S. Wassell, and R. Gilligan. 1999. *Child development for child care and protection workers.* London: Jessica Kingsley.

Darling-Hammond, L. 2006. *Powerful teacher education.* San Francisco: Jossey-Bass.

Darling-Hammond, L., L. Hudson, and S. N. Kirby. 1989. *Redesigning teacher education: Opening the door for new recruits to science and mathematics teaching.* Santa Monica, CA: RAND Corporation.

Darling-Hammond, L., A. E. Wise, and S. P. Klein. 1999. *A license to teach: Raising standards for teaching.* San Francisco: Jossey-Bass.

Davison, B. 2003. Management span of control: How wide is too wide? *Journal of Business Strategy* 24(4): 22.

Deiro, J. 2005. *Teachers do make a difference.* Thousand Oaks, CA: Corwin Press.

deMarrais, K. B, and M. D. LeCompte. 1999. *The way schools work: A sociological analysis of education.* New York: Longman.

Dewey, J. 1990. *The school and society and the child and the curriculum.* Chicago: University of Chicago Press.

Digest (of Education Statistics). U.S. National Center for Education Statistics. Specified years and tables retrieved from http://nces.ed.gov/programs/digest.

Douglas, T. 1995. *Survival in groups: The basics of group membership.* Buckingham, PA: Open University Press.

Dryfoos, J. 1994. *Full-service schools.* San Francisco: Jossey-Bass.

———. 1998. *Safe passage: Making it through adolescence in a risky society.* New York: Oxford University Press.

Duffy, C. 1995. *Government nannies.* Gresham, OR: Noble Publishing.

Duke, D. 2002. *Creating safe schools for all children.* Boston: Allyn and Bacon.

Eisner, E. 2005. Back to whole. *Educational Leadership* 63(1): 14–18.

Elmore, R., P. Peterson, and S. McCarthey. 1996. *Restructuring in the classroom: Teaching, learning, and school organization.* San Francisco: Jossey-Bass.

Epstein, J. L., and M. G. Sanders. 2000. Connecting home, school and community: New directions for social research. In M.T. Hallinan, ed., *Handbook of the sociology of education.* New York: Klewer Academic/Plenum.

Evans, R. 2004. *Family matters: How schools can cope with the crisis in childrearing.* San Francisco: Jossey-Bass.

Eyer, D. 1996. *Motherguilt: How our culture blames mothers for what's wrong with society.* New York: Random House.

Federal Student Aid. 2006. *Teacher loan forgiveness program.* Retrieved February 26, 2008, from http://studentaid.ed.gov/PORTALSWebApp/students/english/cancelstaff.jsp.

Feistritzer, C. E. 2008. Introduction and overview. In C. E. Feistritzer, ed., *Building a quality teaching force: Lessons learned from alternate routes.* Upper Saddle River, NJ: Pearson.

Feldman, J., L. Lopez, and K. Simon. 2006. *Choosing small: The essential guide to successful high school conversion.* San Francisco: Jossey-Bass.

Fibkins, W. 2003. *An educator's guide to understanding the personal side of students' lives.* Lanham, MD: Scarecrow Press.

Fiene, R. 2002. *13 indicators of quality child care: Research update.* Paper presented to Office of the Assistant Secretary for Planning and Evaluation; and Health Resources and Services Administration/Maternal and Child Health Bureau, U.S. Department of Health and Human Services. Retrieved February 21, 2008, from http://aspe.hhs.gov/hsp/ccquality-ind02/.

Finn, J. D. 2002. Introduction and epilogue. In J. Finn and M. Wang, eds., *Taking small classes one step further.* Greenwich, CT: Information Age Publishers.

Finn, J. D., S. B. Gerber, C. M. Achilles, and J. Boyd-Zaharias. 2001. The enduring effects of small classes. *Teachers College Record* 103(2): 145.

Fisher, P. 2003. The prevention of antisocial behavior: Beyond efficacy and effectiveness. In A. Biglan, M. Wang, and H. Walberg, eds., *Preventing youth problems.* New York, London: Kluwer Academic/Plenum Publishers.

Flinders, D., and N. Noddings. 2001. *Multiyear teaching: The case for continuity.* Bloomington, IN: Phi Delta Kappa International.

Forsyth, D. 1999. *Group dynamics.* Belmont, CA: Brooks/Cole.

Fox, M. 2007, November 1. *US healthcare comes up short in survey of 7 nations.* Reuters News Service. Retrieved February 29, 2008, from http://www.reuters.com/article/latestCrisis/idUSN31355765.

Fraley, R. C. 2004. *A brief overview of adult attachment theory and research.* University of Illinois at Urbana-Champaign Web site. Retrieved February 20, 2008, from www.psych.uiuc.edu/~rcfraley/attachment.htm.

Franciosi, R. 2004. *The rise and fall of American public schools: The political economy of public education in the twentieth century.* Westport, CT: Praeger.

Fraser, J. 2007. *Preparing America's teacher: A history.* New York: Teachers College Press.

Fredriksen, K., and J. Rhodes. 2004. The role of teacher relationships in the lives of students. In G. Noam and N. Fiore, eds., *The transforming power of adult youth relationships.* San Francisco: Jossey-Bass.

Funk, P. E., and J. Bailey. 1999. *Small schools, big results.* Report by Center for Rural Affairs, Walthill, Nebraska. (ERIC Document Reproduction Service No. ED 441633) Retrieved December 12, 2007, from ERIC database.

Garbarino, J. 1995. *Raising children in a socially toxic environment.* San Francisco: Jossey-Bass.

Gatto, J. 2001. *A different kind of teacher: Solving the crisis of American schooling.* Berkeley, CA: Berkeley Hills Books.

Gelsomino, K. L., L. A. Kirkpatrick, R. R. Hess, and J. E. Gahimer. 2000. A descriptive analysis of physical therapy group intervention in five Midwestern inpatient rehabilitation facilities. *Journal of Physical Therapy Education,* Spring 2000. Retrieved March 4, 2008, from http://findarticles.com/p/articles/mi_qa3969/is_200004/ai_n8879546/pg_7.

Glasser, W. 1969. *Schools without failure.* New York: Harper and Row.

Glassner, B. 1999. *The culture of fear.* New York: Basic Books.

Gnezda, N. M. 2005. *Teaching difficult students: Blue jays in the classroom.* Lanham, MD: Scarecrow Education.

Goldberg, M. 1998. *How to design an advisory system for a secondary school.* Alexandria, VA: Association for Supervision and Curriculum Development.

———. 2002. *15 School questions and discussion.* Lanham, MD: Scarecrow Press.

Graue, E., K. Hatch, K. Rao, and D. Oen. 2007. The wisdom of class-size reduction. *American Educational Research Journal* 44(3): 670–700.

Gribble, S. C. 1948. *Teacher qualifications and school attendance in New Mexico.* Albuquerque: University of New Mexico Press.

Grissmer, D., A. Flanagan, and S. Williamson. 1997. Does money matter for minority and disadvantaged students? Assessing the new empirical evidence. In National Center for Education Statistics, *Developments in school finance 1997* (NCES 98-212). Retrieved February 20, 2008, from http://nces.ed.gov/pubs98/dev97/index.asp.

Gross, M. 1999. *The conspiracy of ignorance: The failure of American public schools.* New York: HarperCollins.

Guillemette, Y. 2005. *School class size: Smaller isn't better.* C.D. Howe Institute Commentary 215. Retrieved March 16, 2008, from http://www.cdhowe.org/pdf/commentary_215.pdf.

Hagerty, R. 1995. *The crisis of confidence in American education.* Springfield, IL: C.C. Thomas.

Hallinan, M. T. 2004. Race effects on ability group outcomes. In H. J. Walberg, A. J. Reynolds, and M. C. Wang, eds., *Can unlike students learn together? Grade retention, tracking, and grouping.* Greenwich, CT: Information Age.

Hanushek, E. 2003. The importance of school quality. In P. Peterson, ed., *Our schools and our future: Are we still at risk?* Stanford, CA: Hoover Institution Press.

Harber, C. 1996. *Small schools and democratic practice.* Nottingham, UK: Educational Heretics Press.

Hare, A. P. 1976. *Handbook of small group research*. New York: Free Press.

Hare, A. P., H. H. Blumberg, M. F. Davies, and M. V. Kent. 1994. *Small group research: A handbook*. Norwood, NJ: Ablex Publishers.

Harris, D., and D. Plank. 2006. Making policy choices: Is class-size reduction the best alternative? In S. Laine and J. Ward, eds., *Using what we know: A review of the research on implementing class-size reduction initiatives for state and local policymakers*. North Central Regional Educational Laboratory. Retrieved December 17, 2006, from http://www.ncrel.org/policy/pubs/html/weknow/index.html.

Harris, J. 1998. *The nurture assumption: Why children turn out the way they do*. New York: Free Press.

Harrison, P. M., and A. J. Beck. 2006. *Prison and jail inmates at midyear 2005* (NCJ 213133). Bureau of Justice Statistics Bulletin. Retrieved February 26, 2008, from http://ojp.usdoj.gov/bjs/pub/pdf/pjim05.pdf.

Heller, D. 2004. *Teachers wanted: Attracting and retaining good teachers*. Alexandria, VA: Association for Supervision and Curriculum Development.

Helliwell, J., and R. Putnam. 2005. The social context of well-being. In F. Huppert, N. Baylis, and B. Keverne, eds., *The science of well-being*. Oxford: Oxford University Press.

Hewlett, S. A., and C. West. 1998. *The war against parents*. New York: Mariner.

Heywood, C. 2001. *A history of childhood*. Malden, MA: Polity.

Hiatt-Michael, D. B. 2001. Home-school communication. In D. B. Hiatt-Michael, ed., *Promising practices for family involvement in schools*. Greenwich, CT: Information Age.

Hodgson, L. 1997. *Raised in captivity*. St. Paul, MN: Graywolf.

Holmes, J. 1996. Attachment theory: A secure base for policy? In S. Kraemer and J. Roberts, eds., *The politics of attachment: Towards a secure society*. London: Free Association Books.

Holsendolph, E. 2007. Each one, teach one. *Diverse Issues in Higher Education* 24(9): 12–14.

Hong Kong Trade Development Council. 2002, January 11. *Rebound anticipated in 2002, says toy fair survey*. Press release. Retrieved March 3, 2008, from http://www.tdctrade.com/tdcnews/0201/02011101.htm.

Howe, H. 1993. *Thinking about our kids*. New York: Free Press.

Howley, C. 2002. Small schools. In A. Molnar, ed., *School reform proposals: The research evidence*. Greenwich, CT: Information Age.

Hunt, T. 2002. *The impossible dream: Education and the search for panaceas*. New York: Peter Lang.

Huppert, F. 2005. Positive mental health in individuals and populations. In F. Huppert, N. Baylis, and B. Keverne, eds., *The science of well-being*. Oxford: Oxford University Press.

Illinois State Board of Education. 2007. *Special education class size/age range requirements per 23 Illinois Administrative Code 226.720 and 226.731*. Retrieved February 24, 2008, from http://www.isbe.net/spec-ed/pdfs/class_size.pdf.

Infinite Mind, The. 2006. National Public Radio, October 18, 2006.

Ingersoll, R. M. 2003. *Is there really a teacher shortage?* Center for the Study of Teaching and Policy, University of Washington. Retrieved February 20, 2008, from http://depts.washington.edu/ctpmail/PDFs/Shortage-RI-09-2003.pdf.

Jackson, P. W. 1990. *Life in classrooms*. New York: Teachers College Press.

Jacobson, L. 2007. California could tap industry for teachers. *Education Week* 26(42): 26.

Jehlen, A., and C. Kopkowski. 2006. Is smaller better? *NEA Today* 24(5): 24.

Jencks, C., and M. Phillips. 1998. *The Black-White test score gap*. Washington, DC: Brookings Institution Press.

Jepsen, C., and S. Rivkin. 2002. *Class size reduction, teacher quality, and academic achievement in California public elementary schools*. San Francisco: Public Policy Institute of California.

Johnson, G., R. Poliner, and S. Bonaiuto. 2005. Learning throughout the day. *Educational Leadership* 63(1): 59.

Johnson, K. A. 2000. *Do small classes influence academic achievement? What the National Assessment of Educational Progress shows*. Heritage Foundation Center for Data Analysis Report #00-07. Retrieved February 20, 2008, from http://www.heri tage.org/Research/Education/CDA00-07.cfm.

Kaufman, M., and R. Stein. 2006, January 10. Record share of economy spent on health care. *Washington Post*, A01. Retrieved February 29, 2008, from http://www.wash ingtonpost.com/wp-dyn/content/article/2006/01/09/AR2006010901932.html.

Keller, B. 2007. Oft-cited statistic likely inaccurate. *Education Week* 26(41): 30.

Kendler, K. S., and C. A. Prescott. 2006. *Genes, environment, and psychopathology*. New York: Guilford Press.

Kennedy, M. M. 2005. *Inside teaching: How classroom life undermines reform*. Cambridge, MA: Harvard University Press.

Kohl, S. I. 2004. *The best things parents do*. York Beach, ME: Conari Press.

Kozol, J. 2000. *Ordinary resurrections*. New York: Crown.

Krueger, A. B. 2003. Economic considerations and class size. *Economic Journal* 113(485): F34.

Kulik, J. A. 2004. Grouping, tracking, and de-tracking: Conclusions from experimental, correlational, and ethnographic research. In H. J. Walberg, A. J. Reynolds, and M. C. Wang, eds., *Can unlike students learn together? Grade retention, tracking, and grouping*. Greenwich, CT: Information Age.

Kwiatkowski, M. 2002. Class size concerns in higher education. Retrieved July 7, 2006, from http://www.citruscollege.edu/research/reports/class_size_concerns.pdf. (Has since become unavailable. Author retains copy available upon request.)

Landy, S. 2002. *Pathways to competence: Encouraging healthy social and emotional development in young children*. Baltimore: Paul H. Brookes.

Laslett, P. 1984. *The world we have lost: Further explored*. New York: Scribner.

Layard, R. 2005. *Happiness: Lessons from a new science*. New York: Penguin.

Leach, P. 1994. *Children first: What our society must do—and is not doing—for our children today*. New York: Knopf.

Lee, J., and K. K. Wong. 2003. The impact of accountability on racial and socioeconomic equity: Considering both school resources and achievement outcomes. *American Educational Research Journal* 41(4): 797.

Lee, V. E., and D. T. Burkam. 2003. Dropping out of high school: The role of school organization and structure. *American Educational Research Journal* 40(2): 353.

Legler, R. 2000. Implementing a class-size reduction policy: Barriers and opportunities. In S. Laine and J. Ward, eds., *Using what we know: A review of the research on im-*

plementing class-size reduction initiatives for state and local policymakers. North Central Regional Educational Laboratory. Retrieved December 17, 2006, from www .ncrel.org/policy/pubs/html/weknow/index.html.

LeMoine, S., and S. Azer. 2006. *Child care center licensing regulations October 2006: Child-staff ratios and maximum group size requirements.* National Child Care Information Center. Retrieved February 24, 2008, from http://nccic.acf.hhs.gov/pubs/ cclicensingreq/ratios.html.

Levin, H. 2005. *The social costs of inadequate education.* Teachers College Symposium on Educational Equity, a summary by symposium chair. Retrieved March 27, 2007, from http://www.mea.org/tef/social_costs_of_inadequate.pdf.

Lewit, E. M., and L. S. Baker. 1997. Class size. *The Future of Children* 7(3). Retrieved December 17, 2006, from www.futureofchildren.org/usr_doc/vol7no3ART8.pdf.

Littky, D. (with S. Gabrelle). 2004. *The big picture: Education is everyone's business.* Alexandria, VA: Association for Supervision and Curriculum Development.

Lythcott, J., and F. Schwartz. 2005. Professional development in action: An idea with visiting rights. In L. Darling-Hammond, *Professional development schools.* New York: Teachers College Press.

Males, M. 1996. *The scapegoat generation: America's war on adolescents.* Monroe, ME: Common Courage Press.

———. 1999. *Framing youth: 10 myths about the next generation.* Monroe, ME: Common Courage Press.

Mayo, C. 2004. Relations are difficult. In C. Bingham and A. Sidorkin, eds., *No education without relation.* New York: Peter Lang.

McCaskill, E. O., et al. 1979. *A research study about teachers' perceptions of job satisfaction.* (Abstract.) (ERIC Document Reproduction Service No. ED 184205.) Retrieved December 12, 2007, from the ERIC database.

McCluskey, N. 2002. *Sizing up what matters: The importance of small schools.* The Center for Education Reform. Retrieved March 16, 2008, from http://www.edreform .com/index.cfm?fuseAction=document&documentID=863.

McCrery, J. 1997. *Reforming K–12 education through saving incentives: Executive summary.* Joint Economic Committee Study, 105th Congress. Retrieved February 29, 2008, from http://www.house.gov/jec/fiscal/tx-grwth/edreform/edreform.htm.

Meier, D. 1995. *The power of their ideas.* Boston: Beacon Press.

———. 2000a. The crisis of relationships. In W. Ayers, M. Klonsky, and G. Lyon, eds., *A simple justice: The challenge of small schools.* New York: Teachers College Press.

———. 2000b. Can the odds be changed? What it will take to make small schools ordinary practice. In E. Clinchy, ed., *Creating new schools.* New York: Teachers College Press.

———. 2000c. *Will standards save public education?* Boston: Beacon Press.

———. 2002. *In schools we trust: Creating communities of learning in an era of testing and standardization.* Boston: Beacon Press.

MetLife. 2005. *The MetLife survey of the American teacher, 2004–5: Transitions and the role of supportive relationships.* Retrieved February 20, 2008, from http://www .metlife.com/WPSAssets/34996838801118758796V1FATS_2004.pdf.

Miles, K. H. 2000. *Rethinking the use of educational resources to support higher student achievement.* North Central Regional Educational Laboratory "Critical Issue."

Retrieved February 20, 2008, from http://www.ncrel.org/sdrs/areas/issues/envrn mnt/go/go600.htm.

Miles, K. H., and L. Darling-Hammond. 1998. Rethinking the allocation of teaching resources: Some lessons from high performing schools. In National Center for Education Statistics, *Developments in school finance 1997* (NCES 98-212). Retrieved February 20, 2008, from http://nces.ed.gov/pubs98/dev97/index.asp.

Miles, K. H., K. Ware, and M. Roza. 2003. Leveling the playing field: Creating funding equity through student-based budgeting. *Phi Delta Kappan Online.* Retrieved February 20, 2008, from http://www.pdkintl.org/kappan/k0310mil.htm.

Milner, M. 2004. *Freaks, geeks, and cool kids: American teenagers, schools, and the culture of consumption.* New York: Routledge.

Mixing wealth for academic health. 2006. *NEA Today* 24(5): 10.

Mohr, N. 2000. Small schools are not miniature large schools. In W. Ayers, M. Klonsky, and G. Lyon, eds., *A simple justice: The challenge of small schools.* New York: Teachers College Press.

Morisi, T. L. 1994. Employment in public schools and the student-to-employee ratio. *Monthly Labor Review.* Retrieved February 26, 2008, from bls.gov/opub/mlr/1994/07/art5full.pdf.

Munoz, M. A., and P. R. Portes. 2002. *Voices from the field: The perceptions of teachers and principals on the class size reduction program in a large urban school district.* Paper presented at the Annual Meeting of the American Educational Research Association, New Orleans, LA. (ERIC Document Reproduction Service No. ED 466681.) Retrieved December 12, 2001, from the ERIC database.

Napier, R., and M. Gershenfeld. 1985. *Groups: Theory and experience.* Boston: Houghton Mifflin.

National Academy of Education, Committee on Teacher Education. 2005. *A good teacher in every classroom.* San Francisco: Jossey-Bass.

National Association for the Education of Young Children. 1991. *Accreditation criteria and procedures of the national academy of early childhood programs.* Washington, DC: NAEYC. Retrieved December 17, 2006 (as quoted by North Central Regional Educational Laboratory), from http://www.ncrel.org/sdrs/areas/issues/students/earlycld/ea1lk7-1.htm.

National Center for Education Statistics (NCES). 1993. *Public school kindergarten teachers' views on children's readiness for school (NCES 93-410).* Retrieved February 19, 2008, from nces.ed.gov/surveys/frss/publications/93410/index.asp?section ID=5.

———. 1996. *Education indicators: An international perspective (NCES 96-003).* Retrieved February 19, 2008, from http://nces.ed.gov/pubs/eiip/index.asp.

———. 1997. *Private schools in the United States: A statistical profile, 1993–94* (NCES 97-459). Retrieved February 19, 2008, from http://nces.ed.gov/pubs/ps/459t1070.asp.

———. 2001. *Characteristics of the 100 largest public elementary and secondary school districts in the U.S. 1999–2000.* Retrieved February 19, 2008, from http://nces.ed.gov/pubs2001/100_largest/index.asp.

———. 2002. *Special analysis 2002: Private schools: A brief portrait.* Retrieved February 19, 2008, from http://nces.ed.gov/programs/coe/2002/analyses/private/index.asp.

———. 2003a. *Prekindergarten in U.S. public schools: 2000–2001* (NCES 2003-019). Retrieved February 19, 2008, from http://nces.ed.gov/surveys/frss/publications/2003019/index.asp.

———. 2003b. *Characteristics of the 100 largest public elementary and secondary school districts in the U.S. 2001–02* (NCES 2003-353). Retrieved February 19, 2008, from http://nces.ed.gov/pubsearch/pubsinfo.asp?pubid=2003353.

———. 2003c. *High school guidance counseling* (NCES 2003-015). Retrieved February 19, 2008, from http://nces.ed.gov/surveys/frss/publications/2003015/index.asp.

———. 2004. *Condition of education 2004.* Retrieved February 19, 2008, from http://nces.ed.gov/programs/coe/2004/section4/indicator24.asp.

———. 2005. *Special analysis 2005: Mobility in the teacher workforce.* Retrieved February 19, 2008, from http://nces.ed.gov/programs/coe/2005/analysis/index.asp.

———. 2007a. *Status and trends in the education of racial and ethnic minorities* (NCES 2007-039). Retrieved February 19, 2008, from http://nces.ed.gov/pubs2007/minoritytrends/index.asp.

———. 2007b. *Revenues and expenditures for public elementary and secondary education: School year 2004–05 (fiscal year 2005)* (NCES 2007-356). Retrieved March 1, 2008, from http://nces.ed.gov/pubsearch/pubsinfo.asp?pubid=2007356.

National Education Association. 2003a. *Status of the American public school teacher 2000–2001.* Retrieved February 19, 2008, from http://www.nea.org/edstats/images/status.pdf.

———. 2003b. *Status of the American public school teacher 2000–2001: Highlights.* Retrieved February 19, 2008, from http://www.nea.org/edstats/images/statushighlights.pdf.

National Institute of Child Health and Human Development Early Child Care Research Network. 1996. Characteristics of infant child care: Factors contributing to positive caregiving. *Early Childhood Research Quarterly,* 11. Abstract retrieved November 23, 2008, from https://secc.rti.org/abstracts.cfm.

National Research Council. 2004. *Engaging schools: Fostering high school students' motivation to learn.* Washington, DC: National Academies Press.

Newman, K. 2004. *Rampage: The social roots of school shootings.* New York: Basic Books.

Newman, R. E. 2000. *Building urban little schools: Where every child succeeds with dignity.* Cambridge, MA: Brookline Books.

Newman, R. S. 2002. How self-regulated learners cope with academic difficulty: The role of adaptive help seeking. *Theory into Practice* 41(2): 132.

Noddings, N. 1984. *Caring: A feminine approach to ethics and moral education.* Berkeley: University of California Press.

———. 1989. *Women and evil.* Berkeley: University of California Press.

———. 2003. *Happiness and education.* New York: Cambridge University Press.

Noguera, P. 2003. *City schools and the American dream.* New York: Teachers College Press.

North Central Regional Educational Laboratory. 2002, approximately. *Clifton Elementary School, Cincinnati, Ohio.* Retrieved February 26, 2008, from http://ncrel.org/sdrs/areas/issues/envrnmnt/go/go6lk38.htm.

Oakes, J. 2005. *Keeping track: How schools structure inequality.* New Haven, CT: Yale University Press.

Odden, A., and S. Archibald. 2000. *A case study of resource reallocation to reduce class size, enhance teacher planning time, and strengthen literacy: Clayton Elementary School.* Consortium for Policy Research in Education, Wisconsin Center for Education Research, University of Wisconsin-Madison. Retrieved February 21, 2008, from http://www.wcer.wisc.edu/cpre/papers/Clayton%20SF%203-00.pdf.

Odden, A., S. Archibald, and A. Tychsen. 1999. *Farnham Elementary School: A case study of resource reallocation.* Consortium for Policy Research in Education, Wisconsin Center for Education Research, University of Wisconsin-Madison. Retrieved February 21, 2008, from http://www.wcer.wisc.edu/cpre/papers/Farnham%20SF%208-99.pdf .

Orfield, G. 1996. The growth of segregation. In G. Orfield and S. E. Eaton, eds., *Dismantling desegregation.* New York: New Press.

Organisation for Economic Co-operation and Development (OECD). 2003. *GDP per capita USD, using current PPPs, 2003.* Retrieved February 29, 2008, from http://www.oecd.org/dataoecd/55/60/33747039.pdf.

———. 2006a. *Education at a glance 2006.* Retrieved February 19, 2008, from http://www.oecd.org/document/52/0,3343,en_2649_39263238_37328564_1_1_1_1,00.html.

———. 2006b. *Education at a glance 2006: Highlights.* Retrieved February 19, 2008, from sprc.pt/paginas/Propostas/Docs/Education_Glance_2006.pdf.

Otto, H. 1954. *Class size factors in elementary schools.* Austin: University of Texas Press.

Owings, W. A., L. S. Kaplan, J. Nunnery, R. Marzano, S. Myran, and D. Blackburn. 2006. Teacher quality and troops to teachers. *National Association of Secondary School Principals Bulletin* 90(2): 102.

Perkinson, H. 1995. *The imperfect panacea.* Boston: McGraw-Hill.

Pew Report: Latinos more likely than blacks, whites to attend the largest public high schools. 2005. *Diverse,* November 17, 2005. Retrieved February 20, 2008, from http://www.diverseeducation.com/artman/publish/article_5109.shtml.

Pine, F. 2004. Mahler's concepts of "symbiosis" and separation-individuation: Revisited, reevaluated, refined. *Journal of the American Psychoanalytic Association* 52(2): 511. Retrieved March 19, 2008, from http://apsa.org/Portals/1/docs/japa/522/Pine-511-533.pdf.

Plutchik, R. 1981. Group cohesion in a psychoevolutionary context. In H. Kellerman, ed., *Group cohesion: Theoretical and clinical perspectives.* New York: Grune and Stratton.

Poplin, M., and J. Weeres. 1993. Listening at the learner's level: Voices from inside the schoolhouse. *Education Digest* 59(1): 9.

Postman, N. 1996. *The end of education: Redefining the value of school.* New York: Alfred A. Knopf.

Price, D. V., and E. B. Reeves. 2003. Student poverty, school accountability, and postsecondary enrollment: A challenge for educational reform in Kentucky. *Journal of Poverty* 7(4): 21–35.

Pringle, M. 1980. *The needs of children.* London: Hutchinson.

Public Agenda 2000. *A sense of calling: Who teaches and why.* Retrieved December 17, 2006, from www.publicagenda.org/specials/teachers/teachers.htm.

Raywid, M., and G. Schmerler. 2003. *Not so easy going: The policy environments of small urban schools and schools-within-schools.* Charleston, WV: ERIC Clearinghouse on Rural Education and Small Schools.

Ready, D. D., V. E. Lee, and K. G. Welner. 2004. Educational equity and school structure: School size, overcrowding, and schools-within-schools. *Teachers College Record* 106(10): 1989–2014. Retrieved March 19, 2008, from http://epicpolicy.org/node/179.

Reference for Business. 2008. *Span of control.* Retrieved December 17, 2006, from http://www.referenceforbusiness.com/small/Sm-Z/Span-of-Control.html.

Reichardt, R. 2000. *The cost of class size reduction: Advice for policymakers.* RAND Graduate School dissertation. Santa Monica, CA: RAND.

Reid, B. 2006. Finding the right tutor takes legwork, research. *The Arizona Republic* [On-line], Retrieved March 14, 2006, from www.azcentral.com/arizonarepublic/local/articles/0314edtutor0314.html.

Rhee, M., and D. Keeling. 2008. Recruitment and selection. In C. E. Feistritzer, ed., *Building a quality teaching force: Lessons learned from alternate routes.* Upper Saddle River, NJ: Pearson.

Rice, J. K. 2002. Making the evidence matter: Implications of the class size research debate for policy makers. In L. Mishel and R. Rothstein, eds., *The class size debate.* Washington, DC: Economic Policy Institute.

Rishel, C., E. Sales, and G. Koeske. 2005. Relationships with non-parental adults and child behavior. *Child and Adolescent Social Work Journal* 22(1): 19–34.

Robinson, G., and D. Brandon. 1992. *Perceptions about American education: Are they based on facts?* Arlington, VA: Educational Research Service.

Robinson, M. 1984. *Groups.* New York: John Wiley and Sons.

Rockwell, S. 1997. Mentoring through accessible, authentic opportunities. *Preventing School Failure* 41(3): 111.

Rose, H., J. Sonstelie, R. Reinhard, and S. Heng. 2003. *High expectations, modest means: The challenge facing California's public schools.* Public Policy Institute of California. Retrieved February 26, 2008, from http://www.ppic.org/content/pubs/report/R_1003HRR.pdf.

Rothstein, R. 1998. *The way we were? The myths and realities of America's student achievement.* New York: Century Foundation Press.

Safer Child. 2008. *Summer camp.* Retrieved February 24, 2008, from www.saferchild.org/summcamp.htm.

Sands, D., E. Kozleski, and N. French. 2000. *Inclusive education for the 21st century.* Belmont, CA: Wadsworth/Thomson Learning.

Scott, J. P. 1981. Biological and psychological bases of social attachment. In H. Kellerman, ed., *Group cohesion: Theoretical and clinical perspectives.* New York: Grune and Stratton.

Sentencing Project. 2006. *New incarceration figures: Thirty-three consecutive years of growth.* Retrieved February 19, 2006, from http://sentencingproject.org/Admin/Documents/publications/inc_newfigures.pdf.

Shea, R. 2007. Call of duty. *Teacher Magazine* 18(6): 34.

Sidorkin, A. M. 2002. *Learning relations.* New York: Peter Lang.

———. 2004. Relations are rational: Toward an economic anthropology of schooling. In C. Bingham and A. Sidorkin, eds., *No education without relation.* New York: Peter Lang.

Simon, B. S., and J. L. Epstein. 2001. School, family, and community partnerships: Linking theory to practices. In D. B. Hiatt-Michael, ed., *Promising practices for family involvement in schools*. Greenwich, CT: Information Age.

Sizer, T. 1996. *Horace's hope: What works for the American high school*. Boston: Houghton Mifflin.

Slavin, R. E. 1989. Class size and student achievement: Small effects of small classes. *Educational Psychologist* 24(1): 99.

Slentz, K., and S. Krogh. 2001. *Early childhood development and its variations*. Mahwah, NJ: Lawrence Erlbaum.

Smetana, J., N. Campione-Barr, and C. Daddis. 2004. Longitudinal development of family decision making: Defining healthy behavioral autonomy for middle-class African American adolescents. *Child Development* 75(5): 1418–1434.

Smith, W. A. 2008, approximately. Faculty description on University of Utah Web site. Retrieved March 23, 2008, from http://www.ed.utah.edu/ECS/Faculty/William Smith.htm.

Spring, J. 1997. *The American school: 1642–2000*. Boston: McGraw-Hill.

Stearns, P. 2006. *Childhood in world history*. New York: Routledge.

Steinberg, L. 2004. *The ten basic principles of good parenting*. New York: Simon and Schuster.

Stephen, C. 2003. What makes all-day provision satisfactory for three and four year olds? *Early Child Development and Care* 173(6): 577–588.

Steuer, F. 1994. *The psychological development of children*. Pacific Grove, CA: Brooks/Cole.

Strizek, G. A., J. L. Pittsonberger, K. E. Riordan, D. M. Lyter, and G. F. Orlofsky. 2007. *Characteristics of schools, districts, teachers, principals, and school libraries in the United States: 2003–04 Schools and staffing survey.* (NCES 2006-313 revised.) National Center for Education Statistics. Retrieved March 19, 2008, from http://nces.ed.gov/pubsearch/pubsinfo.asp?pubid=2006313.

Sweeting, G. 2004, July 19. Letter from the New York City Independent Budget Office to Leonie Haimson of Class Size Matters. Retrieved February 29, 2008, from http://www.ibo.nyc.ny.us/iboreports/classsizeaug04.pdf.

Swidler, S. A. 2004. *Naturally small: Teaching and learning in the last one-room schools*. Greenwich, CT: Information Age.

Swiss Federal Tax Administration. 2006. *OECD: Total tax revenue (including social security) as percentage of GDP 2004*. Retrieved February 29, 2008, from http://www.estv.admin.ch/e/dokumentation/zahlen_fakten/dok/inter/2006/fisquo.pdf.

Taylor, B. 2003. *What kids really want that money can't buy*. New York: Warner Books.

Texas Center for Educational Research. 2000. *The cost of teacher turnover*. Retrieved February 21, 2008, from http://www.sbec.state.tx.us/SBECOnline/txbess/turnover rpt.pdf.

Texas Department of Family and Protective Service. 2006. *Minimum standard rules for licensed child-care centers*. Retrieved February 24, 2008, from National Resource Center for Health and Safety in Child Care and Early Education, http://nrc.uchsc.edu/STATES/TX/tx_746.pdf.

Toch, T. 1991. *In the name of excellence: The struggle to reform the nation's schools, why it's failing, and what should be done*. New York: Oxford University Press.

————. 2003. *High schools on a human scale: How small schools can transform American education.* Boston: Beacon Press.

"Top of their class." 2001, October 22. *New York Magazine* [On-line]. Retrieved February 21, 2008, from http://nymag.com/urban/articles/schools01/.

Tye, B. B. 2000. *Hard truths: Uncovering the deep structure of schooling.* New York: Teachers College Press.

United Kingdom Office for National Statistics. 2003. *International comparison of total health expenditure.* Retrieved February 29, 2008, from http://www.statistics .gov.uk/healthaccounts/international_comparison_total_health_expenditure .asp.

U.S. Bureau of Economic Analysis. 2007. *State personal income 2006* (BEA 07-11). Retrieved February 29, 2008, from http://www.bea.gov/newsreleases/regional/spi/ 2007/spi0307.htm.

U.S. Bureau of Justice Statistics. 2007. *Direct expenditures by criminal justice function, 1982–2005.* Retrieved February 26, 2008, from http://www.ojp.usdoj.gov/bjs/glance/ tables/exptyptab.htm.

U.S. Bureau of Labor Statistics. 2007. *National compensation survey: Occupational wages in the United States, June 2006.* Retrieved February 28, 2008, from http:// www.bls.gov/ncs/ocs/sp/ncbl0910.pdf.

————. 2008. *The employment situation: January 2008* (USDL 08-0130). Retrieved February 28, 2008, from http://www.bls.gov/news.release/pdf/empsit.pdf.

U.S. Census Bureau. 2008. *USA QuickFacts.* Retrieved February 28, 2008, from http:// quickfacts.census.gov/qfd/states/00000.html.

U.S. Congressional Budget Office. 2005. *The budget and economic outlook: Fiscal years 2006 to 2015.* Retrieved February 29, 2008, from http://www.cbo.gov/ftpdoc.cfm ?index=6060&type=0&sequence=0.

U.S. Department of Health and Human Services, Child Welfare Information Gateway. 2006. *What is child abuse and neglect?* Factsheet. Retrieved March 1, 2008, from http://www.childwelfare.gov/pubs/factsheets/whatiscan.cfm.

West, M. L., S. W. Spreng, S. M. Rose, and K. S. Adam. 1999. Relationship between attachment-felt security and history of suicidal behaviours in clinical adolescents. *Canadian Journal of Psychiatry* 44(6): 578.

Williams, D. 1990. *The dimensions of education: Recent research on school size.* Working Paper Series of the Strom Thurmond Institute, December 1990. Retrieved December 12, 2006, from www.strom.clemson.edu/teams/ced/pubs/DimOed.pdf.

Williams, D. G., and R. R. Land. 2006. The legitimation of black subordination: The impact of color-blind ideology on African American education. *Journal of Negro Education* 15(4): 579.

Williams, R., and C. Pritchard. 2006. *Breaking the cycle of educational alienation: A multiprofessional approach.* Maidenhead, NY: Open University Press.

Wyatt, I., and D. Hecker. 2006, March. Occupational changes during the 20th century. *Monthly Labor Review,* 35. Retrieved February 21, 2008, from www.bls.gov/opub/ mlr/2006/03/art3full.pdf.

Xia, C., and E. Glennie. 2005. Grade retention: A three part series. Policy Briefs. Center for Child and Family Policy, Duke University. (ERIC Document Reproduction Service No. ED 492017.) Retrieved March 15, 2008, from the ERIC database.

Young, D. 1999. *Wayward kids: Understanding and treating antisocial youth*. Northvale, NJ: Jason Aronson.

Zahorik, J. A. 1999. Reducing class size leads to individualized instruction. *Educational Leadership* 57(1): 50–53.

Zigler, E., and M. Lang. 1991. *Child care choices: Balancing the needs of children, families, and society*. New York: Free Press.

Index

abuse, x, 26
Achilles, Charles, 8, 125, 131, 138
administration, 130, 145–146, 151
adults: attachment theory and, 65, 67–68, 76;
    attention and autonomy for children and,
    61–63; consequences of lack of attention
    from, 74–76; dependence on, 63–64;
    grouping sizes for, 7–12; nurturance crisis
    and, 46–47; peer relationships and, 69;
    placing responsibility on, 47; relationship
    load limits of, 73–74, 105–106; role in
    children's play and work of, 70–73;
    withdrawal of, 47–48
advisory model, 159–161
age differences, attachment theory and, 65–67
age-grading, 31–32, 85, 92, 198n1
age specialization, 88–89
Ainsworth, Mary, 61–62, 195
Alexander, Karl, 34–35, 142
Ancess, Jacqueline, 18, 25, 77, 103, 107, 152
anxiety, reducing, 109
apprenticeships, 170–175
Archibald, S., 153
"arousal-relaxation cycle," 71
attachment problems: daycare and, 50;
    preventing, 75–76; solutions for, 48
attachment theory: adults and, 65; age
    differences and, 65–67; attention and

autonomy for children and, 61–63; class
    reduction for early grades and, 124;
    criticisms of, 195–196; mental health and,
    60; in multi-adult classrooms, 154–155;
    non-parental adults and, 67–68; peers and,
    68–70
attention: adult threshold for, 73–74;
    autonomy and, 61–63; children's need for,
    61; consequences of lack of, 74–76;
    dependence and, 63–64; discrimination in,
    108–109; John Dewey on, 78; from peers, 69;
    proving availability of, 182–183; rules and,
    64–65; work and, 70–73. *See also* neediness
attitude, effect of class size on, vii–viii
attrition, 136–137, 166
authority, 154–155
autonomy: attention and, 61–63; dependence
    and, 63–64; rules and, 64–65; for students,
    182; for teachers, 155; work and, 72–73
auxiliary teachers, 86, 129, 131–133, 153–156

baby boom period, 120, 166
Baker, Linda, 131
Barnes, Gary, 137
behavior: causes of poor, 46–47; changing,
    23–24; effect of attention on, 74–76; effect of
    relationship load on, 106, 113–114, 199n1
Benson, Peter, 66, 67–68

Berliner, David: on failing schools myth, 42; on math and science crisis, 45; on performance of public and private schools, 43, 44; on reducing school size, 100; on school and corporate relationship loads, 8; on school funding, 163; on social status and education, 57
Bernstein-Yamashiro, Beth, 24, 26, 104–105
Berry, Christopher, 93, 141
Betts, Julian R., 104
Biddle, Bruce: on failing schools myth, 42; on math and science crisis, 45; on performance of public and private schools, 43, 44; on reducing school size, 100; on school and corporate relationship loads, 8; on school funding, 163
Blackburn, David, 169
Blatchford, Peter, 14, 113, 121–122, 123, 154
Bonaiuto, Susan, 161
Bowlby, John, 61–62, 65
Bracey, Gerald, 28
businesses, 178–179
busing, 139–140

Cahen, Leonard S., 123–124
California, 119–120
Callahan, Raymond, 92
Call Me Mister program, 176
Campione-Barr, Nicole, 64–65
Central Park East Secondary School, 29–30, 130, 153, 162
certification, 166–169
change: in behavior, 23–24; through relationship load reduction, 16–18
childrearing: Deborah Meier on, 40; effect of industrialization and urbanization on, 48–49; importance of family in, 49–51; role of teachers in, 12, 26–28; schools as part of, viii–xi, xiii, 76–77; shared work as part of, 70–73; teacher training and, 121
children: adult withdrawal from, 47–48; attachment to non-parental adults of, 67–68; attention and autonomy for, 61–63; blaming education crisis on, 47; dependence on adults and, 63–64; effect of attachment on development of, 65–67; effect of industrialization and urbanization on, 48–49; grouping size norms for, 3–7; increasing adult attention for, 12; influence of peers on, 68–70; need attention, 61; neglected, 74–75; proving availability of attention to, 182–83; rules for, 64–65;

undoing effects of neglect on, 76; work for, 70–73. *See also* disruptive children; students
choice, of schools, 148–149, 182
chores, 70–73, 94
Christensen, Sandra, 80, 81
Clark, Chap, 47, 105
Clarke-Stewart, Alison, 6, 107
classrooms, 158–159, 200n4
class size: as aspect of relationship load, xi, xii, 79, 83; average, in major cities, 91; calculating average, 198–199n4; compared to daycare groupings, 3–6; effect on academic expectations of, 114–15; effect on discipline of, 106–7, 113–14; effect on personalization of curriculum of, 111–113; effect on teacher of, vii–viii, 14–15; effect on trust and communication of, 80–81; historical arguments over, 78; history of, 92–93; ideal, 94–96; issue of cost and, 19–20, 22–23; math and science and, 44–45; multigrade flexibility for, 156–157; as ongoing issue, 24–25; for prisoners, 11; race and, 54–56; racial achievement gap and, 57–58; as reason for teacher shortage, 36–37; relationship load reduction in, ix–x; small schools and, 28–38, 89–90, 147–148; teacher continuity and, 88–89, 157–158; work and, 70–73
class size reduction: arguments against, 116–126; calculating cost of, 189–90; implementing, 152–53; ongoing costs for, 133–134; projected costs of, 129–131, 185–186, 200n5; reasons for, 1–2; reducing anxiety through, 109; savings associated with, 135–144; timeline for implementation of, 164–165; up-front costs for, 134. *See also* relationship load reduction
Coalition of Essential Schools, 6
coercion, 106–107, 115
Cohen, Elizabeth, 87
Cohen, Rosetta, 89, 130, 155, 183
colleges: class sizes in, 8–9; effect of class size on enrollment in, 59–60; teacher training in, 170, 171
Columbine High School, 39
Comer, James, 52
Commission on Business Efficiency of the Public Schools, 21
communication, 180–182
community, 50, 140, 178–179, 180–181
The Conspiracy of Ignorance: The Failure of American Public Schools, 24–25

construction, of new school buildings, 133–134

continuity: counteracting teacher attrition with, 137; elimination of intermediate-level schools and, 98–99; implementing changes in, 146–149; increasing, 96–98. *See also* teacher continuity

control, 106–107, 115

controversy, 19–20

Coontz, Stephanie, 26, 49–50

corporal punishment, 16

corporate support of schools, 178–79

cost: of alternate teacher recruitment methods, 169; areas for cutting, 138–139; breakdown of ongoing, 133–134; calculating, 189–190; of class size reduction, 152–153; of education in developed countries, 127–128; issue surrounding, of class size reduction, 19–20; of large schools, 134–136; projected, of class size reduction, 129–131, 200n5; of relationship load reduction, xiii, 21–23; of small schools, 90; of special education, 33; up-front, of class size reduction, 134. *See also* savings

Cotton, Kathleen, 81

counselors, 129–130, 159–161, 200n3

crime, 143–144

crisis. *See* fake crisis; nurturance crisis

Crowe, Edward, 137

Cuban, Larry, 22

curriculum: increasing difficulty of, 114–115; personalization and, 111–113; in small schools, 90

Currie, Elliott, 75, 178

Curtin, Leah, 38

Daddis, Christopher, 64–65

Daniel, Brigid, 47, 48, 51

Darling-Hammond, Linda: on cost of large schools, 135; on multigrade flexibility, 157; on necessary teaching force, 131; on reducing pull-out programs, 131; on restructuring school resources, 103; on savings and teacher training, 21–22; on separating special education, 34; on teacher quality, 118; on teacher recruitment methods, 169, 176–177; on teacher shortage, 36; on unattractiveness of teaching profession, 170

Dauber, Susan, 34–35

daycares, xii, 3–6, 50, 69, 187

Deiro, Judith, 48, 76

delivery personalization, 112–113

deMarrais, Kathleen, 46, 84, 107

dependence, 63–64

design personalization, 112–113

Dewey, John, 78, 106

discipline, 16, 106–107, 115, 199n1

disruptive children, 96, 106–107, 113–114

dropouts, 142

Dryfoos, Joy, 12

Duke, Daniel, 39

education: for adults, 8–10; in developed countries, 127–128; effect of urbanness on, 150–151; employment and, 45; imagined simpler era in, 24–25; improvement industry and, 137–138; as part of childrearing, 40; of prisoners, 11; private sector contributions to, 178–179; social justice in, 2; versus special education, 32–34

elementary schools: class size reduction in, 123–125; ideal size for, 101; increasing continuity in, 99; size of public, 149; specialization and, 85

emotions, 24

employees, 7–8

employment, 45

empowerment, 145–146

enrollment, centralized, 157–158

Entwisle, Doris, 34–35

Epstein, Joyce, 57, 79, 80

expulsion, 162

extracurricular activities: in separated schools, 150; in small schools, 90, 100

fake crisis: falling test scores as myth of, 42–43; math and science and, 44–45; overview of, 40–42; private schools and, 43–44; teacher quality and training and, 121

family: importance of, 49–51; poverty and, 56–57

family load. *See* parent load

Feldman, Jay, 147, 183

Finn, Jeremy, 15

Fitzgerald, Linda May, 6

Flanagan, Ann, 57–58

Franciosi, Robert, 118, 119

Fredriksen, Katia, 36–37, 105, 108

full-service schools, 17

Garbarino, James, 50, 74, 105–106

Gatto, John, 100, 137–138

Gilligan, Robbie, 47, 48, 51

Glasser, William, 52, 74

Glennie, Elizabeth, 136
Gnezda, Nicole, 69, 113, 185
Goldberg, Mark, 24
government incentives, 175–176
grade retention, 16–17, 34–36, 135–136, 142, 161
grading, flexibility in class division by, 156–57. See also age-grading
graduation, effect of class size on, 59–60
Graue, Elizabeth, 155
Grissmer, David, 57–58
grouping size: aspects of, ix; effect on discipline of, 106–107; norms for adults, 7–12; norms for children, 3–8. See also relationship load
Gruber, Christian, 6
guardian load. See parent load

Hagerty, Robert, 101, 135
Hallinan, Maureen, 87
Hamilton, Ian, 7
happiness, 60
Harber, Clive, 44, 135, 140
Hare, A. Paul, 10–11
harm, 2
Harris, Doug, 19–20
Harris, Judith, 66, 154
Hatch, Kelly, 155
Hawley Miles, Karen, 19
health care, 200n2
Hecker, Daniel, 166
Heywood, Colin, 49
Hiatt-Michael, Diana, 82
high school(s): dropouts, 142; ideal size for, 99–100; size of public, 149; specialization and, 85
Howe, Harold, 8
Howley, Craig, 101
hyperindividualism, ix

improvement industry, 137–138, 176
incarceration, 11, 143–144
incentives, 175–176
inclusion, 16–17
independence. See autonomy
industrialization, 48–49
Ingersoll, Richard, 36
internships, 170–75
Israel, 143

Jackson, Philip, vii, 125–126
Japan, 127–128
Jehlen, Alain, 83, 94, 147, 148, 183

Jencks, Christopher, 58
Jepsen, Christopher, 119, 164
job market, 44–45
Johnson, George, 161
Johnson, Kirk, 19, 100
Johnson, Lyndon, 8
Julia Richmond Complex, 147
junior high schools: eliminating, 98–99; size of public, 149; specialization and, 85

Kaplan, Leslie S., 169
Keeling, David, 177
Kennedy, Mary, 115
knowledge, levels of conceptualizing, 52–53
Kohl, Susan, 71–72
Kopkowski, Cynthia, 83, 94, 147, 148, 183
Kozol, Jonathan, 11, 22
Krogh, Suzanne, 62
Krueger, Alan, 141–142
Kulik, James A., 35–36

Lang, Mary, 66
Laslett, Peter, 9–10
Layard, Richard, 51
Leach, Penelope, 68–69, 121
LeCompte, Margaret, 46, 84, 107
Lee, Valerie E., 58, 59, 142
Legler, Ray, 173–174
Levin, Henry, 142, 143
Lewit, Eugene, 131
licenses, 171
Littky, Dennis, 38, 100, 136
local control, 18–19
Locke, John, 78
looping. See continuity
lunch, 183
luxury items, 144

Maimonides, 78
Marzano, Robert, 169
math, 44–45, 176
Mayo, Cris, 59
Meier, Deborah: on children's affinity for powerful adults, 155; on covering up education crisis, 41–42; on dealing with trauma, 63; on decline in personal relationships, 12; on driver's education, 11; on ideal school size, 99; mentioned, 1; on myth of education crisis, 40–41; on need for adult attention during work, 124; on reducing school size, 103; on reinventing schools, 9; on schooling and childrearing,

40; on sharing between small schools, 147; on small schools and course variety, 90

mental health, 60

Met, The, 81

MetLife, 105, 137

Mexico, 128, 199n1

middle schools: eliminating, 98–99; specialization and, 85

Miles, Karen Hawley: on alternate teacher recruitment methods, 169; on cost of large schools, 135; on group size for play-like activities, 94; on multigrade flexibility, 157; on necessary teaching force, 131; on reducing pull-out programs, 131; on restructuring school resources, 103; on separating special education, 34

minority groups: class size and, 54–56; improved test scores for, 42; poverty and, 55–57; reducing discrimination against, 58–59. See also race/racism

Mohr, Nancy, 83

"more of the same for each" phenomenon, 13–14

Morisi, Teresa L., 138

motivational seminars, 139

Myran, Stephen, 169

National Academy of Education, 36, 118, 170–171, 172, 198n4

National Education Commission on Time and Learning, 35

National Research Council, 83, 101, 159

neediness, 113–114. See also attention

neglect, x, 74–75, 76

Newman, Robert E., 102, 111, 113

Newman, Richard S., 63

New Teacher Project, 168, 177

Noddings, Nel, 40, 45, 106

Noguera, Pedro, ix

Nunnery, John, 169

nurses, 38

nurturance, x, xiii, 121, 142–143

nurturance crisis: adult withdrawal and, 47–49; crime and, 143–144; effect of industrialization and urbanization on, 48–49; fixing, 187; poverty and, 57; as real educational crisis, 12, 46–47

Oakes, Jeannie, 87

Oen, Denise, 155

Otto, Henry, 92

Owings, William A., 169

parent load: as aspect of relationship load, xi, xii, 79, 83; childrearing argument and, 28

parents: attachment theory and, 65–67; encouraging partnership between schools and, 51–53, 79–82, 180–182; leaving childrearing to, 26–28, 49–51; poverty and, 56–57; relationship load reduction and, ix–x

peers, 68–70

Perkinson, Henry, 31, 85

personalization, 111–113, 186–187

Phillips, Meredith, 58

philosophy of separation: current application of, 84–88; overview of, in education, 40–41; reassignment of auxiliary teachers and, 131–133; in small schools, 90, 148; status quo based on, xi; thinking outside of, ix

Plank, David, 19–20

play, 70–73, 94, 124, 182, 191–193

Poliner, Rachel, 161

Poplin, Mary, 51

"positive interaction cycle," 71

Postman, Neil, 45

poverty: correlation between large relationship load and, 56–57; as criteria for class-size reduction priority, 149–150, 164; effect on graduation and college enrollment of, 59–60; full-service schools and, 17; ideal class size and, 95; ideal school size and, 100–101; private sector contributions to fighting, 179; teacher attention and, 108–109; transportation and, 139–140

Powell, Colin, 24

preschool, 123–124

primate groups, 10

principals. See administration

Pringle, Mia, 62–63

prisons, 11, 143–144

Pritchard, Colin, 68

private schools, 43–44

private sector, 178–179

psychological therapy, 11

"pull out" teacher model, 16–17

Quincy School, 31–32

race/racism: class size and, 22, 54–56; class size reduction and, 153; as criteria for class-size reduction priority, 164; ideal class size and, 95; private schools and, 44; reducing, 16–17; teacher attention and, 108–109; teacher recruitment and, 168, 176; tracking and, 87. See also minority groups

racial achievement gap, 2, 57–60
"Racial Battle Fatigue," 57
Rao, Kalpana, 155
Raywid, Mary Anne, 147, 151–152
Ready, Douglas D., 58
recycling, 23–24
Reichardt, Robert, 130–131, 156
relational knowledge, 52–53
relationship load: classroom control and,
    106–107; dropout rates and, 142; effect on
    students of, 104–105; effect on teachers of,
    105–106; four aspects of, xi–xiii, 79;
    harming students through, 2; historical
    arguments over, 78; interconnectedness of
    aspects of, 82–84; partnerships between
    parents and schools and, 79–82; poverty
    and, 56–57; race and, 54–56; teaching and,
    32. See also class size; grouping size
relationship load reduction: accommodates
    local control, 18–19; administration needs
    after, 151; arguments against, 22–23,
    116–126; author's plan for, viii–xi;
    auxiliary teachers and, 86; benefits of,
    14–18, 53; calculating cost of, 189–190;
    Columbine tragedy as reason for, 39; cost
    of, xiii; effects of, 103–104; empowering
    local personnel for, 145–146; grouping
    size norms and, 3–12; implementing
    school size and continuity changes
    through, 146–149; improved academic
    expectations as result of, 114–115;
    increasing continuity and, 96–98;
    increasing influence of teachers and, 12;
    increasing student acceptance through,
    110–111; as noncontroversial solution,
    19–20; personalization made possible
    through, 111–113, 186–187; as preventative
    solution, 21–22; priority groups for,
    149–150, 164; problems with alternatives to,
    23–28; reasons for, 1–2; reducing anxiety
    through, 109; reducing discrimination
    through, 58–59; simplicity of, 21; small
    schools and, 28–38; teachers' unions and,
    183–184; training needs for, 15–16; yields
    automatic results, 13–14
relationships, 51–53, 181–182
respect, for teaching, 38–39
Rhee, Michelle, 177
Rhodes, Jean, 36–37, 105, 108
Rivkin, Steven, 119, 164
Rothstein, Richard, 42–43
rules, 64–65
Russia, 143

Safe School Study Report to Congress, 39
safety, 39, 136
SAGE experiment, 155
salaries, 19–20
Sanders, Mavis, 57
Sands, Deanna, 62, 84
SAT (Scholastic Aptitude Test), 42, 166
savings, 135–144
Schaefer, Benjamin, 137
Scheer, Samuel, 89, 130, 155, 183
Schmerler, Gil, 147, 151–52
Scholastic Aptitude Test (SAT), 42, 166
schools: as academic and nurturing
    environments, 104–105; aims of, xii; choice
    of, 148–149; compared to daycares, 3–6;
    construction of, 133–134; cost of large,
    134–136; definition of, 82; effect of teacher
    specialization on, 85–86; effect of urbanness
    on, 150–151; empowering, 145–146;
    emulating exceptional, 25; encouraging
    partnership between parents and, 51–53,
    79–82, 180–182; equalizing funding for,
    163–164; finding space for additional
    classrooms in, 158–159; importance of
    relationships in, 51–53; improvement
    industry and, 137–138; local control for,
    18–19; neglect of children and, x; as part of
    childrearing, xiii, 49–51, 76–77; play- and
    work-based, 72–73; private sector
    contributions to, 178–179; second-chance,
    199n2. See also full-service schools; private
    schools; small schools
school size: as aspect of relationship load, xi,
    xii, 79; Columbine tragedy and, 39; effect on
    peer influence of, 68–69; effect on trust and
    communication of, 80–81; history of, 93–94;
    ideal, 99–102; implementing changes in,
    146–149; racial achievement gap and, 58;
    statistics on, 149–150
science, 44–45, 176
"Scientific Management" movement, 92
Scott, John Paul, 10
second-chance schools, 199n2
security, 39, 136
seniority, 184
separation: anxiety, 65–66; special education
    and, 33–34; of students, 16–17. See also
    philosophy of separation
Shelton, James, 148
Sheridan, Susan, 80, 81
Shkolnik, Julian L., 104
Sidorkin, Alexander, 52–53, 72, 84, 121
Simon, Beth, 79, 80

Sizer, Ted, 6–7, 107, 114
Slavin, Robert, 125
Slentz, Kristine, 62
small schools, 28–38; cost of, 134–136, 185–186; cutting costs for, 138–139; effect on class size of, 83; effect on future earnings of, 141; effect on graduation and college enrollment of, 60; as medicine rather than diet, 125–126; policy changes for facilitating, 151–152; self-segregation among, 148; small classes and, 89–90; tracking and, 87–88
Smetana, Judith, 64–65
Smith, William, 57
social groups, 10–11
South Africa, 143
South Korea, 127–128, 165, 199n1
special education: auxiliary teachers and, 131–133; class size recommendations for, 96; cost and separation of, 32–34; ongoing cost projections for, 129; source data for, 191–193; staff reorganizations and, 158; teacher recruitment for, 176
specialization, xi, 83, 84–86, 98–99. See also age specialization
sports teams, 90, 150
Spring, Joel, 31–32
standardized tests, 42, 139, 166. See also test scores
STAR program, 119, 141
Stephen, Christine, 62
Steuer, Faye, 5–6, 100
students: effect of relationship load on, 104–105; effect of school size on, 39; emotions of, 24; equality in attention for, 108–109; harming, 2; increasing acceptance for, 110–111; increasing adult attention for, 12; increasing expectations for, 114–115; separation of, 16–17, 33–34, 90; small classes reduce anxiety of, 109
Switzerland, 128

taxes: disparities in school funding and, 163–164; for education in developed countries, 127–128; ongoing costs of class size reduction and, 133–134; paid by high school dropouts, 142; projected costs of class size reduction and, 129–131, 186
teacher continuity: as aspect of relationship load, xi, xii, 79; class size and, 88–89, 157–158; effect of relationship load on, 141; implementing changes in, 146–149; poverty

and, 56; race and, 55; small classes and, 88–89; specialization and, 83
teacher recruitment: alternate routes for, 166–169, 199n1; government incentives for, 175–176; for hard-to-fill areas, 176; history of, 165–166; internships and apprenticeships for, 170–175; public relations for, 176–177; reappropriating counselors for, 159–161, 200n3; staff reorganizations and, 166; traditional routes for, 169–170
teacher(s): attachment theory and, 67–68; attention-paying threshold for, 73–74; attrition, 136–137; aversion of potential, 37–38; discipline and, 106–107; effectiveness of one versus many, 153–156; effect of relationship load on, vii–viii, 14–15, 105–106, 152–153; empowering, 145–146; emulating exceptional, 25; encouraging partnership between parents and, 79, 180–182; equality in attention from, 108–109; increasing acceptance of, 58–59, 110–111; increasing influence of, 12; licensing issues for, 171; of math and science, 45; motivational seminars for, 139; multigrade flexibility for, 156–157; perceived laziness of, 23–24; prequalifications for, 176; proving availability of, 182–183; public and private school turnover for, 44; reducing relationship load on, viii–xi; role in childrearing of, 26–28; salaries for, 19–20; shortage of, 36–37; small classes reduce anxiety of, 109; in small schools, 89, 151–152; specialization of, xi, 83, 84–86; student neediness and, 113–114; time breakdown for, 201n1; training for, 15–16, 118–123, 169–170. See also auxiliary teachers; teacher continuity; teacher recruitment
teachers' unions, 183–184
Teach for America, 170
teaching: difficulty of, 32; discipline and, 106–107; reasons for avoiding, 37–38, 170; respect for, 38–39, 118–120; time breakdown for, 201n1
test scores, 42–43, 141. See also standardized tests
therapy, 11, 38
Toch, Thomas, 115
tracking, 34–36, 87–88, 148, 161–162
training, for teachers, 15–16, 118–123, 169–170
transportation, 139–140
Troops to Teachers, 168–169

trust, 80–81, 180–182
tutoring, 125–126, 139, 176
Tye, Barbara, 18, 138, 178–179

ULS proposal, 102
unions, 183–184
United Federation of Teachers, 184
universities, 8–9, 170, 171
Urban Academy, 30–31
urbanization, 48–49, 150–151
Urban Little Schools (ULS) proposal, 102

violence, 39
Vonnegut, Kurt, vii
vouchers, 28–29

Wagner, Tony, 29–30, 47–48, 87–88, 122, 153

Walberg, Herbert, 36
Wassell, Sally, 47, 48, 51
Weeres, Joseph, 51
Welner, Kevin G., 58
Wenglinsky, Harold, 44
Williams, Richard, 68, 101, 135
Williamson, Stephanie, 57–58
work: adult attention for children's, 70–73;
    adult environments for, 7–8; class reduction
    for early grades and, 124; ideal class size for,
    94
Wyatt, Ian, 166

Xia, Claire, 136

Zahorik, John, 112
Ziglar, Edward, 66

Garrett Delavan is a secondary teacher in the Salt Lake City public schools.